States and Markets

Susan Strange

Basil Blackwell
New York

First published in the United States of America in 1988 by
Basil Blackwell Inc.
Suite 1505, 432 Park Ave South,
New York, N.Y. 10016

Library of Congress Cataloging-in-Publication Data

Strange, Susan.
  States and markets.

  Bibliography: p.
  Includes index.
  1. Industry and state. 2. Capitalism. 3. Authority.
4. Economic history—1945—. 4. Economic history—
1945—. 5. International economic relations.
I. Title.
HD3611.S78 1988   337   88–10358
ISBN 1–55786–012–2
ISBN 1–55786–013–0 (pbk.)

Printed in Great Britain

Contents

Tables and Figures

Figures

Tables

Acknowledgements

Consciously or unconsciously, so many people have helped me write this book that I would find it hard to remember and list them all by name. Mostly I must acknowledge colleagues and students at the London School of Economics and other places I have visited over the past decade or so in which I have tried by trial and error to introduce university students at all levels to the study of international political economy. One of the first was an evening class of mature Master's students in the London programme of the University of Southern California, meeting at Chatham House. Two of the most recent have been an undergraduate class at the University of California in Davis and a Master's class at the Bologna Center of the Johns Hopkins School of Advanced International Studies. In between I have profited from teaching or advising students at the University of Southern California in Los Angeles, at the University of Minnesota, the Australian National University, the European University Institute and the International University of Japan, not to mention of course the students from all over the world who have come to the London School of Economics, finding there a truly international school in which students by long tradition over almost a century have developed to a fine art the habits of questioning authority and challenging the wisdom of their teachers. To them — and particularly to research students with whom it has been my privilege to come in contact — I owe a specially great debt.

Then there is an extensive invisible college of other scholars in other countries and universities who share my interest in this subject even though there are many things on which we do not always agree. I would like to make special mention of Roger Tooze, Gautam Sen, James Mayall, Peter Wiles at the LSE and Bob Kudrle, Jonathan Aronson, John Zysman, Marcello de Cecco, Michael Hodges, David Wightman, David Calleo, Bob Keohane, David Baldwin, Bob Cox and Jonathan Hall.

In the closing stages of putting the book together I have had cheerful and efficient help from Kate Grosser as research assistant, Margaret Bothwell as secretary and typist and Heather Bliss as editor. To all of them, my appreciative thanks.

Prologue: Some Desert Island Stories

It was a dark and stormy night. A ship was steaming laboriously through mountainous seas whipped by gale-force winds. Suddenly there is a terrific explosion amidships. All the lights go out. Whatever the cause, it has wrecked the power system. On board there is panic. People rush about in all directions, shouting and screaming and bumping into one another. Everyone is trying to get to the lifeboats. The deck begins slowly to tilt to one side. The explosion must have torn a hole in the side. Panic gets worse. Some of the lifeboats, clumsily handled, get stuck in the davits. Some capsize in the heavy seas. Only three get safely away before the ship, with one last shuddering lurch, sinks beneath the stormy water. This is the story of what happened to the people in the three lucky lifeboats.

In one of the lifeboats, there is a group of people who, by accident, all followed Martin, one of the ship's officers. He kept his head and took charge of the launching, helped by three of the crew, Mike, Jack and Terry. Among the handful of passengers with them are two lovers, John and June; and a mother, Meg, and her children, Ken and Rosy.

For three days and nights, blown by the storm, they have a fearful journey. For some reason the radio won't work. They have no idea where in the wide ocean they are. Water's getting short when, well into the third night adrift, they hear breakers. Miraculously escaping the reef, they land exhausted on a beach, and all fall asleep on the sand, happy to be alive.

In the morning, they explore the shore of their desert island. They find fresh water, coconut palms and fish in the lagoon. Martin, still in charge, sees that the lifeboat is safely pulled up the beach and organizes the building of a rough shelter. After some days Martin gets everyone together one evening and tells them he has been exploring the hills behind. He says he has seen tracks that look human. 'Friends,' he says, 'we may be in danger. We must cut down some trees and build a stockade. We must fashion some spears, organize a watch and send out some patrols.'

There's a bit of discussion about that. John and June, happy in a lovers' idyll, don't much want to work on the stockade. They have other ideas. Meg would rather hunt for fruit and nuts and start a garden for vegetables. But the crew are used to taking orders from Martin and their agreement carries his plans. Gradually, the little group get used to doing as they're told.

Meanwhile, the second lifeboat to get away from the ship also reaches the island — but lands in another part. They do not meet. So far as each group knows, they are the only survivors. This boat has a very different group aboard. It's a bunch of young students, led by Jerry, a bit older than the rest. It's he who got them together, organized the launch and managed to get the lifeboat safely away. As it happened, there were no officers or crew in the boat — and no professors either. In the three days and nights at sea they are being blown about, as ignorant as the first group about where they are. They talk endlessly, as students will, about their predicament and what they'll do if they ever find land. Idealistically, they agree with Jerry that it would be a great idea to organize a commune. To each according to their needs, from each according to their ability. Equality in taking decisions; the same rules for everybody.

When they wake on the beach that first morning ashore, they set happily to work gathering coconuts and fishing in the lagoon. After a few days, the first problems start to arise. Two lovers, Bob and Betty — just like John and June in the first lifeboat — are apt to wander away from their allotted jobs and go off together hand-in-hand into the woods. The others feel they are slacking. Then there are other long arguments about who is to fish and who is to work on the coconuts and the shelter. Joe, a practical fellow who brought along a toolbox, claims he ought to get extra rations or extra free time because, with his saw and axe, he can do as much in an hour as the others in a week. Amos is big and hefty and likes to work. Should he be rewarded? Meanwhile, the camp site not only has no stockade, it has no latrines. No one wants that particular job, so it begins to get a bit squalid and smelly. But everyone still believes the commune is a good idea.

The people in the third lifeboat land on yet another part of the same island. They too think they are the only survivors. This time the group includes some old people and many more mothers and children, as well as members of the crew. These include some of the ship's cooks, Jack the head steward, and the ship's purser, a silent, tough character who says 'Call me Mac'. But, at first, with this group, there is no one who takes charge. Everyone cracks their own coconuts and catches and cooks their own fish.

After some days, the mothers are complaining that a diet of coconuts upsets the kids' stomachs but they can't leave them to go fishing. The older people sit around looking lost and miserable. No one's building a shelter, let alone latrines. Then Jack has a suggestion. Instead of the bartering of fish for coconuts that's growing up, why not use the bag of nails that somehow was found among the lifeboat's stores as money? To start with everyone will be given an equal share of nails and they can be used to buy or sell fish, coconuts, fruit and personal services, like hut-building or mending clothes. To make life easier until rescue comes, he suggests, everyone ought to contribute two nails a week to Mac who will act as guard and take care of security and sanitation, and one nail a week to old Uncle Tod, who's lame and not too well but offers to organize a sort of school for the kids so the mothers can fish or hunt.

The market starts out well, though some problems do arise. The price of fish in nails is so good, everyone wants to go fishing. But how to decide who uses the lifeboat? A bargain about who has first claim, when and for how long, has to be negotiated among them. The diet of grilled fish and coconuts begins to pall. It would be good to grow some crops, but how can the growing period be financed? Someone kills a wild goat. Should it be divided equally or sold to the highest bidder? Aunt Jane falls ill. Who's to look after her? How are these collective decisions going to be taken? But at least the group is sheltered and fed, and even the old people believe that, though rescue may be slow to come, they'll be able to manage.

* * *

The next part of the story is about what might happen if, and when, the three groups find out that they're not, after all, the sole survivors from the sinking ship. This is where the reader joins in, and the desert-island stories become an allegory of political economy. We have three groups, each dominated by a different social value. Martin's group gives priority to order and security; it is a fortress society. Jerry's group of students gives priority to justice and equality; it is trying hard to work as a community. Jack's group gives priority to wealth, to efficiency in production; it is a market society. 'Ah, I see,' says the sophisticated reader at this point, 'you are setting up three competing models. The fortress society is a realist model; the commune is an idealist model and the market society is an economic model. The economists would find that most familiar. Students of politics would recognize the realist model and the sociologists would be more familiar with the idealist model.' In simpler terms, you might say that the three represented the nationalist, the socialist and the liberal approaches to the authority-market relationship that is at the heart of political economy.

There are two games, both quite instructive, that we can play at this point. One is to ask people what they think will happen when the groups encounter each other. How will each group react to the others? How, you ask, would they carry on and finish the story — always assuming that it really is a conventional desert island and that it's some time before the castaways are 'rescued'? That game can tell you something about other people's perceptions of reality, of their own experience of the real world, their particular interpretation of history and human nature. You will find, I think, that not everyone agrees about what is most probable.

They will do so even less if you play a different game and ask, not how people think the story really would end, but how they would *like* it to end. Honestly played, that should tell you something about their normative preferences, their aspirations, their idea of what constitutes a 'happy ending'. People do in fact attach different values to order and security, to wealth and to social harmony and the search for a just society.

Let me suggest a few alternative scenarios. One is that, as Martin's fortress group has put security first and organized itself for defence against a real or imagined enemy, so it is their patrols that first find out about the others. 'We can't afford to let Jack's lot get too rich, and we can't risk the mothers and the lovers slipping away to join the students', says Martin, 'we have to act first.' Catching both unprepared, Martin issues an ultimatum: 'Join us, or else ...'. From then on the story depends on whether either or both give in and accept the military authority, or whether either or both resist, even to the point of fighting if necessary. The story can also take different turns according to whether, after the takeover, the other two groups are treated magnanimously as equals, albeit in an authoritarian but secure and orderly society, or whether the victors are corrupted by power and treat the others as servants or exploit them as 'colonies'.

A different scenario starts with the students one day hunting wild goats. Venturing far from the camp, they accidentally catch sight of Martin's stockade. They figure out what they think is going on and decide they had better prepare for the worst. Freedom and equality have to be compromised. Socialism has to wait. Once organized, though, they are strong enough to issue *their* ultimatum: be liberated or we attack.

Yet another scenario lets one of the market group accidentally make the same discovery that they are not alone on the island. A meeting is called and, reluctant to lose their evidently higher style of living, they decide to double their 'security tax', appointing Mac to organize an army of paid volunteers. This team plans and carries out a surprise night attack on Martin's stockade when the watchman is asleep. So, in this scenario it is they who liberate the group from Martin's iron rule, at once increasing the size of the market and the opportunities for specialization in the division of labour. Easier still would be a second takeover of the commune, increasingly squalid and ideologically divided among themselves.

All three scenarios contemplate the possibility of violence, even among people who — literally — were once in the same boat. Is that realistic, or pessimistic? Is a peaceful co-existence among the three groups a possibility? And if so, in this miniature society of states, do the leaders begin to play a primitive game of diplomacy — making alliances, and perhaps subsequently breaking them — with one or the other group? Will they make promises of mutual defence? Will they go in for discriminatory trading?

One obvious lesson is that different societies, in ordering their

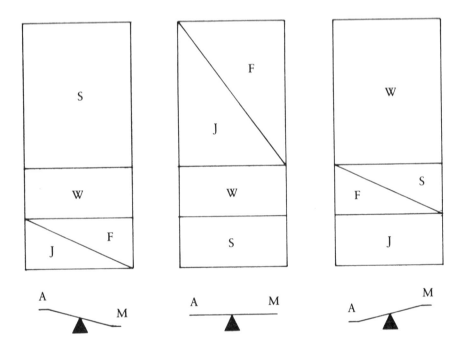

(where A = authority, M = market)

Figure A   Value preferences of three lifeboats (where S = security, W = wealth, J = justice and F = freedom to choose

political economy, will give different values priority over others. One, perceiving an external threat and/or under militaristic authority, will put security before the creation of wealth and will give a low priority to freedom for individuals or opposition groups. Even democratic states at war restrict the citizen's freedom in all sorts of ways. We can represent this crudely in Figure 1 as Model *A*. It also follows that, in the see-saw nexus between authority and market, market will tend to take the lower position.

Another society will value the creation of wealth above security and freedom (using a broad definition that includes economic freedom from the pinch of poverty and want). In Model *B* we see the see-saw tipped the opposite way, with the state (or other authority) interfering as little as possible with market forces. The use of money in this model enhances wealth through the division of labour and has in it the seed of a financial power structure through the creation and use of credit.

In yet another (as in the students' commune where freedom and justice for the individual are given joint priority) both market and authority are shrunk in importance and more evenly balanced, and the pursuit of security and wealth are given secondary importance. I have represented this equally crudely in Model C.

In an international economy in which authority is diffused and not centralized, and in which power is unequally distributed among states, the dominance of a state basing its political economy on any one of the three models naturally will, if it is able, try to bias the global political economy towards the same pattern. Capabilities, in military power in pursuit of security, in production power in pursuit of wealth, in the ability to appeal for the compliance of others on the basis of ideas and beliefs, will affect outcomes. But, the tales are trying to say, the judgement of outcomes, as of goals, is a subjective matter. Theories of international political economy are rooted in personal preferences, prejudices and experience. It is all up to the reader. My stories are like Lego, the little Danish-made building blocks that fit together in endless variation to make whatever you will. Like toys, you can learn something from them even if you do not take them very seriously.

Part I

The Study of International Political Economy

Chapter 1

The Conflict of Values and Theories

This is not a conventional textbook. Students are often given books to read which tell them what they are supposed to know, or else what they are supposed to think. This is not like that. It is going to suggest to you a way to think about the politics of the world economy, leaving it to you to choose what to think. It will leave you free to be an arch conservative or a radical Marxist, to think about the world problems from a strictly nationalist point of view or, more broadly, as a citizen of the world. You can be a free trader or a protectionist. You can favour monetarist discipline or Keynesian pump-priming. You can even decide that technological change is going too fast and needs to be slowed down because 'small is beautiful', or you can look forward to a brave new world in which technology can actually help solve some of the endemic problems that accompany the human condition. Before you there is not a set menu, not even an *à la carte* menu, but the ingredients for you to make your own choice of dish and recipe.

This is partly because I believe profoundly that the function of higher education is to open minds, not to close them. The best teachers are not those who create in their own image a crowd of uncritical acolytes and followers, obediently parroting whatever they say or write. The best are those who stimulate and help people with less experience in and exposure to a subject than themselves to develop their own ideas and to work them out by means of wider reading, more informed discussion and more disciplined thinking.

At the very start, we must clarify our ideas about the nature of theory in social science.

Theory in social science

There is a great deal of confusion about the nature of theory concerning the working of the international system, political and economic. This has resulted in a lot of 'theoretical' work which is not really theory at all, in the sense in which that word should be used and is defined in dictionaries (i.e. 'a supposition explaining something, especially one based on principles independent of the phenomenon to be explained', *Concise Oxford Dictionary*).

I preface my approach to international political economy by making four negative assumptions about what is *not* theory and three positive assumptions about what *is* theory.

The negative assumptions

Firstly, a great deal of social theory is really no more than description, often using new terms and words to describe known phenomena, or to narrate old stories without attempting theoretical explanations. Putting one event after another without explaining the causal connection, if any, cannot count as theory. Sometimes there are indeed theories underlying the narrative which are so taken for granted that they are not even made explicit.

Secondly, some so-called theory in international studies merely rearranges and describes known facts categories or in new taxonomies. This is not to say that a fresh taxonomy may not be necessary to the elaboration of a new theory. But the taxonomy by itself does not constitute an explanation and therefore does not qualify *per se* as a theory. The same is true of using new terms or words to describe known phenomena.

Thirdly, simplifying devices or concepts borrowed from other social sciences or fields of knowledge have often had their pedagogic uses in teaching, for getting across to students or readers a certain aspect of individual social behaviour. Examples are the story of the prisoners' dilemma, or a demand curve, or the graphic representation of the concept of marginal utility. But none of these by themselves explain the paradoxes or puzzles of the international system. Their current appeal to some teachers, I suspect, is that they offer a politically and morally neutral explanation (indeed, an exculpation) for the recent failures and inadequacies of the international organizations dominated by the United States in which post-war America put so much faith. Their appeal to students lies in their simplicity; it confirms what their common sense already tells them, which is that individuals are apt to act selfishly. But they are simplifying devices, not theories of social behaviour. They do not help to explain the actions of corporations, of political parties or of states in a global political economy. They do not even constitute evidence that would be relevant to a theory — in the way in which a map of the world might be relevant evidence for, say, a theory of continental drift and the existence of Old Gondwanaland. Moreover, those in the other disciplines who have developed such pedagogic devices are usually under no illusion as to their usefulness to policymakers or the possibilities of their practical application to real-life situations.

Lastly, the development of quantitative techniques applied to international studies has not advanced theory. The choice of what is to be counted is too arbitrary and the determination of what is causal and what is coincidental is too subjective to provide a basis for explanation. For the most part such methods have been used only to substantiate platitudes and to reinforce conventional wisdom concerning historical patterns of state behaviour in relation to other states.

Positive assumptions

The first is that assumption theory must seek to explain some aspect of the international system that is not easily explained by common sense. It must serve to explain a puzzle or a paradox where there is some aspect of the behaviour of individuals, groups or social institutions for which a simple explanation is not apparent. It is not necessary to look for a theory to explain why people try to leave a burning building. It *is* necessary to find a theory to explain why they patronize shops on one side of the street more than the other. International relations started with the puzzling question: why did nation-states continue to go to war when it was already clear that the economic gains made in war would never exceed the economic costs of doing so. Theories resulted. International political economy today addresses another puzzling question: why do states fail to act to regulate and stabilize an international financial system which is known to be vitally necessary to the 'real economy' but which all the experts in and out of government now agree is in dangerous need of more regulation for its own safety? Theories result. By contrast, the common use of the term 'information revolution' does not usually reflect good theory. While it notes rapid technological change, it does not postulate a clear causal connection, supported by logic or evidence, between that technological change and social change — change in political or economic relationships so great as to result in a redistribution of power and/or wealth. It does not, therefore, advance our understanding or add anything to our capacity to make causal connections and to see the consequential effects of certain phenomena.

Second, theory need not necessarily aspire to predict or to prescribe. This is where social science differs from natural science. Natural science can aspire to predict — though it does not always or necessarily do so. Much science, from astronomy to microbiology, enlarges understanding of what happens without being able to offer conclusive explanations of why it happens. Social science can never confidently predict because the irrational factors involved in human relations are too numerous, and the permutations and combinations of them are even more numerous. The one social science that has most notably aspired to predict is economics. But its record of success is so abysmal that it should make all those that seek to emulate the economists and to borrow from them try something else. Economists are particularly bad at prediction when it comes to the world economy because many of the basic theories regarding international trade and exchange rates are based on assumptions that no longer hold good in the present state of the integrated world market economy.

As to prescription, that is a matter of choice. Whether the theorist chooses to proceed from explanatory theory to policy prescription is up to him or her. He or she need not necessarily apply theory to policy-making, since policy-making necessarily involves value judgements and risk assessments that are exogenous to theory and that are better made by practical policy-makers than by irresponsible academic theorists.

Thirdly, theory should be scientific only in the sense that the theorist respects the scientific virtues of rationality and impartiality and aspires to the systematic formulation of explanatory propositions. The title 'social science' is only justifiably used to remind us that, although our subject lies closer to our emotions than the origin of rocks or the composition of molecules, and although it has to do with subjectively important questions concerning power and wealth, we must nevertheless still try to preserve a 'scientific' attitude to our studies. Indeed, many of the problems regarding theory and social science stem ultimately from the inferiority complex of social scientists towards natural scientists and, more specifically for us, the inferiority complex of political economists towards the apparent rigour of economic 'science'.

The nature of international relations

These prefatory remarks are particularly necessary because I think the literature of contemporary international political economy has, firstly, been too much dominated by the American academics and has therefore been permeated by many hidden and even unconscious value-judgements and assumptions based on American experience or on American national interests; and, secondly, because the contemporary literature, with certain rare exceptions, has been predominantly directed at far too narrow a set of questions.

Let me explain that last point a little. You will find that most of the conventional textbooks and most of the more specialized works of an analytical nature are directed primarily at what is properly called the *politics of international economic relations*. What that means is that it is directed at those problems and issues that have arisen in the relations between nations, as represented by their governments. The agenda of topics for discussion follows closely the agendas of inter-state diplomacy concerning major economic issues. These would include issues like the rules of the game in trade, the terms on which investments are made across national frontiers, the ways in which currencies adjust to one another and balance of payments deficits are financed, and the ways in which credit is made available through international capital markets and by international banks. These are some of the issues that have dominated international economic diplomacy over the last twenty years or so. You could call them the West–West issues. They have engaged the attention of the affluent industrialized countries of North America, Western Europe and Japan — roughly speaking the members of the Organization for Economic Co-operation and Development (OECD).

Since the mid-1970s or a little earlier, some writers about the politics of international economic relations have added what could be (and often are) called North–South issues. These include the amount and conditions on which aid — development assistance, so-called — in the form of grants or concessional loans are made available by rich countries to poor ones; the means by which volatile commodity prices could be stabilized and possibly raised; the means by which technology can be acquired by governments and enterprises in poor countries from governments and enterprises in rich ones; the ways in which new and insecure states can insulate themselves from the pervasive dominance of Western ideas and values purveyed by wealthy and powerful Western media — films, television, radio, newspapers and wire services, not to mention advertising. Even though the South — the poor, developing countries — has not had much success on any of these issues, they have been added to the formal agenda of international economic relations. They have thus been added to the list of things that students of international political economy are supposed to know about.

Then there are the East–West questions, issues arising out of the relations between the OECD countries on the one hand and those of the Soviet bloc — or more widely, members of the organization popularly known as Comecon (more properly titled the CMEA, or Council for Mutual Economic Assistance) — led by the Soviet Union. Though often separate, these East–West relations could be bracketed with OECD relations with the other great socialist country, the People's Republic of China (PRC). These issues are different in that there is still little real attempt at an East–West dialogue as there has been, however unproductive, at a North–South dialogue. The policy questions here have been mainly debated not between the OECD group and the CMEA group but between the dominant power on each side and its respective allies.

Logically, the politics of international economic relations should also complete the circle of combinations by including issues between the East and the South, between the major socialist countries and the less developed countries, or LDCs. But these links are often excluded, chiefly because there is neither much interest in, nor much information on them, in the United States.

Even at their most extensive, the 'directional' or 'azimuthal' agendas that exist are still far too restrictive and so do not really qualify as the study of political economy. The literature on the politics of international economic relations reflects the concerns of governments, not people. It tends always to overweight the interests of the most powerful governments. Scholars who accept this definition of the subject thus become the servants of state bureaucracies, not independent thinkers or critics.

What I am suggesting here is a way to synthesize politics and economics by means of structural analysis of the effects of states — or more properly of any kind of political authority — on markets and, conversely, of market forces on states. As Martin Staniland has rightly observed, it is not enough to say (as I and many others have done) that politics takes too little notice of economics or conversely, that economics takes too little notice of politics (Staniland, 1985). Realizing that there is a connection between the two is not enough. As Staniland says, appreciating that in poker there is a connection between a card game and winning money is not the same as knowing how to play poker and win the game! Many people have written of the need to achieve a synthesis. Few have achieved one.

The main problem in attempting such a synthesis lies in the very nature of economics and politics. Economics — as every first-year student is told — is about the use of scarce resources for unlimited wants. How best to make use of those scarce resources is fundamentally a question of efficiency. The question is, 'What is the most efficient allocation of resources?' Supplementary to it are a whole lot of related questions about how markets behave, which government policies are best, and how different parts of the economic system function — always in terms of their efficiency or inefficiency. 'Market failure' of one kind or another, for example, is the subject of much economic inquiry and research.

Politics, though, is about providing public order and public goods. In some universities, indeed, the department of politics is actually called the department of government. Students of politics are expected to know about conflicting theories of what sort of order is best, and how it is to be achieved and maintained. They are usually expected to know a good deal about the political institutions of their own country — and of some others. Some may choose to specialize in the study of world politics. But here too the ruling questions tend to concern the maintenance of order and peace and the provision of minimal public goods, together with the management of issues and conflicts arising between them. The study of trade relations between states, for example, is frequently justified, explicitly or implicitly, on the grounds that these may give rise to conflicts of interest, and perhaps to trade wars, and that these may spill over into military conflicts. There is very scant historical evidence to support such an assumption, but the reason for including such issues in the study of world politics is revealing. Almost all the standard texts on international politics assume the maintenance of order to be the prime if not the only *problématique* of the study.[1]

The consequence is that each discipline tends to take the other for granted. Markets are studied in economics on the assumption that they are not going to be disrupted by war, revolution or other civil disorders. Government and the panoply of law and the administration of justice are taken for granted. Politics, meanwhile, assumes that the economy will continue to function reasonably smoothly — whether it is a command economy run according to the decisions of an army of bureaucrats or a market economy reflecting the multiple decisions taken by prudent and profit-maximizing producers and canny consumers. Politics in the liberal Western tradition recognizes a trade-off between order and liberty and between security and justice — if you want more of the one, you may have to sacrifice some of the other. But only rarely does it take in the further dimension of efficiency — the ability of the sustaining economy to produce the wealth necessary for both order and justice. If you want both more wealth *and* order, must justice and liberty be sacrificed? That *problématique* is addressed by the radical left; especially has this been true of the Latin-American writers of what is called the bureaucratic–authoritarian school who have suggested that there is a connection between political systems and party alignments in developing countries and the expansion of a capitalist market-oriented economy and the income distribution patterns that it tends to generate. But on the whole it is still true that most political science assumes a rather static economic backcloth to politics and that the dynamism so apparent in the real economic world is too often overlooked (Strange, 1970: 304–15).

That cannot be said of many distinguished writers who have come to political economy from outside the main streams of liberal economics and politics. Robert Cox, for instance, came from the study of industrial, labour–management relations and the comparative study of labour movements in different countries. He has followed up some seminal and much-quoted articles with a magisterial work, *Production, Power and World Order* (1987), that seeks to analyse the connections between the three levels of the world system, the social and economic relations resulting from production structures, the political nature of power in the state, and, overall, the nature of the prevailing world order. Development economists like Gunnar Myrdal, Dudley Seers, Gerald Helleiner, Arthur Lewis, Walt Rostow, Hans Singer and Al Hirschman — not to mention Raul Prebisch — have been well aware of the impossibility of divorcing politics from economics. So have the historical sociologists like Michael Mann, Jonathan Hall, Christopher Chase-Dunn and others, following a mainly French tradition drawing on the work of Francois Perroux and Fernand Braudel. We also owe great debts to the economic historians who have followed the trails blazed by Max Weber, Joseph Schumpeter, Karl Polanyi, Simon Kuznets and Carlo Cipolla. Not least in their contributions to the further development of international political economy are the business historians on the right — Alfred Chandler, John Dunning and Leslie Hannah — and the radical historians on the left — Immanuel Wallerstein, Michael Barrett Brown, Ernst Mandel, Fred Block and Teddy Brett.

But for the rest, all we have, so far, are competing *doctrines* – sets of normative ideas about the goals to which state policy should be directed and how politics and economics (or, more accurately, states and markets) *ought* to be related to one another. This is enough to satisfy ideologues who have already made up their minds. They may be realists who want to think narrowly about the means and ends of national policy at home and abroad; or they may be liberal economists who want to think about how the world economy could be most efficiently organized, or they may be radicals or Marxists who want to think about how greater equity and justice could be achieved for the underdogs.

What we need is different. It is a framework of analysis, a method of diagnosis of the human condition as it is, or as it was, affected by economic, political and social circumstances. This is the necessary precondition for prescription, for forming opinions about what could and should be done about it. For each doctrine has its own custom-built method of analysis, so planned that it leads inevitably to the conclusion it is designed to lead to.

Thus it is that students of world politics or of international political economy are often asked to choose between three set menus.[2] The way the subject is often presented to them does not allow them to pick an appetizer from the realists, a main course from the liberals and a dessert from the Marxists or radicals. Nor is there any real debate between the authors of the set menus. Each begins their analysis from a particular assumption that determines the kind of question they ask, and therefore the answer they find. They are like three toy trains on separate tracks, travelling from different starting-points and ending at different (predetermined) destinations, and never crossing each other's path.

What we should *not* try to look for, because it does not exist and therefore cannot be found, is an all-embracing theory that pretends to enable us, even partially, to predict what will happen in the world economy tomorrow. The ambition in the social sciences to imitate the natural sciences and to discover and elaborate 'laws' of the international system, patterns so regular they govern social, political and economic behaviour, is and always has been a wild goose chase. Much valuable time and strenuous effort has gone into it and most of both the time and the effort could have been better spent on re-learning some of the basic axioms about human vice and human folly, about the perversity of policies and the arbitrariness of coincidences. This is not to say that a social 'scientist' should not be as fiercely uncompromising in the search for truth as any physicist or geologist. But it is a different kind of truth and it is not best served by aspiring to the unattainable or promising that which cannot in the nature of things be delivered.

What we have to do, in short, is to find a method of analysis of the world economy that opens the door of student or reader choice and allows more pragmatism in prescription; and, secondly, a method of analysis that breaks down the dividing walls between the ideologues and makes possible some communication and even debate between them.

I believe it can be done. We have to start by thinking about the basic values which human beings seek to provide through social organization, i.e. wealth, security, freedom and justice. We can then recognize that different societies (or the same societies at different times), while producing some of each of the four values, nevertheless give a different order of priority to each of them. All societies need to produce food, shelter and other material goods; but some will give the production of wealth in material form the highest priority. All societies will be organized to give the individual some greater security from the violence and abuse of others, both from others within that society and others from outside it. But some will put order and security first. Indeed, the two great advantages of social organization over life in individual isolation is that association with other humans both increases the possibility of wealth and adds to personal security. Social organization does, however, entail certain choices regarding freedom, or the individual's right to choose; and regarding the relative justice of one set of arrangements over another. An isolated individual like Robinson Crusoe has no problems with these two values of freedom and justice; the only limits on his freedom of choice are set by nature and his own capability. His own liberty is not constrained or compromised by someone else's. Nor does any question of justice arise — except perhaps between his claims to life or resources and those of plants or animals — for there is no other human claimant on resources whose claims need to be arbitrated.

Once you have a society, therefore, you have arrangements made which provide *some* wealth, *some* security, *some* element of freedom of choice for the members or groups of them, and *some* element of justice. These basic values are like chemical elements of hydrogen, oxygen, carbon and nitrogen. Combined in different proportions, they will give quite different chemical compounds. In the same way, a cook can take flour, eggs, milk and fat and make different kinds of cakes, pancakes, biscuits or cookies by combining them in different ways and different proportions.

Societies therefore differ from each other in the proportions in which they combine the different basic values. That was the simple but important point behind the desert-island tales in the prologue. Ideal societies, too, will differ, just as real ones do, in the priority given to particular basic values and in the proportion in which the different basic values are mixed. Plato and Hobbes wanted more order; both lived in troubled and chaotic times. Rousseau and Marx wanted more justice; both were offended by the inequalities they saw around them. Adam Smith, Maynard Keynes and Milton Friedman all thought — despite their differences — that it was important to generate more wealth. Hayek and John Stuart Mill wanted more freedom – though the trouble with freedom is that, more than the other values, it often involves a zero-sum game: more freedom for me means less for you; national liberation for one ethnic group may mean enslavement for others.

Thus, whether we are anthropologists studying a society remote in every way from the one we are familiar with, or whether we are comparative political economists comparing, let us say, socialist societies and market societies, or whether we are international political economists studying a world system that is both a single global social and economic system and, coexisting with it, a series of national societies, we can in each case apply the same analytical method of political economy. What values, we can ask, do these arrangements rate the highest? And which do they rate the lowest? Secondary to that, there are the old questions of all political analysis, 'Who gets what out of it? Who benefits, who loses? Who carries the risks and who is spared from risk? Who gets the opportunities and who is denied an opportunity — whether for goods and services or more fundamentally a share of all the values, not only wealth, but also security, the freedom to choose for themselves, some measure of justice from the rest of society?'

The definition, therefore, that I would give to the study of international political economy is that it concerns the social, political and economic arrangements affecting the global systems of production, exchange and distribution, and the mix of values reflected therein. Those arrangements are not divinely ordained, nor are they the fortuitous outcome of blind chance. Rather they are the result of human decisions taken in the context of man-made institutions and sets of self-set rules and customs.

It follows that the study of international political economy cannot avoid a close concern with causes. Consequences today — for states, for corporations, for individuals — imply causes yesterday. There is no way that contemporary international political economy can be understood without making some effort to dig back to its roots, to peer behind the curtain of passing time into what went before. Of course, there is no one 'correct' interpretation of history. No historian is an impartial, totally neutral witness, either in the choice of evidence or in its presentation. But that does not mean that history can be safely ignored. Nor should it be too narrowly or parochially conceived. There may be just as much for Europeans and Americans to learn from the political and economic history of India, China or Japan as from that of Western Europe and North America. One important lesson that is too often forgotten when the history of thought — political thought or economic thought — is divorced from the political and economic history of events, is that perceptions of the past always have a powerful influence on perceptions of present problems and future solutions. Happily, I think, this acute awareness of the historical dimension of international political economy has now taken as strong a hold in American scholarship as it has always had in Europe. Because Europeans live in places where they are surrounded by reminders of the past — a past that stretches back, not a few hundreds of years, as in even the longest white-settled parts of the United States, but thousands of years — it is easier for Europeans to remain sensitive to this historical dimension. Now, a generation of American political economists share that sensitivity.

Thirdly, besides present arrangements and past causes, international political economy must be concerned with future possibilities. In my opinion, the future cannot be predicted; but it cannot be ignored. What, the political economist must ask, are the options that will be open in future to states, to enterprises, to individuals? Can the world be made wealthier? Safer and more stable and orderly? More just than it used to be? These are important and legitimate questions. Such questions inspire the interest of many people in the subject. Some of these people will not rest until they think they have found the answers. Others, less sure, will be content to clarify the issues and the options, knowing that their personal opinion of optimal solutions will not necessarily carry the day in the real world of politics and markets, but feeling that nevertheless they have a moral responsibility to attempt a cool and rational analysis based on reading, listening and thinking. Although final decisions may be taken in the real world on the basis of value preferences and power relationships, perceptions and ideas also play some part and these at least can be susceptible to rational presentation of the costs and risks of alternative options. To my mind, the difference between the normative, prescriptive approach to international political economy and the reflective, analytical approach is a matter of personal temperament and individual experience, training and so forth. There is no right or wrong about it. The study of international political economy, like that of international relations and foreign policy, has room for both.

The way things are managed, how they got to be managed in that particular way, and what choices this leaves realistically open for the future, these three aspects or *problématiques* of political economy are implicit in the semantic origins of the word 'economics'. It derives from the Greek *oikonomia*, which meant a household — typically in the ancient world, not a small nuclear family but rather a patriarchal settlement of an extended family and its slaves, living off the crops and flocks of the surrounding land. The management of the *oikonomia* thus included the choices made in cropping and in breeding, in the provision of security from attack or robbery, in the customary relations between men and women, old and young, the teaching of children and the administration of justice in disputed matters. In other words, it was rather more about politics than economics.

'Political economy' as a current term in French, Italian or English only came into general use towards the end of the eighteenth century, when it came to mean, more narrowly and specifically, that part of political management that related to the prosperity of the state and the ordering — as we would say — of its 'economic' affairs. It was, in this more restricted sense, related to the nation-state of modern times, that Adam Smith, whose *Wealth of Nations* appeared in 1776, understood the term. In fact, before Adam Smith, the French had shown a more active interest than the English in political economy. French rulers and writers had already perceived the close connection between the wealth of the nation and the power of the state. Like Thomas Jefferson in America, the French physiocrats of the eighteenth century thought that agriculture was the basis of national wealth and saw the management of agriculture as the first *problématique* of political economy. Adam Smith, on the contrary, saw trade and industry as the basis of national wealth, narrow mercantilism as the chief obstacle to its growth and the *problématique* of political economy as how best to achieve this while defending the realm and managing the currency. History proved Smith right and the physiocrats wrong, so that it was in Scotland and England that the main debates of political economy in the next century were conducted, not in France.

And it was the British too who were mainly responsible for letting the term 'political economy' fall into disuse for more than half a century, until about the 1960s. The subject had become so complex and arcane that when a book appeared in 1890 that set out to explain what went on in economic matters in simple, everyday terms that anyone could understand, its author, Alfred Marshall, coined a new word to distinguish it from political economy. He called his book *Principles of Economics*. Only in the 1960s did the study of political economy (outside of radical left-wing circles) once again become both popular and legitimate. And then it was more because of a concern with the management of the world economy than with the management of particular national economies. A seminal book by an American economist, Richard Cooper, appeared in 1968 called *The Economics of Interdependence*. It developed an argument in favour of multilateral co-operation, especially by industrialized liberal democracies led by the United States, on the grounds that the full benefits of international economic integration and interdependence in trade and finance would be lost if there were a failure so to coordinate national policies as to find an agreed and efficient way of managing the world economy[3].

Cooper's lead was followed more readily by American scholars interested in international organization than by his fellow economists. By the early 1970s, they began to ask why it was that the apparently stable and set 'rules of the game' that had prevailed in international economic relations in the 1950s and 1960s seemed to be less and less observed in the 1970s. The erosion of what came to be called — in a rather strange use of the word — international 'regimes' became the dominant *problématique* of international political economy in the United States. As defined by Stephen Krasner in an edited collection of papers devoted to this theme, regimes were 'sets of explicit or implicit principles, norms, rules and decision-making procedures around which actor expectations converge' (Krasner, 1983).

Krasner's original argument in introducing the papers was that regimes were an intervening variable between structural power and outcomes — an argument much closer to mine than to much of the subsequent American work on the subject of different international regimes. The latter has often tended to take the way things are managed in the international market economy as given, without enquiring too much into the underlying reasons of why it was certain principles, norms and rules and not others that prevailed. Or, if research did ask the 'why' questions, the range of possible explanations was too narrowly drawn. An influential study by Keohane and Nye of US–Canadian and US–Australian relations in the 'issue-areas' — another term drawn from international relations — of money and ocean management called *Power and Interdependence* listed the change in states' relative political power, or in other words the political structure, as a possible explanation for regime change, but omitted changes in economic power and in economic structures, paying attention only to economic processes, which was a much narrower factor altogether (Keohane and Nye, 1977).

Concentration on international organizations and on the politics of international economic relations has tended to let inter-governmental relations overshadow the equally important transnational relations, that is to say, relations across national frontiers between social and political groups or economic enterprises on either side of a political frontier, or between any of these and the government of another state. Corporations, banks, religious leaders, universities and scientific communities are all participants in certain important kinds of transnational relations. And in such transnational relations, the relationship across frontiers with some governments will be far more important in determining the outcomes in political economy than will relations with other governments. For example, it is a recognized fact in business circles that decisions taken by the US Supreme Court, and sometimes by lesser courts, or by some federal or state agency of the United States, may be of crucial importance far beyond the border of the country. The 'global reach' of US government is one of the features of the contemporary international political economy that is easily overlooked by too close attention to international organizations and so-called international regimes.[4]

If the omission or underrating of transnational relations — especially economic relations — was one important deficiency of political economy based on the regimes' *problématique*, another serious one was that it did not absolutely require the researcher or the student to ask whose power those 'principles, norms, rules and decisionmaking processes' most reflected. Nor did it insist on asking about the sources of such power: was it based on coercive force, on success in the market and on wealth, or on the adherence of others to an ideology, a belief system or some set of ideas?

By not requiring these basic structural questions about power to be addressed, and by failing to insist that the values given predominant emphasis in any international 'regime' should always be explicitly identified, the presumption has often gone unchallenged that any regime is better than none. It is too often assumed that the erosion or collapse of a set of norms or rules is always a bad thing, to be regretted, and if possible reversed. Such an assumption takes the *status quo ante* the erosion to be preferable to the *ex post* situation. But that assumption unconsciously overweights the value of order and stability over the other values, and especially the order and stability of international arrangements for the world economy designed and partially imposed in the period after 1945. It is easy enough to see why. These post-war 'regimes' were set in place by the United States taking a lead where no other state could do so. It was natural for American scholars to assume that these arrangements were admirable and well-designed, without questioning too closely the kind of power they reflected or the mix of values they inferred as desirable — not only for the United States but for all right-thinking people the world over.

By contrast, the approach that I am proposing, by concentrating on the authority–market and the market–authority nexus, and by directing attention to the four basic values of security, wealth, freedom and justice, ought to succeed in highlighting the non-regimes as much as the regimes, the non-decisions and the failures to take a decision, which, no less than active policy-making have affected — and still affect — the outcomes of the international political economy.

It is also more likely to reveal the 'hidden agenda' of issues that are of little interest to governments, where there is no international agreement, no organization, no secretariat to publicise the question and not necessarily any accepted norms or principles around which actor perceptions converge. The failure to do this — which also reveals the bias in favour of the status quo — is one of the major weaknesses of the regimes approach. For, among the many different ways in which power may be exercised in the international political economy — a question to which we now turn in the next chapter – the power to keep an issue off the agenda of discussion or to see that, if discussed, nothing effective is done about it, is not the least important.

Chapter 2

Power in The World Economy

It is impossible to study political economy and especially international political economy without giving close attention to the role of power in economic life. Each system of political economy — the political economy of the United States compared with that of the Soviet Union, the political economy of the states of Western Europe in the eighteenth century compared with the highly integrated political economy of the world today — differs, as I have tried to explain, in the relative priority it gives to each of the four basic values of society. Each reflects a different mix in the proportional weight given to wealth, order, justice and freedom. What decides the nature of the mix is, fundamentally, a question of power.

It is power that determines the relationship between authority and market. Markets cannot play a dominant role in the way in which a political economy functions unless allowed to do so by whoever wields power and possesses authority. The difference between a private-enterprise, market-based economy and a state-run, command-based economy lies not only in the amount of freedom given by authority to the market operators, but also in the context within which the market functions. And the context, too, reflects a certain distribution of power. Whether it is a secure or an insecure context, whether it is stable or unstable, booming or depressed, reflects a series of decisions taken by those with authority. Thus it is not only the direct power of authority over markets that matters; it is also the indirect effect of authority on the context or surrounding conditions within which the market functions.

In the study of political economy it is not enough, therefore, to ask where authority lies — who has power. It is important to ask why they have it — what is the source of power.[1] Is it command of coercive force? Is it the possession of great wealth? Is it moral authority, power derived from the proclamation of powerful ideas that have wide appeal, are accepted as valid and give legitimacy to the proclaimers, whether politicians, religious leaders or philosophers? In many political economies, those who exercise authority, who decide how big a role shall be given to markets, and the rules under which the markets work will derive power from all three sources — from force, from wealth and from ideas. In others, different groups will derive different sorts of power from different sources. They will have rather different power-bases and will be acting upon the political economy at the same time but possibly in opposed directions.

The point is only that it is impossible to arrive at the end result, the ultimate goal of study and analysis in international political economy without giving explicit or implicit answers to these fundamental questions about how power has been used to shape the political economy and the way in which it distributes costs and benefits, risks and opportunities to social groups, enterprises and organizations within the system. Many writers on political economy will avoid making their answers explicit, either because they do not see how important it is to their conclusions, and especially policy recommendations, or because they assume that readers share their implicit assumptions about who has power and why, and how it is used. But if, like me, you are trying to write about political economy in a way that will be useful to people who have very different value preferences, and who do not necessarily agree about what kinds of power are really important and decisive, then it is particularly important to try to clarify the assumptions about power that underlie a particular view, such as mine, of the nature of the international political economy and how it works. That is what I shall try to do in this chapter. I shall try to draw a kind of sketch-map of the landscape as I see it, explaining in the process why it is that I have given particular attention in the rest of the book to what I see as the most outstanding features of the landscape, both those of the first order (as in Part II, Chapters, 3, 4, 5 and 6), and those of a still important but secondary order (as in Part III, Chapters, 7, 8, 9, 10 and 11). Whether the reader is trying just to understand why the international political economy results in the particular who-gets-what, the particular mix of basic values that we can observe around us, or whether he or she is seeking solutions and policy descriptions to change the system does not matter. Both have to start with an examination of power.

Structural and relational power

The argument in this book is that there are two kinds of power exercised in a political economy — structural power and relational power — but that in the competitive games now being played out in the world system between states and between economic enterprises, it is increasingly structural power that counts far more than relational power. Relational power, as conventionally described by realist writers of textbooks on international relations, is the power of A to get to B to do something they would not otherwise do. In 1940 German relational power made Sweden allow German troops to pass through her 'neutral' territory. US relational power over Panama dictated the terms for the Panama Canal. Structural power, on the other hand, is the power to shape and determine the structures of the global political economy within which other states, their political institutions, their economic enterprises and (not least) their scientists and other professional people have to operate. This structural power, as I shall explain it, means rather more than the power to set the agenda of discussion or to design (in American academic language) the international regimes of rules and customs that are supposed to govern international economic relations. That is one aspect of structural power, but not all of it. US structural power over the way in which wheat or corn (maize to the British) is traded allows buyers and sellers to hedge by dealing in 'futures'; even the Soviet Union, when it buys grain, accepts this way of doing things. Lloyds of London is an authority in the international market for insurance; it allows big risks to be 'sold' by small insurers or underwriters to big reinsurance operators, thus centralizing the system in those countries and with those operators large enough to accept and manage the big risks. Anyone who needs insurance has to go along with this way of doing things. Structural power, in short, confers the power to decide how things shall be done, the power to shape frameworks within which states relate to each other, relate to people, or relate to corporate enterprises. The relative power of each party in a relationship is more, or less, if one party is also determining the surrounding structure of the relationship.

It seems to me that this is a much more useful distinction for the understanding and analysis of power in political economy than the distinction between economic power and political power. We may say that someone has economic power if they have a lot of money to spend: they have purchasing power. They may also have economic power if they have something to sell which other people badly want. Such economic power will be all the greater if they are the only ones able to sell it, if, in short, they have monopoly or oligopoly power. They may also have economic power if they can provide the finance or investment capital to enable others to produce or to sell a service. Banks, by controlling credit, have economic power. Equally, we can say that people have political power if they control the machinery of state or any other institution and can use it to compel obedience or conformity to their wishes and preferences from others. The trouble with this distinction, however, is that when it comes to particular situations — particularly in the international political economy — it is very difficult (as some later examples will show) to draw a clear distinction between political and economic power. It is impossible to have political power without the power to purchase, to command production, to mobilize capital. And it is impossible to have economic power without the sanction of political authority, without the legal and physical security that can only be supplied by political authority. Those with most economic power are no longer — or only very rarely — single individuals. They are corporations or state enterprises that have set up their own hierarchies of authority and chains of command in which decisions are taken that are essentially political more than economic. I do as the company president or the managing director says, not because I shall gain economically, but because he has the authority to command me, a middle manager or a shopfloor worker. Mine not to reason why — just as if he were the general and I am a private soldier.

The next part of the argument is that structural power is to be found not in a single structure but in four separate distinguishable but related structures. This view differs from the Marxist or neo-Marxist view of structural power which lays great stress on only one of my four structures — the structure of production. It differs from Robert Cox's interpretation of structural power which also attaches prime importance to the structure of production (Cox, 1987). Cox sees production as the basis of social and political power in the society. The state, therefore, is the embodiment in political terms of the authority of the class or classes in control of the production structure. States, however, live in an anarchical world order. The image, or model, in that interpretation is a club sandwich, or a layer cake, in which production is the bottom layer and world order the top layer, with the state in between both, responding to change both in the world order and in the production structure on which it is based. My image is rather of a four-faceted triangular pyramid or tetrahedron (i.e. a figure made up of four planes or triangular faces). Each touches the other three and is held in place by them. Each facet represents one of the four structures through which power is exercised on particular relationships. If the model could be made of transparent glass or plastic, you could represent particular relationships being played out, as on a stage, within the four walls of the four-sided pyramid. No one facet is always or necessarily more important than the other three. Each is supported, joined to and held up by the other three.

These four, interacting structures are not peculiar to the world system, or the global political economy, as you may prefer to call it. The sources of superior structural power are the same in very small human groups, like a family or a remote village community, as they are in the world at large. The four sources, corresponding to the four sides of the transparent pyramid, are: control over security; control over production; control over credit; and control over knowledge, beliefs and ideas.

Thus, structural power lies with those in a position to exercise control over (i.e. to threaten or to preserve) people's security, especially from violence. It lies also with those able to decide and control the manner or mode of production of goods and services for survival. Thirdly, it lies — at least in all advanced economies, whether state-capitalist, private-capitalist or a mix of both — with those able to control the supply and distribution of credit. Such control of credit is important because, through it, purchasing power can be acquired without either working for it or trading for it, but it is acquired in the last resort on the basis of reputation on the borrower's side and confidence on the lender's.

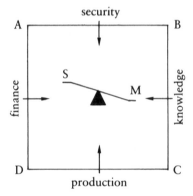

Or, in three dimensions

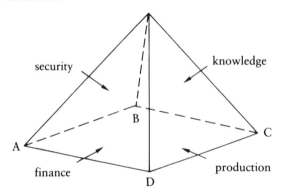

But since each structure affects the other three, but none necessarily dominates:

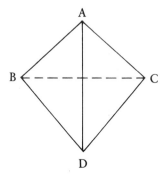

Here, ACD represents the production structure; ABD the security structure; ABC the finance structure; and BCD the knowledge structure.

Figure 2.1 Four structures around the state–market see-saw

Fourthly and lastly, structural power can also be exercised by those who possess knowledge, who can wholly or partially limit or decide the terms of access to it. This structural power in particular does not easily fit into the layer-cake, club-sandwich model because it may very easily lie in part beyond the range and scope of the state or any other 'political' authority. Yet its importance in political economy, though not easy to define or describe, is not to be underrated.

The bottom line, or conclusion, of this approach to the question of power in the international political economy seems to me to throw serious doubt on an important assumption of much contemporary writing on international political economy, especially in the United States. The assumption is that the United States has lost hegemonic power in the system and that this is why, in plain terms, the world economy is in such a state of instability, uncertainty and even disorder that economic forecasts are unreliable, if not impossible; it is why there is such widespread gloom and even despair over the prospects of solving contemporary problems of international economic relations. But, to me, using this model or analytical framework, the conclusion seems inevitable that the United States government and the corporations dependent upon it have *not* in fact lost structural power in and over the system. They may have changed their mind about how to use it, but they have not lost it. Nor, taking the four structures of power together, are they likely to do so in the foreseeable future. Not all readers will agree with this conclusion of mine. But even if they do not, I would still contend that their assessment of power in the international political economy will be more realistic if they adopt a structural approach such as, or similar to, the one outlined above and developed later in the book than if they stay with conventional notions of relational power — still less if, with the theoretical economists, they try to ignore power altogether.

The rest of this book is an attempt to explore and develop each of these aspects or sources of structural power in the world political economy. It is essentially an attempt to break right away from the politics of international economic relations approach which I find biased and constricting. It tries to develop an alternative approach based on the four fundamental sources of structural power. Once these are understood, it can be shown that certain subjects of discussion in international political economy, such as trade, aid, energy or international transport systems, are actually secondary structures. They are not as they are by accident but are shaped by the four basic structures of security, production, finance and knowledge. If I wanted to write a long, exhaustive text, I would have added a further section dealing with some of the different sectors of the international economy, for example cereals, fish, timber, minerals, cars, arms, computers, textiles, toys, films, advertising, insurance or databank services. But since the whole purpose of the book is not, like most texts, to instruct readers in what I think they should know about international political economy but to demonstrate by example the sort of questions I think they should address in studying it, I did not think an exhaustive series of sectoral studies was either necessary or (if the book were to b? kept manageably short) desirable.

Four sources of structural power

Before proceeding to illustrate with examples this notion of four-sided structural power, it may be helpful to elaborate a little the four sources just listed from which it is derived. They are no more than a statement of common sense. But common sense has often been obscured by abstruse academic discussion about the nature of 'state' or by definitions of 'power' so abstract, or so narrowly based on the experience of one place, one society, one period of human experience, that a re-statement of the fairly obvious seems necessary. (Readers confident of their own common sense can easily skip the next few paragraphs.)

First, so long as the possibility of violent conflict threatens personal security, he who offers others protection against that threat is able to exercise power in other non-security matters like the distribution of food or the administration of justice. The greater the perceived threat to security, the higher price will be willingly paid and the greater risk accepted that the same defence force that gives protection will itself offer another kind of threat to those it claims to protect. Within states, it has been those that felt themselves most insecure, that perceived themselves as 'revolutionary' states challenging the accepted order and the prevailing ideology of their time or region that have been most prepared to pay the costs and accept the risks of military government and 'state security' forces such as secret police.

Who decides what shall be produced, by whom, by what means and with what combination of land, labour, capital and technology and how each shall be rewarded is as fundamental a question in political economy as who decides the means of defence against insecurity. As Cox and a great many radical and left-wing writers have demonstrated, the mode of production is the basis of class power over other classes. The class in a position to decide or to change the mode of production can use its structural power over production to consolidate and defend its social and political power, establishing constitutions, setting up political institutions and laying down legal and administrative processes and precedents that make it hard for others to challenge or upset. Now that an ever-growing proportion of goods and services produced throughout the world are produced in response, in one way or another, to the world economy and not to local needs, tastes or demands, the structural power over production has become the base for social and political changes that cut right across national frontiers. The old territorial frontiers of the state used also to separate, far more than they do now, not only the national culture and language from that of neighbours, but also national social structures and the national economy. Now, the territorial limits of state power remain but the other frontiers are crumbling so that structural power over production geared to a world market becomes that of increasing cultural, linguistic and ideological influence.

The third leg, or facet, of structural power is, admittedly, rather more peculiar to advanced industrialized economies, whether socialist or capitalist, than it is to small communities or less developed economies. But finance — the control of credit — is the facet which has perhaps risen in importance in the last quarter century more rapidly than any other and has come to be of decisive importance in international economic relations and in the competition of corporate enterprises. It sometimes seems as if its complex manifestations are too technical and arcane to be easily understood even by those professionally engaged in banking and finance. Yet its power to determine outcomes — in security, in production and in research — is enormous. It is the facet of structural power least well understood by the Marxists and radicals who have written most cogently about structural power over production. Many of them still entertain the old-fashioned notion that before you invest you must accumulate capital by piling up this year's profit on last year's, that capitalism somehow depends on the accumulation of capital. What they do not understand is that what is invested in an advanced economy is not money but credit, and that credit can be created. It does not have to be accumulated. Therefore, whoever can so gain the confidence of others in their ability to create credit will control a capitalist — or indeed a socialist — economy. So large have the financial requirements of industry and even of agriculture become in a high-technology age that there would have been none of the economic growth the world has seen in the past four or five decades if we had had to wait for profits to be accumulated. They could *only* have been financed through the creation of credit.

Fourthly, and finally, knowledge is power and whoever is able to develop or acquire and to deny the access of others to a kind of knowledge respected and sought by others; and whoever can control the channels by which it is communicated to those given access to it, will exercise a very special kind of structural power. In past times priests and sages have often exercised such dominance over kings and generals. It is a structural power less easy to keep control over, more subtle and more elusive. For that reason priesthoods in every religion have hedged their power even more jealously than military castes and ranks of nobility. Keeping the laity out and in ignorance has been a necessary means of preserving structural power over them. Today the knowledge most sought after for the acquisition of relational power and to reinforce other kinds of structural power (i.e. in security matters, in production and in finance) is technology. The advanced technologies of new materials, new products, new systems of changing plants and animals, new systems of collecting, storing and retrieving information — all these open doors to both structural power and relational power.

What is common to all four kinds of structural power is that the possessor is able to change the range of choices open to others, without apparently putting pressure directly on them to take one decision or to make one choice rather than others. Such power is less 'visible'. The range of options open to the others will be extended by giving them opportunities they would not otherwise have had. And it may be restricted by imposing costs or risks upon them larger than they would otherwise have faced, thus making it less easy to make some choices while making it more easy to make others. When Mother or Father says, 'If you're a good boy and study hard, we'll give you a bicycle for your birthday', the boy is still free to chose between studying hard and going out to play with friends. But the choice is weighted more heavily in favour of studying by the parents' structural power over the family budget. To take another example from international political economy, the big oil companies had the power to look for oil and sell it. The oil states in the 1950s and 1960s could offer them concessions. But the royalties the companies could offer on production in return gave them structural power over the governments. The governments could choose to forego the extra revenue. But it was so large in relation to any other possible source of income that the range of choice, the weighting of options, was substantially changed by the structural power over oil production and oil marketing. It was only when the oil-producing states gained access to knowledge about the oil business, and when they had used the royalties from the companies to consolidate their financial power, that they could offer a partial challenge to the companies' structural power over production. Until then, as the examples of Iran in 1951 and Indonesia later indicated, the cost of expelling the companies was, for most, unacceptably high.

Another point about my four-faceted plastic pyramid image is that it is significant that each facet touches the other three. Each interacts with the others. It should also be represented as balancing on one of the points, rather than resting on a single base. There is a sense in which each facet — security, production, finance and knowledge-plus-beliefs is basic for the others. But to represent the others as resting permanently on any one more than on the others suggests that one is dominant. This is not necessarily or always so.

For example, the realist school of thought in international relations has held that in the last resort military power and the ability to use coercive force to compel the compliance of others must always prevail. *In the last resort*, this is undeniably true. But in the real world, not every relationship is put under such pressure. Not every decision is pushed to such extremes. There are many times and places where decisions are taken in which coercive force, though it plays some part in the choices made, does not play the whole, and is not the only significant source of power.

Some examples

Let me suggest a few illustrations of the way in which structural power can be derived simultaneously from more than one source, from more sides than one of the plastic pyramid. In 1948, the United States had only recently demonstrated in Europe its superiority in conventional force over any other European power except the Soviet Union. And at Hiroshima and Nagasaki it had demonstrated that its *unconventional* power was superior to the Soviet Union and all others through its (temporary) monopoly of atomic weapons of mass destruction. But that kind of strategic power was not enough by itself to set the wheels of economic life turning again in Western Europe. Without the productive power to supply food and capital goods for the reconstruction of European industry, and without the financial power to offer credits in universally acceptable dollars, the United States could not have exercised the power over the recipients of Marshall Aid that it did. Nor was American structural power based only on dominance of the security structure, the production structure and the financial structure. Its authority was reinforced by the belief outside America that the United States fully intended to use its power to create a better post-war world for others as well as for its own people. Roosevelt had pronounced the Four Freedoms as America's war aims, had invited the United Nations to San Francisco as an assurance that the United States would not again, as in 1920, change its mind. President Truman had followed up in his inaugural address to the Congress with the firm promise of American help to peoples seeking freedom and a better material life. Moral authority based on faith in American intentions powerfully reinforced its other sources of structural power.

A very different example of the power derived in part from the force of ideas would be that exercised within and beyond Iran after the fall of the Shah by Ayatollah Khomeini and his followers. The idea that the Shah, out of greed and lust for power, had fallen captive not only to a foreign country but to a culture and a materialistic belief system alien and inimical to traditional Islamic values had contributed powerfully to the collapse of his government and his own exile. But the power of the ayatollahs in defending and promoting Islamic virtues would have been constrained if they had not also gained control over the state and the armed forces sufficient to confirm their authority both within the country and beyond. Undoubtedly, the power of ideas was indispensible but it could only be used to affect outcomes in conjunction with military capability and economic resources.

Structural power, derived in part from ideas, in part from coercive force and in part from wealth, is not confined to states and those who seize the power of government. For example, the Mafia has used the threat of violence — and violence itself — to ensure obedience within its ranks. It has extracted a kind of tax from those it claimed to protect. But its strength over a surprisingly long period also owed much to beliefs rooted in an older, simpler and harder society — beliefs in the importance of loyalty to the family and to the *capo*, and of honour in personal relations. Its durability as a force in the international political economy should not be underrated. Although great secrecy shrouds the details of Mafia operations, enough is known about its connection with the international trade in narcotics, in arms and in finance to make it an importance source of non-state authority. Yet it would not be so if there had not been weaknesses in the state-based structure for the control of drugs and arms deals or the regulation of financial transactions across frontiers.

The weaknesses of the basic structures as well as their strengths influence power relations between states and between other organizations. Take, for example, the remilitarization of the Rhineland by Hitler in 1936. This had been declared a demilitarized zone by the Treaty of Versailles after World War I. It was supposed to act as a kind of cushion or shock-absorber in the security structure for Europe, making it more difficult for Germany to start a second European war. When Hitler marched troops into the zone, he was aware that mere denunciation of the 'unequal' treaty was not enough. He had done that many times before. The show of force was necessary to demonstrate the weakness of the structure and to add to it. The fact that the troops met with no opposition was not because France was lacking in military might. Indeed, at that moment French forces were probably superior to Germany's in men and in aircraft. It was weak because France and Britain were divided in the realm of ideas and specifically on the question of the wisdom of the Versailles settlement. Britain still hoped that direct negotiation with Germany and diplomatic manoeuvring with Italy to outflank her would combine to avoid war. Differences in the perception of the problem and in beliefs about what to do about it robbed former allies of structural power in matters of security. Their inaction in 1936 enhanced Hitler's perception of their lack of will to resist and allowed him far more important military victories in Austria and Czechoslovakia at relatively low cost. Perceptions, not only of relational power, but of the solidity or otherwise of structures are often crucial to outcomes.

A different kind of example, this time of the use of coercive structural power in relation to the market, would be the use of Anglo-American naval power in World War I and again in World War II to interfere with the conduct of trade by neutral countries. The targets were innocent, peaceful traders, who wanted to sell their goods to the enemies of Britain and the United States. Their ships were stopped by the naval patrols of the two allies and if their masters could not produce a valid 'navicert' — a document guaranteeing that the voyage and the cargoes had been authorized by British or American authorities at their port of origin and that they were not destined for the enemy — they were subjected to forcible seizure of both ship and cargo. The relational power of Allied warships over neutral merchant ships was the basis or necessary condition for the setting of a highly partial security structure within which trade could be carried on. It was accepted and traders conformed to the rules laid down by the two great naval powers, so that it came briefly to resemble a regime or power structure. And the regime was dismantled, not when Britain and American structural power at sea declined but when, after hostilities ceased, the allies decided that they no longer needed to use their power in the security structure to distort and interfere with the market.

Limits of social science

It would not be difficult to find plenty more examples from the political and economic history of the world to show the importance of different kinds of structural power in affecting outcomes both in distributional terms and in terms of the mix of values in the system, to show how relational power can be translated into structural power and how hard it is in practice to distinguish between political power and economic power. It only seems necessary to develop some new way of looking at political economy, and to illustrate it with a few examples, because so much writing in the social sciences today has failed to adjust mentally to the 'globalization', to use a popular term, of economic, political and social affairs. My attempt may not be the best, and probably can be improved upon by others. But the limitations of the major social sciences that have claimed to interpret the politics of the world economy are so serious that they insistently call for new perspectives and analytical frameworks.

But what, the reader may ask, are these limitations and why have they so constrained the development of international political economy? These are two large questions. Without going into a very large digression, I can only offer a rather brief answer to each of them.

Mainly, the limitations arise out of the past history of three important social sciences — economics, political science and international relations. Both of the first two developed earlier in this century on the assumption that national frontiers divided different political and economic systems so they could be studied and analysed for all practical purposes in isolation from each other, or else comparatively, as if they were distinct species of animal, or breeds of dog or horse. The third, international relations, was so focused on the *problématique* of war and peace in which the main 'actors' or protagonists were nation-states that it had difficulty handling any other question than that of world order — as shown by the titles of even quite recent textbooks in international politics. By the time world events caused students to ask urgent questions about the problems of the world economy, academic specialization and interdisciplinary jealousies had raised such barriers between the three social sciences that when students tried to study simultaneously some economics, some political science, some international relations, they often found it hard to fit the three together. They complained, with justification, that the jigsaw did not make a whole picture.

One important reason for this, of course, was the exclusion of considerations of power from the study of economics. By this means, theory could be developed that was 'parsimonious', 'rigorous', 'elegant' — all words of praise much used by contemporary economists. This deliberate myopia caused K. W. Rothschild some years ago to observe:

> As in other important social fields, we should expect that individuals should struggle for position; that power will be used to improve one's position in the economic game; and that attempts will be made to derive power and influence from economic strongholds. Power should therefore be a recurrent theme in economic studies of a theoretical or applied nature. Yet if we look at the main run of economic theory over the past hundred years, we find that it is characterized by a strange lack of power considerations. [Rothschild, 1971:7]

So it is that anything that upsets or goes against economic theory is apt to be referred to as an 'exogenous factor' — often as an 'exogenous shock', especially shocking to economists unprepared by nature to expect power factors to intervene, whether from governments or operators in the market. And behaviour that is not consistent with the premises of economic theory then, of course, becomes condescendingly and disapprovingly referred to as 'irrational', however sensible it may seem to the ordinary person.

Some economists, it is true, have tried to break out of this unreal straightjacket by contributing to the development of public choice theory in which actors try to maximize their gains and minimize their costs. But the insights gained — so it seems to me — are often constrained by the presumption of economic analysis that people invariably try, first and foremost, to get everything on the cheap, and that cost is the ultimate determinant of all behaviour. All in all, it is a pity that applied or descriptive economics has been so badly out of favour in the profession for nearly fifty years. For the above strictures apply far less to those economists who have worked in development economics or in any specialized branch — agricultural economics or transport economics, for example — that requires attention to the real world and to the political factors or the historical experience that actually influences outcomes. It is impossible for development economists to see markets for exportable commodities, for instance, without noting the political forces at work on and in them. To quote from a development economist:

Economic reasoning often ascribes to markets a spontaneity of origin and a determinism in operations that originate from economic necessity . . . Yet if markets are viewed as creatures of social and political systems, then their operations, given certain economic parameters and technical constraints, can be understood as being induced or suppressed through political decisions and institutional mechanisms, both at the national and international level. [Vaitsos, 1976:114]

Vaitsos rightly pointed out that markets for different sorts of things, being the creation of decisions and institutions that vary from sector to sector and from time to time, will not easily conform to an analysis that excludes political power and interest.

Moreover, the adage 'once bitten, twice shy', which popular wisdom accepts as a powerful characteristic of human behaviour, cannot be fitted into economic theory. There are some kinds of lags between cause and effect — like the famous J-curve that delays the benefits of devaluation while the costs of dearer imports are quickly felt — which economic theory has tried (not too successfully) to grasp and explain. But the variant effects of recent experience on economic behaviour is something that eludes the profession. Perceptions of future risks — as insurers know — are governed in part by past experience, good or bad, and weighed alongside the expected costs. Equally, the perception of future possibilities — for a better life, for example — will be sharpened by hardship so that opportunities will be more eagerly seized by the poor and hungry than by the rich and comfortable.

Political scientists, meanwhile, have tended to assume that power is exercised within a given social and economic structure, even subject to certain constitutional limitations and institutional influences. Even the best work in comparative politics tends to focus on the similarities and differences — more often, the differences — between individual states or national systems of decision-making than on the common factors emanating from the world economy — such as the greater mobility of capital, of technical know-how, of disease and of ideas. The model used to such effect by Dahl (1961) in analysing different kinds of decision-making power in the government of New Haven, Connecticut, had its limitations when applied by Cox and Jacobson (1974) to decision-making in international organizations. For, even though these have formal statutes or constitutions, the freedom of states to opt out, to veto or withhold consent (or money), makes for a much more fluid and less structured exercise of power than is to be found in local government. National legal systems will therefore tend to be taken as given, even though political scientists in reflecting on the differences between states will see that law can institutionalize and legitimize both power derived from coercive force and/or power derived from unequal wealth, or for that matter power derived from a general consensus about national aspirations, ideals and values.

While the economists have ignored power and the political scientists have been more interested in how it was exercised inside states, many scholars in international relations have shown too narrow a concern with relational power of one state over another. Too often, they have ignored or refused to contemplate structural power, or the power to define the structure, to choose the game as well as to set the rules under which it is to be played. It is as if you said, 'This man has power in relation to this woman because he can knock her down', ignoring the fact of structural power in a masculine-dominated social structure that gives the man social status, legal rights and control over the family money that makes it unnecessary even to threaten to knock her down unless she does as she is told. Secondly, they narrowed their concern with power to power exercised between states, to the exclusion of other groups or organizations. It consequently tended to reify and to treat as one homogeneous unit the states that were its subject matter.

Thirdly, it narrowed its field of vision of the resources that conferred power to those that could be used and were relevant to inter-state relations. The classic example of this was a book called *The War Potential of States* by Klaus Knorr. This listed territory, population, raw materials, weapons, financial reserves, and so forth — but had to conclude that it was difficult to add them all up to see who had most power or to foretell the combination of assets that in international conflicts would be most effective.[2]

Not all schools of thought concerned with international relations, naturally, have been guilty on all three counts. The Marxists and the dependency schools in the Third World (and especially Latin America) were well aware of the importance of structural power, though they have tended to limit their interpretation of it to the structures of production and trade (see Chapter 4). The pluralists looked beyond state–state relations and pointed to non-state actors such as transnational corporations and international organizations. But then they tended to ask only whether these supernumerary players were likely to help or to hinder State *A* against State *B*. What role, they asked, did non-state actors play in the foreign policy game? They only rarely looked beyond inter-state relations to ask what other kinds of structural power the non-state actors might have at their disposal. The Nye and Keohane framework only takes structural power in at secondhand as it were, by looking at the rank ordering of states in international regimes or organizations. This will often mirror the relative importance of states in the world economy. But it only reflects the structural power of states, not of other entities; and it can often be a rather distorting mirror, as when some states are excluded from an organization for historical or political reasons or when voting systems reflect a power distribution of the past rather than the present.

These various astigmatisms in the vision of the three major social sciences concerned with the international political economy have undoubtedly hindered its proper development. They have been handicaps for research and for teaching. As a result, some of the more useful contributions to the development of the subject have come from outside the three disciplines, from lawyers, historians and sociologists — especially in recent years the sociologists, who, when they discarded the search for some simple general theory applicable to all human societies, began to look to the histories of society, not only in Europe but also in Asia and the Middle East for clues to the common problem of who has power in society, what are the sources of such power and to what ends is it used.[3]

States showed themselves sharply aware of the intangible, unquantifiable resources of social cohesion and a strong civil society that could more than make up for a state's deficiencies in size of land or people or even its store of military armament. Their vision of resources was thus sometimes more comprehensive, being ready to include a state's degree of self-sufficiency in food or in energy, or the security of its means of access to both of these and to raw materials. Some would include control over communications systems or sea and air transport, the command of technical skills or of the respect and sympathy of nationals in other states — for example, the socialist countries' support for Cuba or Switzerland's reputation for stability and impartiality.

On this point, too, the pluralists extended their field of vision. In Nye and Keohane's *Power and Interdependence*, for example, the difference between susceptibility (being open to damage from the world system) and vulnerability (susceptibility qualified by the ability to limit the damage) is usefully developed to enlarge the analysis of comparative power of states in the system. But the viewfinder is still only taking in the susceptibility or vulnerability of *states*. And among the four factors listed as determining outcomes in the system, political power is treated as a structure (the 'overall power structure in the world') derived (p.21) from 'the distribution of power resources among states', and sometimes modified by the two other factors — the power of states within issue areas, and the power of states as modified by international organization. But these authors refer only to economic *process* or, to put it plainly, how things worked out for states in the trading system or under the rules agreed in an international regime. The analysis for practical purposes was more or less blind to the distribution of power in all four *structures* of the international political economy.

A network of bargains

Starting with structures, though, is only half the battle. The next important question is where to go from there, how to proceed with the analysis of a particular situation so as to discern in more detail where a government, a political movement or a corporate enterprise has a range of feasible choices, and what possible scenarios might follow, depending on which choices are made. My proposal, based on some experience of trying to write monetary and financial history in a world context and to look at sectors of agriculture, industry and services also on a global scale, is that you should look for the key bargains in any situation, and then decide which might, and which probably will not, be liable to change, altering the range of choices for all or some of those concerned.

The basic bargain to look for first is often a tacit one, that between authority and the market. One of the simplest and earliest examples would be the tacit agreement between kings and princes in medieval Europe and the participants in the great trade fairs, or in local town markets given a special licence or charter by the king in return for a payment of tax. The rules gave access and in some cases guaranteed the maintenance of minimum public order; the buyers and sellers profited from the trade. Non-state authorities can make such basic bargains too. At Wimbledon, the British Lawn Tennis Association sets the prices of entry for spectators, lays down the rules for the selection of players and reserves some seats for its own members and those of affiliated tennis clubs. If it reserved all the seats, or too many of them, the bargain with the market — the general public — might break down. If its rules excluded too many good players, again, the market might shrink and undermine the bargain. The Olympic Games network of bargains is even more complex because governments become involved in deciding on political grounds whether athletes may compete and in financing their participation.

Even in a command economy, there is, behind the veil of bureaucratic control, a kind of bargain between authority in the form of state ministries, and market in the form of consumers and producers. To maintain the authority of the state, a bargain has to be struck with the producers — managers and workers — to reward them sufficiently and to give effective enough incentives for them to produce the goods and services that will sell to consumers. Some waste of unsold goods, unused resources can be tolerated — as, in different ways, it can in a private enterprise system. But too much waste will put a strain on the bargain with the consumers. When there is discontent with the way the bargains are working out on the part of *both* producers and consumers, as there was in Poland in 1973 and again in the early 1980s, authority is in trouble. Martial law and coercive force may have to be used to back up the unsatisfactory bargain. In that particular case, two of the weak links in the network of bargains were, firstly, the inability of Solidarity, having brought the workers out on strike, to get them back to work again and, secondly, the inability of the government to produce the necessary food and consumer goods to back up any deal on wages and the workers' purchasing power. It was, unfortunately, a situation made worse by the intervention of the United States. Imposing sanctions and taking no action to restore the flow of Western bank credit only further weakened the strength of both partners in the two key bargains.

One set of bargains — inevitably in a system in which political authority is so concentrated in the hands of many states — is that made between the governments of states. But those bargains, as countless specialized studies have demonstrated again and again, depend heavily on the durability of some internal, domestic bargains, especially in the most structurally powerful states. Sometimes these will be between political parties. Sometimes they will be between the government and the local representatives of sectoral interests or the leaders of organized labour. They can also (though less often) be with organized groups of consumers or environmental conservationists. Identifying whose support, political, financial or moral, is indispensible to the partners in the key bargains is often an essential stage in analysis of a dynamic situation. It was the static nature of a great deal of work on the bureaucratic politics model, incidentally, that was its great weakness. The US Treasury or the Department of State may be a powerful bureaucracy in the policy-making under one Secretary and one President. It did not always follow that it survived death, resignation or the next election.

Work that has been done by political scientists on the subject of neo-corporatism is particularly instructive in this context. Neo-corporatism is the practice in democratic states within the world market economy of hammering out a trilateral bargain regarding the management of the national economy between the agencies of government, the representatives of management in industry, banking, agriculture and trade, and the representatives of labour and, in some cases, farmers. It has been most fully developed and has proved most successful in the smaller European states, and in a somewhat different and less well understood form in Japan and Taiwan and less successfully in South Korea. Austria takes the neo-corporatist prize, followed by the Netherlands and Sweden. The success of annual negotiations over wages and prices requires two things: some flexibility in government policy to accommodate and to mediate successfully between capital and labour, and some confidence on the part of both capital and labour that each of the other two parties will deliver the promised goods. The bargaining therefore becomes easier as time builds such confidence, but more difficult as external forces — interest rates or oil prices, for example — make it more difficult to put promises into practice. The essential ingredient is common consent given to the survival of the nation-state as a distinct entity, as autonomous as possible in its international political and economic relations and the conduct of its domestic affairs. Such consent, and the willingness to sacrifice short-term special interests to the long-term collective national interest, seems to be less necessary in larger countries, and especially in those with a large domestic market as a base for industry. It seems less necessary — and also perhaps more difficult — in the larger members of the European Community like Britain, France, Germany or even Italy for the government to seek neo-corporatist solutions. Both state and market appear to offer that much more status to the state bureaucracy, more opportunity to the managers of industry and more security to labour. Even more clearly is this the case with the United States.

Another set of bargains in which the world economy of today is of increasing importance and significance is the rather peculiar tacit bargain between central banks and commercial banks. It cannot, in the nature of banking, be too explicit. Bankers say there is a moral hazard if they are ever able to be too sure that the central bank will bail them out, no matter what they have done. On the other hand, unless they have some confidence in the willingness of the central bank as lender of last resort to come to their aid in times of crisis, they are unlikely to heed its warnings or obey the spirit as well as the letter of its prudential regulations at other times. That is a particularly delicately balanced bargain.

With corporations, whether private or state-owned, as well as with banks, the bargains struck will not only differ in character from country to country but also from sector to sector. The international oil business — as earlier references have already hinted — is a particularly complex cat's-cradle of interlocking bargains. In the 1960s, for instance, there were the bargains between the seven biggest oil companies to maintain an effective cartel, exerting authority over the market. There was also the network of bargains between the companies and the host-states in which oil was found and produced. And there was an important financial bargain between the oil companies and the government of the United States, imitated in practice by those of other consumer countries. It allowed the companies effective freedom from the demands of the internal revenue for tax provided they continued to apply their large profits to investment in exploration, thus raising the chances of further discoveries of new oilfields. Assuring a continued flow of crude petroleum adequate to meet the needs of a fast-growing world economy was a vital link in the network of bargains. Only very rapid demand in the market and the unexpected resolution of the dissatisfied host states found out the weak links in the network.

The great advantage of paying attention to bargains, it seems to me, is that it is more likely to result in feasible prescription for policy-makers in business or in government and politics than other approaches. Making pretty blueprints for the reform of international organizations may be a beguiling pastime. It seldom cuts much ice with the relevant governments. The last years of the League of Nations were spent in drawing blueprints; only a few years after, it looked in retrospect like fiddling while Rome burnt. Equally irrelevant in the real world is the elaboration of abstract economic theory, when it is based on unrealistic assumptions, such as 'Let us assume infinitely living households with perfect information on market conditions'. In real life, durable conditions in political economy cannot be created which ignore the interlocking interests of powerful people. The problem — which never has an easy, quick or permanent solution — is to find that balance of interest and power that allows a working set of bargains to be hammered out and observed.

Part II

Structures of Power in the World Economy

Chapter 3

The Security Structure

The security structure in a political economy is the framework of power created by the provision of security by some human beings for others. The protectors — those who provide the security — acquire a certain kind of power which lets them determine, and perhaps limit, the range of choices, or options available to others. By exercising this power, the providers of security may incidentally acquire for themselves special advantages in the production, or consumption of wealth and special rights or privileges in social relations. Thus the security structure inevitably has an impact on the who-gets-what of the economy. It cannot be left out. For instance, in tribal societies or in a feudal security structure, the chief and his warriors or the feudal baron and his soldiers supply security to the women and the peasants, and in return not only acquire powers as lawgivers and judges but also social privileges in food, physical comforts and freedoms which are denied to others.

Security is, after all, the most basic of basic human needs. If someone kills you, you immediately *have* no further needs. In fear of death, most human beings are ready to sacrifice wealth, to abandon social status or political position, and to accept injustice and the loss of freedom. Anyone who was unlucky enough to be in Hiroshima, or in Berlin in 1945, who was in Petrograd in 1917, in Saigon when the Americans left in 1975 or in Beirut in 1986 will have seen how people in danger quickly change. Their preoccupation is with survival. Their demand curves shift dramatically. Other values pale into insignificance beside the need for security.

The analysis of a security structure, whether it relates to a local community in some big city today, to another kind of society in the distant historical past or to world society in modern times, will ask the same sort of basic question: Who provides security to whom? Against what perceived threat or threats? What price or terms are exacted for this security? Looked at from the other side, from the point of view of the 'consumers' of security, the questions would be somewhat different. To whom does a state, a corporation, a social group or an individual look for greater security? How much security is provided? Again, on what terms?

In the international political economy of modern times, the security structure is built around the institution of the state. The state claims political authority and the monopoly of legitimate violence. But the state does not exist in isolation. It exists alongside others, in a society of states. All claim political authority and the monopoly of legitimate violence within — and also sometimes beyond — their territorial boundaries. The relations between states therefore have great importance for the security structure, and for the world economy. One of the major issues with which we must deal therefore is how well or badly this international political system, this world of states, provides security to the world economy. Economists may choose to ignore the question. The political economist cannot.

There are four other general systemic questions that must also be considered:

(1) whether the provision of security varies with the nature of the individual states who are the players in this international political system;
(2) whether the provision of security is affected by the role of markets, by industrialization, and the stage of economic development;
(3) whether what you might call the 'geometry', or pattern, or state-state relations is significant, i.e. whether the security structure is more or less effective if, in the society of states, there are many small ones, or two dominant states or, perhaps, an oligopoly of half a dozen Great Powers. This is an old question for students of international relations but still an important one;
(4) whether and how the structure is affected by technological change, especially in the weapons with which states are armed.

Note that these questions are not directed at the security of any particular state. What choice of defence policy the government of a state, whether it is India or West Germany, should adopt is the concern of strategic studies, just as the choice of a policy for its relations with other states is the concern of foreign policy analysts. This chapter, and this book, are directed rather at the framework within which those national choices are made. It may not be possible always to find simple answers to the five major questions listed above, but it is important that they should at least be asked. This is partly because of the separation of economics from politics but also because of the way in which the study of international relations has tended in many places to divide into 'strategic studies' on the one hand and the 'politics of international economic relations' on the other.[1] The strategists who are familiar with the security problems and issues in the international political system too seldom read or speak to people with an interest in trade or finance; while those interested in economic relations seldom enter into dialogue with the strategic experts. While acknowledging that states will play a larger part in determining the nature of the security structure, international political economists should still be as much concerned, firstly, with how that structure affects the distribution of security between individuals, social groups and corporate enterprises as well as it does the distribution of security among states. And they should also be concerned with how the structure affects the priority given to order or security as compared with the other three major values of organized human society — wealth, equity and freedom.

Defining security

Security from sudden unnatural death may be the most basic of human needs, as pointed out earlier, but it is not the only kind of security to which human beings aspire. There is security from slow death by starvation, and security from disease, from disablement, or from all sorts of other hazards — from bankruptcy to unemployment. If we think only of states, we confine analysis of security to threats to the survival of the state, of which war and conquest are the most extreme but not the sole threat. But if we think of the international political economy, this comprises enterprises and individuals, and the factors affecting their survival are rather more various and complex. It may be helpful therefore to try to clarify a little what we mean by a security structure, and how we could most usefully classify different kinds of threats against which individual people, or social groups or states, seek some measure of security. How they seek it tells us something about the security structure. Whether they find it tells us something about the distributive character of the framework of power described as a security structure.

Security can be threatened by natural forces or by human agency. And the threat to security can be local or global, selective or general. At first glance, you might think that there is very little that can be done to give people security against the elemental forces of freakish nature — earthquakes, hurricanes, volcanoes, floods, mudslides or forest fires. But in fact all mankind is not equally insecure from these threats, especially where recurrent and therefore anticipated natural disasters are concerned. The Japanese learn to build earthquake-resistant buildings. The Americans develop an elaborate hurricane warning system. The technology of flood control is well known — but not as well applied in the Ganges delta, for instance, as in the Mississippi, Nile or even the Indus. One of the features of 'advanced' countries is that they have eliminated or controlled dangerous wild animals: there are tigers still in India, but no more wolves in Europe.

Most of the threats to individual security, however, are threats coming from some human agency. These range from threats coming from other individuals (whether criminals, lunatics, or carriers of serious diseases), to threats from organized crime, civil war or revolution, local or regional wars, up to threats of major nuclear war — a threat which puts in jeopardy the whole world, all mankind and all life on earth.[2]

The latter is perhaps the one major universal threat, affecting all mankind equally and indiscriminately. All other threats are unevenly distributed and unevenly coped with by authority. Whether directed at particular individuals (assassination or kidnapping, for instance) or particular groups (whether political, or religious), threats will occur unequally, very unevenly and by design as well as by the accidents of history or geography. And they may be direct threats to the life and safety of a person or a group of people, or indirect threats to the means of life (to water supplies, food supplies, fuel and energy supplies, even to shelter and various factors of production or forms of property).

But apart from natural disasters and individual acts of disruption it is fair to say that almost all the other threats to people's security arise, in one way or another, from conflicts of authority. And it is not, intrinsically, the coexistence of a multiplicity of authorities in a political economy that may threaten the structure of security. It is disagreement between them about the limits of their respective authority.

This disagreement may be between two states, or between a state and a provincial government (as in the American Civil War), or between a state and some lesser authority such as a labour union, a religious sect or a criminal gang. The state-centred model of politics which dominates so much political science has made a sharp but essentially false distinction between threats to security that arise within states (crime, terrorism) and threats that arise from other states (i.e. war, strategic embargoes or blockades).

But if the international political economy is looked at as a whole rather than simply as a society of nation-states, then it is apparent that the conflicts of authority giving rise to threats to security can come from *any* situation where two authorities conflict because they do not, tacitly or explicitly, agree to coexist side by side, and where the weaker source of authority is held to exceed the limits tolerated by the stronger.

Thus, security can be threatened by conflict between the authority of the Soviet Union and that of the United States or China; or it may be threatened by conflict between the authority of a criminal leader over his gang with the authority of the state embodied in the person of a local police chief. In both cases, there can be peaceful coexistence, or there can be head-on conflict. This rather obvious common sense observation helps to explain the paradox that coexistence of authorities can be at the same time both a source of security and a source of insecurity. The balance of power (to use terms familiar to students of international relations) can thus be a power for peace or a cause of war. Mutual nuclear deterrence can be part of the structure of security *and* at the same time the greatest potential threat to security.

At the level of the state, the study of political science being concerned with the effort of the state to maintain order in society has tended to make a clear distinction between 'legitimate' and 'illegitimate' threats to security — from rebel or terrorist forces and from the state's army or police. Yet, for the individual the result may be the same if the police shoot you by mistake, or if a bankrobber shoots you by mistake. This false distinction is something that, for clarity of analysis, political economy might well discard. Normative judgements can be made afterwards. But if we pose the questions suggested earlier, we at least start from an analytically neutral definition of the situation in terms of the degree of security or insecurity.

The same bias in political science and in law is found in the different treatment of threats to economic security resulting from revolution and civil war and those resulting from organized piracy and banditry. The effect of both on production structures and on trade is much the same. Indeed, sometimes it is quite hard to tell revolutionaries from bandits. There were successful bands of outlaws in nineteenth-century Russia, as in China, Bolivia or the Balkans, some of which started as groups of political dissidents and then turned to robbery to survive. Equally, there were robbers, like the famous Giuliano in Sicily in the 1940s, who started as simple robbers but found themselves heading a political protest, and were hunted down by the authorities as enemies of the state. And perhaps it is only the subtle ideology of nationalism and the nation-state that makes such a rigid distinction between taxation when it is legitimized by the authority of the state and other forms of enforced contributions to the costs of protection against threats to security, such as those levied by the Mafia and other counter-societies, sometimes no more arbitrarily.[3]

It then becomes apparent that some of the more stable counter-societies go further and emulate the other functions of a state. Chinese secret societies, for instance — some of the most persistent and well-organized of all known counter-societies — not only tax their members, but make rules, administer justice and exact punishment. They create internal welfare systems, looking after sick or old members, even bringing up children. A stable counter-society — organized Judaism, for instance — does not necessarily threaten security or jeopardize economic activity in any way. Provided always that the boundaries between it and the 'legitimate' authority are clear and unchallenged, the two can coexist. This has been the case with the Kibbutzim in Israel, with the Mafia and the police in some American cities, and in the 'no-go' areas of Belfast left by the British Army to the authority of the Irish 'provos'.

An important axiom for political economy follows from this observation. It is that the security structure is jeopardized not by the existence of counter-societies in themselves but only when one authority challenges the domain or rights of another and when that challenge is accepted. Then violence is apt to ensue. The challenge can come from either side. The lesser authority — a counter-society or a dissident political or ethnic group — may try to extend its authority. If the greater authority resists the attempt, conflict is apt to ensue. Or else the greater authority will decide for one reason or another to assert or reassert its authority over the lesser one — whether over territory, as with a Chinese warlord or the Irish provos, or over some matter of ideology or of economic rights and responsibilities, including the responsibility to pay taxes. Again, conflict ensues only if the lesser authority then accepts the challenge and resists. In either case, the outcome depends on a crucial calculation by the challenger in the first place and the challenged in the second of the gains that might be achieved, the risks of loss involved if conflict does ensue and the costs of defending their respective authority.

Security in a system of states

It is precisely the same uncertainty over the limits of authority at the borderline that is the major weakness of the security structure based on a multiplicity of territorial states. The only difference — but it is a big one — is that states have this in common, that they all claim a monopoly of legitimate violence and that they acknowledge reciprocally each other's right to the claim. It follows therefore that the security structure fails when they decide to challenge the authority of another state. At other times, they operate a kind of collective alliance against the lesser authorities with which all of them to some degree have to deal. From time to time, of course, they will decide to intervene, to aid the insurgents or harbour the revolutionaries who challenge the authority of another state. What they are doing then by giving such aid is to run the risk of conflict with the other state. (Their wish to maintain the freedom to make such challenges is the reason why, although they normally have extradition treaties with other states in confirmation of their shared interest in fighting crime, such treaties usually exclude 'political' crimes — and leave to each state the right to decide how it interprets 'political'.)

The risk in the system lies not in the coexistence of states *per se*. It lies in the risks that come with that coexistence, risks resulting from the uncertainty over how far the stronger state can extend its authority, and over the point at which the weaker state feels it has to resist and turn to fight.

This of course is why the security structure of the world economy has been weakened as much by the decline of empires or of formerly powerful states as by the rise of aggressive new states. Whenever there has been such a decline, whether of the Roman Empire, the Ottoman Empire, the Manchu Empire in China or the European empires in Africa, the decline has been accompanied by conflictual challenges from other states and by conflict among other states for the territory and resources of the former imperial power. It is only because much recent history has been written by the victors that the threat to international security from the increased power of a rising or resurgent state like Germany or Japan in the interwar years has been more often stressed than the threat from a declining state, like Austria or the Ottoman Empire before 1914.

In reality, the break-up of empires, the decline of a former great power, opens up more possibilities of misperception and thus of unintended conflict than the usually slower and more gradual rise of new powers. It was the decline of the Manchu Empire in China and the subsequent inability of the Nationalist government to control the warlords in border regions that tempted Japan into the occupation of Manchuria in 1931. It was the summary and ill-prepared retreat of Britain from India in 1947 that led to inter-communal violence and the deaths of millions at the dawning of independence and to continuing conflict and hostility between the successor states thereafter. As Jervis and many other writers on international security and the history of international relations have observed, it is misperception that is a more common source of breakdown in the security structure than any other.[4] Misperception by North Korea of the significance of the United States withdrawal of troops from South Korea was a major reason for the outbreak of the Korean War in 1950. And it was misperception by both Britain and Argentina of each other's intentions towards and interest in the Falklands/Malvinas that led to that bloody, anachronistic and unnecessary conflict in the 1980s.

The inevitable question, though, is whether there is any other basis for a security structure that would limit violent and destructive conflict between coexisting political authorities. The present one may be imperfect, but is there any practical, conceivable alternative? There are two conceivable possibilities: a world state or empire, and a world organization of states better and more effective than either the League of Nations or the United Nations. Neither, however, seems practicable.

A world empire, whether ruled from Washington, Moscow or Beijing, would certainly eliminate international conflict. Any resistance to the central authority could be called civil, not inter-state, war. But resistance there would be if history is any guide. Every single bid for domination over neighbours that looked as if it might lead to setting up a world empire has met with fierce, and growing, resistance. Even when, as in the case of Napoleon and Stalin, the bid could be clothed in a universalist ideology of liberalism or socialism it has met with deep suspicion and strong opposition. Long before these potential world empires controlled even half of the surface of the earth, the opposition proved too strong for them.

And the root of opposition, its source of strength and staying power, has been nationalism. The very insecurity of the system, paradoxically, seems to increase the individual's need for a sense of some identity in an insecure and dangerous world. And the sense of identity is still most successfully offered by the nation-state — even when the 'nationalism' is somewhat false and artificially contrived. Moreover, loyalty to the state — on which the whole mutual recognition and protection system of inter-state relations finally depends — has tended to increase rather than decrease as individuals perceive their heightened need for security and the state's heightened power to provide them with social and economic security as well as the security of public order. Even though not all states can as yet provide their citizens with social security, the fact that the rich ones do so encourages people in other states to think that they too will be so provided as soon as their states' economies grow rich too. Therefore, although people know that the state can also constitute a threat to their individual security, the lack of an alternative and the trade-off of present enjoyment of state-provided security against the future risk of state-engendered insecurity tends to reinforce the existing international state system.

All the same reasons make the second alternative of a world organization more effective than the League or the United Nations even less easily achieved. For if there is resistance to a world empire when those who want it carry a sword — that is, a violent threat to security — there is likely to be even less chance of change when the advocates of world government come empty-handed, armed only with reason. Everyone knows that the present security structure is both dangerous and costly to the point of wanton wastefulness in the production of superfluous armouries of missiles. But the knowledge has not been enough to make even small dents in popular attachment to the state as the provider of security. There was no public outcry between the wars when the responsibilities of states towards the League of Nations were slowly whittled away to nothing by the collective decisions of national representatives. Nor was there any outcry when, at Dumbarton Oaks and then at San Francisco, the member-states of the United States protected their precious independence of action by inserting in the Charter two key articles. One was Article 2, paragraph 7 which reserved to the members all matters that they considered to be matters of domestic jurisdiction. The other was Article 51 which preserved for them the right to individual or collective self-defence — thus reopening the door to a security structure based on alliance and counter-alliance rather than on collective responsibilities for the maintenance of peace between states. The fear that either the world organization would merely be the tool of one or other great power (as indeed it was the tool of the United States in the early 1950s) or that it would be ineffectual — as both the League and the UN have proved to be in the face of repeated grave threats to international peace and order — have been enough to kill any realistic hopes of managing a transition from the present security structure to a multilateral or confederal one.

Despite the idealistic dreams of peace parties, of academic international lawyers and world system enthusiasts, it has to be admitted that popular convictions have changed little in the last hundred years. National sentiments and prejudices are still the most easily aroused — in the United States, in Britain, in the Soviet Union — and the least easily laid to rest. It looks as though we are stuck with a security structure based on the nation-state. Whether there are factors that make it more or less effective or more or less risky is another question.

Are some states more peaceful?

The illusion that some states are more peaceful than others is a kind of intellectual phoenix that rises time and time again from its own ashes. It has always been — and always will be — an unfortunately seductive piece of political ideology. For the security structure the significant difference between states lies not in the political ideas they profess but, as Martin Wight (1946) wrote some forty years ago, in whether they are satisfied, conservative, status-quo powers or whether they are dissatisfied with the structures of power and therefore feel themselves to be have-nots, dedicated to radical change in those structures. As observed earlier, the conjunction of two such authorities in conditions of uncertainty as to the relative strength of the will to resist in the first group and the will to bring about change by force if necessary is a potent recipe for war.

The belief that monarchies were more belligerent and republics more peace-loving was a delusion strongly associated with both the French and the American Revolutions. It was given philosophical weight and popular appeal by Rousseau's rather unscientific and ahistorical notions of how men behaved in a state of nature, whatever that might be. It was borne out neither by the campaigning strategies of Napoleon nor by the policy of the United States towards the American Indian states. (The ideological element in the latter case is revealed by the refusal to acknowledge the tribes as political entities even though formal treaties were concluded with them as if they were states, and by the fiction of US law that denied legal personality to all American Indians for most of the nineteenth century.)

Notwithstanding the record, it was a delusion shared by Woodrow Wilson, a professor of history who became President of the United States, who took his country into World War I and then insisted on the principle of self-determination as a basis for the post-war settlement, partly on the grounds that nations permitted to organize themselves as liberal democratic states would be less prone to indulge in secret diplomacy, destabilizing alliance building and aggression against their neighbours. Breaking up the former enemy monarchies, he thought, would in itself improve the security of Europe. In fact what it produced was a group of rather weak successor states whose independence depended on the support that was or was not forthcoming from Britain and France, and on the changeable policies of the Soviet Union.

And while Wilson was thinking that democratic republics would improve security, socialists in many countries and not only the Soviet Union believed that socialist states would behave more peacefully than capitalist ones. The belief rested on the Leninist interpretation of Marx, which argued that the declining rate of profit in a capitalist state drove its government to seek cheaper raw materials and cheaper labour as well as new markets by acquiring colonial possessions. Competition between capitalist imperialists over colonial territory would lead to increased risk of war. Nor was the notion that capitalist states inclined to bellicosity confined to Marxists. Between the wars, many New Dealers and social democrats also believed that allowing the profit motive to rule in the international market for arms had fostered arms races and contributed to conflict between states. The example of the notorious Sir Basil Zaharoff selling guns and submarines to Greeks and Turks alike popularized the idea that capitalist governments licensed the 'merchants of death' to profit from warmongering.[5] Even in 1939, after the Molotov-Ribbentrop pact, partitioning Poland once again, many left-wingers still fell for the Soviet propaganda line that the war with Germany was a war between imperialists. It took some of them until the 1960s and the deterioration of Sino-Soviet relations over their common frontier in eastern Asia to recognize that socialist states could also be motivated by mutual fear and suspicion.

In the meantime, in developing countries, yet another version of the myth that some states were inherently more peaceful than others had taken root. It, too, is less credible now than when Nehru first proposed his Five Principles of Coexistence in the late 1940s. Joined by Tito of Yugoslavia and Nasser of Egypt, Nehru led the Nonaligned Movement (NAM) of neutral states, most of them newly liberated from colonial status. The presumption of the NAM was that the world's security was being threatened by conflict between the two armed camps of allies organized by the superpowers, and that the more that states could be persuaded to refuse alignment with either superpower, the less the risk of conflict. The implication was that such neutral bystanders were themselves more inherently peace-loving and mutually tolerant than the great powers. It too lost credibility as India itself fought with Pakistan, as Indonesia fought with Malaysia and as conflicts proliferated in Africa, and later the Middle East (Willetts, 1978).

Industrialization and war

While the two latter myths about the greater propensity of some kinds of state to threaten international security identified the older developed states as the culprits, another kind of logic has suggested that, on the contrary, industrialization in the production structure might improve the chances of stability and peace in the security structure. More developed, industrialised states might have less incentive in going to war.

Two early thinkers along such lines were Auguste Comte in France and Norman Angell in Britain. Comte believed that greater productivity in agriculture and in industry would so modify the harsh pressures of scarcity on national societies that governments would no longer need to conquer territory in order to acquire wealth. About the same time, Norman Angell was stating a similar argument based on the assumption of rational choice in the making of foreign policy. As the costs of war had escalated, so had its destructiveness. Rational calculation would show that it was a 'great illusion' — the name of his most famous book — that any national economic interest could possibly be served by going to war. However, Angell, more perhaps than Comte, doubted that policy choices in international relations were always made rationally — and his doubts were proved tragically justified when the Great War (as they called it then) began in 1914 (Angell, 1909; Miller, 1986).

The question nevertheless remains, for irrational fears, misperceptions and human error can still start wars, even though the wealth brought by industrialization makes them less worthwhile. It was a question that continued to tease the late Raymond Aron, perhaps the most distinguished writer on international relations of his generation. Twice in his long and productive life, Aron challenged Comte's optimism. But in 1978 he was still no more sure than he had been in 1958 how to assess the effects of industrialization on the security structure. He could see that it had by no means eliminated war because it had not eliminated the thirst for power, and war was still one means of acquiring power. The balance of deterrence between nuclear powers remained precarious and vulnerable, and the proliferation of nuclear weapons brought new risks of catastrophe (Aron, 1958; 1978).

Ten years later, the internationalization of production (as described in a later chapter) introduced a new factor into this old debate. If the wealth of a developed state depends more and more on the investments made by its banks and corporations in other countries, and less and less on its industrial productivity at home, will not its government be aware that this wealth is even more vulnerable than its industry, and is more directly jeopardized by war? War tends to wipe out old debts. Victors do not necessarily acquire spoils from the vanquished as they did when control over territory was the basis of national production. The 'security community' perceived by Deutsch in the 1950s as uniting the members of the Atlantic alliance in such a way that they would not contemplate war against each other may have rested on a cross-investment and cross-frontier production rather than on the intensity of cross-frontier communication counted on by Deutsch (Deutsch, 1968).

Industrialization, however, has also been a key factor in the final question posed at the beginning of this chapter — how the security structure has been affected by the technological changes in the weapons with which states arm themselves. Without manufacturing capacity, and without the access to the scientific knowledge of how nuclear warheads are made, the proliferation of nuclear weapons — widely regarded as a major weakness in the security structure — could not have taken place. Both superpowers have been keenly aware that it was not in their interest that other states should acquire nuclear weapons. But their efforts to use control over the technology and materials necessary for nuclear power stations as a lever to get others to promise not to use their help for military purposes and to submit to international inspection have failed. The Nuclear Non-Proliferation Treaty of the 1960s still binds over a hundred states. But not only was the deal refused from the very beginning by several important states, including China, France, South Africa, Israel and India and Pakistan, it has increasingly lost credibility. By the 1990s, it seems probable that the number of states admitting to possession of nuclear weapons of some kind, or known to possess them, will have multiplied, weakening to some unknown degree the structure of security. That is surely more significant for the system as a whole than the declaration by some states that they are 'nuclear-free' — either by multilateral agreement, as in the 1969 Treaty of Tlatelolco between the states of Latin America, or by unilateral declaration, as in the case of New Zealand. Such declarations are made when statesmen perceive that their country enjoys relative security, so that if they disavow any intention of allowing nuclear missiles or submarines to be based in the country, the declaration may marginally add to its already rather low risk of involvement. Such possibilities are not equally open to the European states.

Patterns of balance and security maps

The economic power of Japan, and the re-emergence of a rapidly-industrializing China into active international politics has recently revived the old question of which kind of balance of power makes for more security — a seesaw balance between two superpowers such as has dominated the global security structure for the past forty years, or a 'chandelier' balance in which equilibrium is maintained between a group of five or six great powers, such as dominated world security in the years before 1914.

It is in many ways a false problem, for the number in the balance is not the only variable. An important factor in the multiple balance, for instance, is the degree of flexibility in other participants if any one of the others appears to be losing or gaining 'weight' in the balance, and so upsetting the equilibrium. A multiple balance may have more ways of compensating for changes in relative (or perceived relative) power than a bipolar balance. The fact that the multiple balance of pre-1914 Europe failed and that last-minute diplomacy was unable to stop the accelerating slide into general mobilisation and war from about June 1914 onwards can be ascribed to other factors (Joll, 1914; Lowes Dickinson, 1916). For instance, the solidification of British relations with France from 1902 onwards removed the limited flexibility of an important balancer, while the Germans' perception of their increased weakness in military manpower after France brought in three-year conscripts seems to have led Bethman Hollweg to gamble on the probability that if Austria were encouraged to resist Russian backing for Serbia after Sarajevo, either the Russians would back down, weakening the Franco–Russian side of the chandelier, or a war could be as quickly won as the wars of the 1860s and 1870s. Perhaps it was the rapidity of economic change, and of military and naval technology, that added significant destabilizing factors. For until about five years before 1914 it had certainly seemed as if the Concert of Europe was a rather efficient security structure, allowing bilateral or peripheral wars to be fought without dragging in the whole continent — the Franco–Prussian and the Crimean for instance — and allowing competition for colonial territory which, notwithstanding Marxist theories, only rarely led to confrontations like that between Britain and France at Fashoda. Much more often, the colonial powers collaborated in exploiting the inhabitants of weaker continents — Latin America under the Monroe Doctrine excepted. They banded together in the Boxer expedition to teach China a lesson of subservience, and they conducted repeated multilateral peacekeeping summits to prevent the European domination of North Africa from leading to a European war. The care taken by the European powers in multiple balance of power to avoid stepping on each others' toes, to demarcate clear spheres of influence and to use diplomacy to avert crisis was on the whole rather more striking than the times when their mutual fears threatened to get out of hand.

But an equally strong case can be made for the durability of a bipolar balance. This has constituted the mainstay of the security structure for states since the breakdown of the wartime alliance between the United States and the Soviet Union in the winter of 1947/48 and the final collapse of hopes that some agreement could be reached between them to put some peacekeeping forces at the disposal of the United Nations

Security Council. Despite the mutual accusations and the competitive build-up of arms, peace has been kept between the superpowers for forty years. Head-on conflicts have been averted — as over Berlin in 1948, over Hungary/Suez in 1956, over Cuba in 1962 and over Iran/Afghanistan in 1978–80. There have been successive risks of local conflicts escalating, as when MacArthur contemplated crossing the Yalu river in the Korean War, over the Congo intervention in 1960, or through Soviet support for Nicaragua or American support for the Afghan tribesmen. Mutual Assured Destruction may indeed have seemed a MAD way to keep peace, but even the experts could think of no other.

But by the mid-1980s it was becoming increasingly costly. Difficult as it was sure to be, there were strong economic incentives for both superpowers to reach agreement on a reduction of nuclear armouries and the negotiation of a more stable bipolar balance. Nor have the costs been only economic and financial. Looked at as a security structure in which the power is held by the providers of security, a price has also been paid by the 'protected' in terms of a loss of other values — free choice, in particular. Within each of the blocs, and in their immediate vicinity, the superpowers have allowed very limited autonomy. Poles, Hungarians and Czechs have paid in terms of the choices denied them, as have Guatemalans, Sandinistas and Panamanians. By contrast, the superpowers have shown growing indifference to conflicts that did not seem to threaten or upset the balance between them. It almost seems as though the Concert of Europe, because of the wider spread of its collective interests, was rather more active in the role of world policeman than the Soviet Union and the United States have been — at least in the 1980s. For both, the relations between them seemed to be more important than intervening in unsettled 'neutral' regions to prevent conflicts — as in the Falklands or, in the earlier stages of the Iraq war, the Persian Gulf.

There is always a danger of security being regarded in highly subjective terms. The nineteenth century was relatively peaceful for Europe — but much less so seen from Africa. For this reason, the political economist might find it worth trying to represent the security structure of the world economy by drawing a series of maps, each showing the incidence of different kinds of threats to security at different times to different people. This is no more, indeed, than is attempted by political risk analysts — those latest well-paid advisers to banks and corporations operating in a global economy.

Geologists can draw maps showing the earthquake zones and the volcanic zones of the physical world, places where the pressure of tectonic plates gives greatest risk of instability. Meteorologists can draw maps of areas of climatic extremes, and of high liability to the passage of hurricanes. So the political economist could draw security maps showing areas of high, low or uncertain security from various kinds of threat. Like the geographer's map, they could be drawn with isobars of 'security pressure', or incidence dots of the kind used by demographers or economic geographers.

The world map of liability to individual crime and violence, for example, might show less variation between countries than it did within countries. Los Angeles and parts of New York City have a much higher incidence of murder and robbery-with-violence than Tokyo but only a few miles beyond, life can be much more secure. The efficiency of most governments in preventing crime varies more in big cities than in the countryside. And only when crime is mixed up with civil and political unrest, as in Belfast or Beirut, is the level of insecurity apt to be so high as to interfere seriously with economic life, with investment, production and trade.

Nor is there great variation in the risks to security from full-scale nuclear war. The probability is that, once started, it would spell total disaster and death for everyone — 'nuclear-free' or not. The security map for that risk is almost uniformly grey all over.

It is in the middle of the continuum between highly local threats to individual security at one end and universal threats to all life at the other that the maps would show most variation. There would be some very black or dark grey areas of high risks, of civil war or revolution, and other pale grey areas of very low risk. To sum up, the idea of drawing such maps, however rough and subjective they may be, would at least serve the purpose of broadening the debate over the sources of security and power conferred by the ability to increase it, and over the kinds of security sought by states, by corporate enterprises, by other social groups and by individuals.

Prospects

World economic order will greatly depend, in the future as in the past, on developments in the global security structure. Choices open to states in their economic policies and to corporations and social groups will be determined by what happens to the security structure. Whether it becomes more or less stable, or remains a mixture of positive and negative features, it is certain to have a direct and strong impact on future patterns of production, finance and ideas, and secondary effects on trade, transport, the supply sources of energy and the provision of welfare.

No one, I hold, can predict which of the conceivable scenarios, short of nuclear catastrophe, will be played out in the years ahead. One optimistic scenario, popular after the signing of the 1987 Intermediate Nuclear Forces treaty, sketches a trend towards superpower *détente*, arms limitation and co-operation (or at least mutual restraint) in regional conflicts, whether in Africa, Central America or the Middle East. Less optimistic scenarios sketch the seizure of a significant lead by one superpower over the other — as, for instance, through the Strategic Defence Initiative or its Soviet counterpart. The imminence of weakness provokes aggression and pre-emptive strikes ensue. Another scenario envisages the rise of various threats from within and without to the Soviet–American balance of power, thus increasing rather than decreasing instability in the security structure. One such threat could arise from internal conflict in the Soviet Union between the conservatives and the reformers, complicated by rising nationalism in the Asian provinces. Disorder, or the danger of disorder, at home and in Eastern Europe would harden policy attitudes towards the United States. Conversely, mounting American difficulties in managing Central American disorder and controlling the Hispanic diaspora northwards, might have an equivalent effect on American attitudes.

Or else, there exist external threats to the security structure based on a Soviet–American balance of power. A more active military role by China or by Japan or by both is not at all inconceivable and could easily introduce new destabilizing variables into the structure.

The crumbling restraints already noted on the spread of nuclear weapons to conflict-prone states, especially in the Middle East, is widely acknowledged as a grave weakness for which no clear solution is apparent. Nor is it only the spread of highly destructive nuclear weapons that is already eroding the security structure and could do so more seriously. In many parts of the world civil disorder and local wars and revolts threaten security because modern conventional weapons — from missiles to automatic guns — are much more easily available. A vast unregulated market for small arms has been allowed to grow, making it easier for political dissidents and minorities to challenge the centralized monopoly of violence. Meanwhile, at the next level, restraints on the international sale of arms have weakened markedly as arms exports have come not only to increase the economic security of the state through their contribution to the balance of payments, but to reduce the costs of national security by spreading and diluting development costs to small armed forces over a larger market.

Against these negative developments, we have some positive factors to weigh in the balance. The changed competition between states makes the acquisition of land less important and of market shares more important. Armaments are useful for the conquest of territory, less so for the sale of goods and services. The use of nuclear and other weapons of mass destruction diminishes with victory and leaves only a man-made desert of no possible economic or political value. Then again, the spreading perception in the global knowledge structure of the universal consequences of nuclear war is slowly building social and political pressures on governments to moderate not only their acts but even their language.

From year to year, perceptions of the relative importance of positive versus negative factors, of the probability of one scenario compared to another are bound to change in the future as they have done in the past. It will not only be the objective but also a subjectively perceived nature of the security structure that will react upon the structure of finance, production and knowledge.

Chapter 4

The Production Structure

A production structure can be defined as the sum of all the arrangements determining what is produced, by whom and for whom, by what method and on what terms. It is people at work, and the wealth they produce by working. They may be helped by animals, or by machines. Their efforts may be supplemented by a bountiful Nature. But it is about how people at work are organized and what they are producing. The production structure is what creates the wealth in a political economy.

Production has been the foundation, the base, of almost all political economies. Only in very few places, in very rarely favourable climates, has it ever been possible for people to have enough to eat, enough clothes and enough shelter without working. All organized societies therefore are built on the foundation of a production structure, on the wealth produced by people at work. Because there is such a close connection between the locus of power in society and the production structure, no political economist can afford to ignore it. For instance, when a social group loses power — the senators of ancient Rome, African tribal chiefs, Japanese *samurai* — big changes are apt to follow in who produces what and how they are organized — and consequently in *cui bono*, in who benefits. Equally, when the production structure changes — because the irrigation system built up on a great river breaks down, because a machine has been invented to take the place of hand labour, or because women join the work-force and work for money instead of staying at home — big changes are apt to follow in the distribution of social and political power, and sometimes the nature of the state and the use of authority over the market.

There have been two very profound changes in the production structure in the last two centuries and it is important to think about why each of them happened and what consequences have followed — and in the second case — are likely to follow in the international political economy. The first change was the change to a capitalist, market-oriented mode of production in the states of North-Western Europe, a mode so much more successful and dynamic than other capitalist, market-oriented systems that it came to dominate the economic development of the rest of the world. By 'capitalism' in this context, we understand a system in which markets for goods and services allow the forces of demand to influence what is produced, so that innovation in products and processes and the application of capital to the means by which they are produced are both rewarded.

The second change has been the gradual, uneven but apparently inexorable supplanting of a production structure geared primarily to serve national markets to one geared primarily to serve a world market. As Peter Drucker, the grand old man of management studies, has put it, today the world economy is 'in control', superseding the macroeconomics of the nation-state on which much economy theory, whether Keynesian, monetarist or Marxist, still anachronistically focuses (Drucker, 1986). It is the internationalization of production that is the second crucial stage. Many writers have focused on the rise of the 'multinational' corporation (so-called), and have sought to find explanations for the change in the nature of this dominant production-organizing institution (Skocpol, 1979), but multinationals are only the visible expression of a deeper change as — in medieval Italy — the *condottieri* and their mercenaries were the visible expression of political change from a feudal state based on clan loyalty to a city-state based on wealth. The internationalization of production is no longer nowadays confined to the giant corporations that are annually listed by *Fortune*, *Expansion* or even *South* magazines. Today, more and more small and medium-sized companies, and state-owned as well as privately-owned enterprises, are engaged in production directed by a global strategy for design, production and selling to a world market.

The change has been somewhat obscured by the uneven way in which it has taken place; the supersession of the national economy by the global production structure has proceeded rather faster in some parts of the world than in others, where it has met with more resistance. The Russian Revolution of 1917 and the Chinese Revolution of 1949 each arrested and reversed the absorption of two major national economies into the world capitalist, market-oriented system. Both substituted an authoritarian political structure capable of annihilating opposition and imposing on national societies a command economy, a production structure directed by the agencies of the state, backed when necessary by military force.

Nor have they been the only ones to resist the change. Between those two economic counter-revolutions, there were at least three other serious attempts to resist in the inter-war period — the National Socialist revolution in Germany, the Fascist revolution in Italy and the Franco revolution in Spain — all of which had in common the determined, forceful use of state power to insulate the national economy from the outside world. Each raised barriers of trade controls and bilateral bargaining, exchange and financial controls and controls over the movement of people to prevent too great an involvement with the world market economy. Since World War II, and for almost a quarter of a century, many of the developing countries — India, for example, and countries in Latin America — jealous of their political independence and resentful of the economic power and social influence of foreign multinationals, adopted import-substituting strategies of economic development that slowed down their absorption into the world market — and also, it seems, slowed their economic growth.

Today, however, the resistance of even the great socialist countries seems to be weakening. Import substitution in developing countries is discredited, while the power of the transnational corporations seems to be growing.

A great many writers have been intrigued by the question of what political implications there are in this process of change in the production structure, of why and how it came about and what social consequences have ensued. These writers have come from many different starting-points: from industrial relations, like Robert Cox; from social history, like Michael Mann, Jonathan Hall and Christopher Chase-Dunn; from economic history, like Immanuel Wallerstein, Angus Maddison and Arthur Lewis; from political science, like Jean Baechler, Christian Stoffaës in France and Ed Morse in America; from economics, like Arghiri Emmanuel, Charles-Albert Michalet, Mancur Olson, Charles Lindblom and Dudley Seers; and, not least, from business studies and business history, like Raymond Vernon, Alfred Chandler and John Dunning.[1] It is invidious and difficult to pick out names, aware as one must be of the limits to what any one person has read. The point is only that the questions are important enough to have teased many good minds, and that the student who does not try to range beyond his or her familiar well-trodden field in the whole big farm of the social sciences is going to miss much. You learn by looking over the fence. It is also clear from what has already been written that there is hardly a single writer who does not see a direct connection between the first major change in the production structure and the second. A starting-point, therefore, might well be the question, 'Why did capitalism and a production structure geared to the market start in Western Europe and not in China, in India or the Islamic world?' Just the attempt to answer the question leads to some interesting ideas about the sources of change, and the resistances to change in the production structure that may be very relevant to contemporary issues of international political economy.

Why Western Europe?

Whole books have been devoted to answering the puzzle of why it was the societies of North-Western Europe that from the sixteenth century onwards began to forge ahead economically and not China (Hall, 1985; Mann, 1986). Obviously, there are two parts to the puzzle: what drove Europe forward, and what held China back. For when Marco Polo visited China in the fifteenth century he found an empire that had already lasted nearly 2,000 years, and that seemed to have both the

political strength and the capacity for innovation that economic development needed. Unlike the societies of Africa, or America at the time, the
Chinese were already using paper, gunpowder, the wheelbarrow and cast-
iron tools. Agricultural methods were more advanced than in Europe.

There are four factors that social and economic historians identify as
answering the first question of why Europe forged ahead. They are,
separately, political division; social and cultural unity; and two kinds of
mobility: social and vertical mobility; and geographical and horizontal
mobility.

The second factor explaining why the feudal production structure of
medieval Europe should have been replaced so quickly (by Chinese and
Indian standards) by a mercantile and industrial production structure was
Europe's cultural unity. The European feudal production structure, like
the Chinese, was based primarily on agriculture, but on the whole was
much less secure. The feudal lords and barons were less good at providing
order than the Chinese bureaucratic empire. The only uniting authority
that extended from Ireland to Bohemia and from Italy to Denmark was
the Church. And the Church's authority over the production structure was
rather greater than that of the temporal rulers of states or the local lords
and barons.[2] The cultural and social unity provided by the Church
created a primitive kind of common market in Europe. It also made possible
the accumulation of capital — especially by the great religious orders. As
the Church's authority declined, the emerging nation–states inherited from
it an economy already pregnant with the growing points of technical change
and a commercial structure ready for exploitation by a nascent merchant
class.

The combined effect of the feudal security structure and the feudal-
Christian production structure was that the mass of people were persuaded
to consume less than they produced, yet to continue working hard both
in towns and in the country. As Jean Baechler wrote, it was one necessary
condition of capitalist development that the labourers reduced their leisure
and rest-time to the minimum compatible with survival. Baechler's other
necessary conditions were that the producers should be strongly motivated
by the pursuit of profit, not in order to enjoy worldly goods but simply
for profit itself; that the intellectual activity of society was directed to
science; that science was applied to lowering the costs of production and
that there was always sufficient demand to absorb the output so produced.
None of these four conditions must be subjected to limitation of any kind
— neither cultural, moral or religious, nor intellectual or political. His
argument was that, compared with others, Western society from the eighteenth century to the twentieth had come nearest to fulfilling these necessary
conditions.[3]

The industrialized production structure that emerged in the period, faster
in some countries, more slowly in others, was characterized by the ever-
growing capacity of the entrepreneurs to finance the new forms of industrial

manufacture and by the ever-growing recruitment, usually from the countryside, of workers to man the machines. As Marx put it, in his usual rather turgid way, 'Accumulation reproduces the capital–labour relation on a progressive scale, more capitalists or larger capitalists at this pole, more wage-workers at that'.[4] The process gave more power to a new class of industrialists and their financiers and less to the wage-earners until they began to organize in labour unions and to use democratic political systems, whenever they could, to defend themselves. What Marx omits, in concentration on the reproduction, as he put it, of capital and of labour power, is the element of demand stressed by Baechler.

The social change that supplied that demand and accompanied the domination of capitalists over wage-labourers was of course the emergence in the countries of North-Western Europe especially of the new middle class, the rich farmers, the traders, lawyers and small entrepreneurs, who no longer depended for their livelihood on the monarchical state but who owed it instead to a changing production structure. It was these people who started the English Revolution and fought the Civil War against Charles I. And it was these people who were behind William of Orange in the Netherlands and England in the Glorious Revolution of 1688 and who started the French Revolution and later the European revolutions of 1830 and 1848.

The fourth factor was the horizontal or geographical mobility that allowed the European economies to surmount the problem of multiplying populations which might otherwise have seriously delayed and slowed down the economic transformation to modern capitalism. It did this in two ways. It allowed some of the surplus population so feared by the Reverend Thomas Malthus when he wrote his *Essay on the Principle of Population as it Affects the Future Improvement of Society* in 1798 to spill out into the 'new' lands of America and Australia. And it allowed these same European emigrants to settle and to produce the cheap food to feed the factory workers back home.

Numbers matter

This question of population in relation to production is so central in any political economy, whether of England in the eighteenth and nineteenth century or of the world economy and especially the Third World in the twentieth, that it merits a short digression from our consideration of the origins of the present production structure. Production of wealth is a relative matter: relative to the number of people needing to be fed, clothed, sheltered and supplied with other goods and services. Can production keep pace with population? This is not always an easy question: for what may be enough to feed a multitude where everyone has an equal share may not be enough where some groups insist on extra large shares, on the right to waste production, or on factors of production going into sophisticated artefacts and luxuries rather than into basic needs of food and shelter.

This was one of the points missed by Dr Malthus when he concluded gloomily that there was no solution in Britain to the inadequacy of production in relation to population. Given 'the passion between the sexes', he argued, disapprovingly, there was an inherent conflict between the rate of population growth and the rate of production growth. Human population grew, like rabbit population or fly population, at a geometric rate, but food production grew only at an arithmetic rate: an extra acre of cultivated land only produced the same amount of bread as any other acre. His friend the economist David Ricardo pointed out that it might even, in reality, produce less than other acres because the best land is always used first and the quality of what later economists called 'the marginal land' tends to fall, as does its unit productivity. So, since men and women could not resist the temptations of sexual intercourse, population growth was limited only by the means of subsistence. The only check lay in vice and misery debilitating potency and the female capacity to produce. Malthus concluded — as do the advocates of *triage* theories today — that poor relief was futile and destined to be ineffective in relieving human misery. *Triage* was a principle originally developed by French army doctors for the allocation of scarce medical resources in battle. If the choice lay between treating those so badly hurt that they would probably die anyway, and those so slightly wounded that they would probably live anyway; or those for whom quick treatment meant altering their chance of survival, then it was rational from a military–economic point of view to treat the third group first and, if necessary, abandon the first and second groups. Adapted to the global problem of aid for economic development, the advocates of *triage* have suggested that it is not necessary to give official aid to those countries already far enough along the path of economic growth that they can cope with population growth (as Japan has done). Aid should therefore be concentrated on those who have just a chance of doing so, given enough financial, managerial and technical help, while it would be wasted on the poorest because they have no hope, whatever happens, of closing the gap between numbers and output, between population and production.[5]

One reason for the apparent hopelessness of systems of poor relief in Malthus's time and later was that the agricultural revolution of the seventeenth and eighteenth centuries had been directed not simply at producing more barley bread and oat porridge for everyone, but at producing more and cheaper meat and wool for those who could afford them. 'Turnip' Townsend's objective was cheaper animal, rather than human, feed.[6] The depopulation of the Scottish Highlands was brought about by political, not economic factors — because the lairds wanted to increase their cash incomes by allowing sheep to run loose over their clansmen's tiny crofts. Agricultural improvement in France was similarly skewed to a more inequitable distribution of production, through the choices imposed by a ruling class on the peasants about the content of production, as well as about its amount.

The other and more commonly noticed weaknesses in Malthus's argument were, firstly, that it assumed an irreversible downward trend to diminishing returns for additional inputs in agricultural production; and, secondly, that it assumed an unalterable human ability to limit rates of reproduction. In the short run, an even more important blind spot was to ignore the possibilities of European populations solving the problem of insufficient production through emigration and imported food. The Scottish clansmen were not the only ones to take ship to the United States, Canada, Latin America and Australia, there to grow wheat to sell to Europe.

As the demographers calculate, some 50 million Europeans left Europe for other continents between 1846 and 1930. By the early twentieth century, industrialized Western Europe had not only shed some of its people; it was also being partially fed and supplied not only from its own limited acres, but from those of other continents with whom it traded. By these means, Europe was able to achieve with comparative ease the difficult transition from a population profile typical of a basically agricultural production system to one characteristic of a predominantly industrial and service system of production.[7]

The Asian experience

Despite its head-start at the beginning of the sixteenth century, China did not manage a similar transition. One reason for this was that its population problem was much greater — 450 million against 300 million — and was eased neither by the exodus of so large a proportion of the population to other lands, nor by the import of cheap food. From the sixteenth century to the mid-nineteenth century, China's population also exploded, doubling or trebling in numbers. Large-scale starvation and endemic famine were avoided by a combination of agricultural productivity and intensification and population control by female infanticide. But the production structure failed to follow Europe into an industrial revolution. Max Weber's reason for that failure was that bureaucracy in China killed off capitalism. Subsequent scholarship has only refined and elaborated this judgement. The empire had already lasted so long by the seventeenth and eighteenth centuries that its survival had become an end in itself. That survival was assured through the support of a mandarin class of administrators recruited by examination and therefore owing loyalty directly to the state rather than to a particular family or group. Jealous of their own privileged position, they also naturally governed in such a way as to block the rise to power of any rivals — the military or the navy, for instance. Jonathan Hall calls this 'capstone' government, as if it were a monolithic block sitting on top of society (Hall, 1985). Confucian beliefs in the land as the source of all virtue, plus the fact that revenue for the state came from the land, made for policies directed towards agriculture and a healthy peasantry. Peasants, being tied to the land and separated physically from each other, have to be pushed hard before they challenge the social and political order. Horizontal linkages would be easier between a merchant or a military class but the formation of rival concentrations of power was always carefully opposed by the capstone state.

There was, of course, much more to the story than that. A cumbersome and inefficient tax system left the state — like many empires — better at blocking than initiating change. Geographical isolation fostered the enormous arrogance of Chinese culture towards the rest of the world. It also meant that, free of any sense of serious threat even after European settlement and the Opium Wars of the 1840s, the political incentives for economic change that were so powerful a force in seventeenth- and eighteenth-century Europe simply did not exist in China.

If the bureaucracy of the state was the major barrier to change in the Chinese production structure, in India it was religion and religious beliefs that so influenced social relations as to inhibit change and mobility and to discourage enterprise and innovation. The salient characteristic of Hindu society for centuries was that a man's economic role was determined by his caste, and that, being born into one caste, he could not change either his social status or his role in the production structure. He was either a brahmin, a soldier, a trader, a farmer, or he might be unlucky enough to be an untouchable, the caste destined to perform the unpleasant, dirty and menial tasks that other people were keen to avoid. The barriers maintaining the distinctions between castes were sustained by religious authority, and the belief that breaking them brought penalties to a man's soul. All this was, of course, sustained by the self-interest of those in the higher castes. The religious authority vested in the brahmins, according to social historians, proved durable through all kinds of invasions and political changes precisely because it was not too closely associated with the political authority of the state. It was therefore largely independent of those who held political or military power. It could survive the Mogul Empire and the British Empire and still rule the way in which the work was organized. In Hindu society, the separation of powers was carried to an extreme, the state being totally secular and the religious authority sustained by belief able to maintain a set of rules regarding diet, personal hygiene and marriage that people feared to break far more than they feared the power of their political rulers — as the British discovered to their cost in the Indian Mutiny of 1857.[8]

The only challenge to Hindu society that might have succeeded was another religion – Buddhism. But though adopted by rulers, its total concentration on the salvation of the soul robbed it of any interest in offering an alternative set of rules for daily life to that of Hinduism. At the same time, the authority of the brahmins was not based only on birth and religious scholarship; they had close contact with people in villages and they provided essential social services, combining the roles of teacher, judge, technical adviser and community leader. These services and an open, non-exclusive attitude to other religions provided the kind of social cement that, in a vast sub-continent with poor communications, the political authority based on military force could not.

That such a socially rigid society created far too rigid a production structure to allow innovation and development is easy to understand. There were also some additional interventions by the state which obstructed capitalist enterprise. Jonathan Hall, for instance, notes that the Mogul Empire taxed Hindu traders at 5 per cent, but Muslim traders at only 2.5 per cent. They also caused land to revert to the state on the death of the landlord, so that there was inevitably more incentive for the conspicuous consumption observed by European visitors and far less for agricultural improvement, capital accumulation and investment (Hall, 1985: 82–3).

Moreover, the evidence of historians is clear that the poverty of India had more to do with the relation between population and production than it had to do with British rule. By the time the East India Company's role was taken over after the 1857 Mutiny by the British Government's India Office, India's per capita income was well past its peak. A century before, it had fallen to only two-thirds that of England. The British may not have made India rich but neither was it they who made it poor. They were spread too thin to make very much difference. The good effects and the bad of British rule probably cancelled each other out. They may have suppressed the textile industry to protect Lancashire but they did (for mainly strategic reasons) build the most comprehensive railroad system outside of Europe or America. This helped to counter the endemic problems of drought, crop failure and famine. At the same time, their concern for their own health brought cleaner water and better drains to some cities. This may have been one major factor unintentionally intensifying the pressures of population growth.

The American century

If the triumph of the European capitalist production system over all other rivals was the first globally important change, the second, which grew out of it, was the development of a global production system, gradually taking over and supplanting separate national production structures. That change has been in large measure an American achievement. It was made possible, firstly by economic leadership passing from Europe to the United States in the course of the first half of the twentieth century; and, secondly, by the permissive attitude of the American state towards business — and more particularly, towards the giant corporations that were the first to emerge as genuinely transnational corporations designing goods for a world market, producing in several countries at once and directing their financial and marketing strategies to the world economy and not just to the national economy of the United States. The example of US-based transnationals has now been followed by the Europeans, Japanese and Koreans, Latin Americans and others. The result was that by 1985 international production — production by transnationals outside their home base — actually exceeded the volume of world trade, and in fact by then a large and growing proportion of world trade was intra-firm trade, transactions conducted between branches of the same transnational corporation but across state frontiers.

The two questions that call for explanation, therefore, are: why did America forge ahead of Europe in industrial production? And why did the transnational corporation come to dominate and reshape the global production structure? The first is a question of economic history on which much has been written and must include political as well as social and economic factors. The second has also been much written about but is much more disputed. Let me try to summarize the answers given to both questions.

The answer to the first question could be summed up as three Ds — debt, dominance and demand. These were the factors which laid the basis for American economic growth and which, aided by two world wars, allowed an inviolate America to overtake a war-torn Europe. The United States was the major beneficiary of British overseas investment in the nineteenth century and could never have managed the rapid physical occupation of the continent and the enormous physical investments made in agriculture and industry without the finance provided by the City of London (and, to a lesser extent, Paris). Foreign debt, involving (just as it does now) periods of effective default on past loans, was then as now a major engine of economic growth. The finance, however, would never have kept coming through the nineteenth century as it did if it had not been for the political dominance of the United States over the North American continents. To the South, French, Spanish and then Mexican opposition was weak; and to the North, except for one rather brief frontier dispute, there was no serious danger of an attack from Canada, either under British rule till 1867 or thereafter. The security structure of the continent was therefore stable enough to bring a steady capital inflow not seriously interrupted even by the Civil War of the 1860s.

The demand factor also was essentially more political than economic. The early American industrialists, manufacturing clothes or covered wagons, ploughs or guns, were producing for a market under one federal authority. Moreover, it was a market that, aided by immigration, was always growing and in which the liberal democratic political system allowed such social mobility that income was much more evenly distributed in society than at the same period in the European countries. The poor factory workers may not have been much better-off in Chicago than in Manchester, but they could more quickly hope to join a large and relatively affluent middle class of eager consumers. This was the big difference between Henry Ford, for example, and his European competitors like Rolls Royce, Mercedes Benz and Lancia who, until the advent of Volkswagen and Morris, were mostly producing for a wealthy but much smaller class of potential car-owners. This contrast between a mass market and a class market reflected the different income distributions of the two continents, so that it was not so much — as Chandler (1977) and other business historians have pointed out — the innovation of the mass *production* system (vilified by the Marxists as 'Fordism') that accounted for rapid American economic growth, as the innovation of mass *distribution* systems, making sure that what was produced in quantity could be sold in quantity.

The other important factor, accounting for more rapid American economic growth in the twentieth century, was, of course, the country's longer neutrality and security from invasion in both world wars. World War I had turned the United States from a major international debtor into a major creditor, owed vast war debts by Britain and France and able to let capital flow to Europe, especially to Germany in the 1920s. While the United States manufacturers had a large single mass market to exploit their European counterparts after 1918 found their markets further split and reduced by the Wilsonian principle of self-determination and the substitution of little successor states for the former Austro–Hungarian and German Empires. World War II had even more drastic results for the US economy, boosting industrial production by over 44 per cent between 1941 and 1944. As shown in Figure 4.1 much of the increase went into production for the military. In constant dollars, the value of military contracts rose from about $18 billion in 1941 to about $88 billion in the peak year 1943. A veritable reserve army of the unemployed, which numbered as much as 13 million at the outbreak of the war, was put to work (Vatter, 1985: 22). And, on the management side, the stimulus of fat defence contracts developed in US corporations new managerial skills at directing and controlling from company headquarters production facilities located in several places, often far from each other and from headquarters. Because the parent company was legally responsible for observing national labour and safety laws and had to maintain product standards if it wanted to

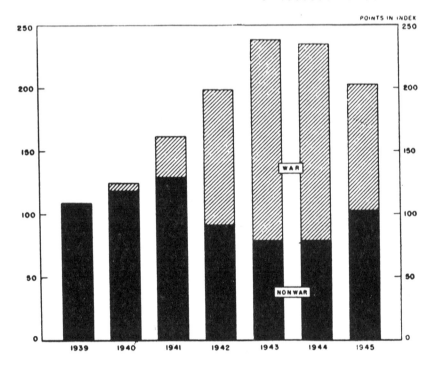

Source: Vatter (1985) p. 16
Figure 4.1 US war production, 1939–45

get more fat, cost-plus defence contracts, it had a powerful incentive, according to Melman, for developing management methods suited to centralized decision-making for dispersed production plants — methods which, after the war, could easily be adopted to running a series of foreign affiliates (Melman, 1970).

Given that the US economy came out of World War II so much stronger and more productive than the economies of either Europe or Japan, there is still the question of why this dominance should have resulted not only in massive exports from the United States — which in the short term it did, thanks to aid and credits supplied by the US government as a means of fighting the cold war — but also in an outward spread of US companies from America to Canada, Europe and Latin America. They bought local companies, and they set up local production facilities. They began to change from national production for national markets to international production for a world market. Their lead was followed by hundreds of non-American enterprises, even state-owned enterprises, convinced that this was the only way to survive against American competition.

The 'multinational' and its theorists[9]

Today, outside the Soviet bloc and China, there are almost no really big businesses — the French Crédit Agricole and the British National Coal Board being two possible exceptions — that are not transnational. The foreign operations of the top companies in the world represented 30 per cent of total sales in 1970, 40 per cent in 1980 — the most marked rise being in chemicals, ships, cars and aircraft, metals and electronics. The 350 largest enterprises in the world have over 25,000 foreign affiliates. One quarter of the whole work-force of the industrialized countries — 25 million people, according to a recent UN report — worked in international business. And, as European, Japanese and now Third World enterprises quickly followed the big American corporate move to organize production abroad, so the American-controlled share of international business, though still growing in absolute terms, fell from two-thirds before 1970 to less than half in the 1980s.

The French writer Charles-Albert Michalet usefully identified two kinds of international business: there are, he said, the *relay affiliates*, which simply reproduce abroad the same kind of production operation organized by the parent enterprise at home, and there are the *workshop affiliates*, where the parent arranges for certain operations, possibly drawn by cheap labour or low taxes or both and made possible by cheap, quick transport, to be done in foreign 'workshops' (Michalet, 1976). Although many developing countries were tempted in the late 1970s and early 1980s to encourage the latter, by opening free economic zones (FEZs), it seems likely that the relay affiliates will now grow more rapidly, attracted especially to those LDCs with potentially large domestic markets and a literate, skilled work-force. In some recent cases car companies (for instance) have arranged that their whole production of certain parts, or even the production of entire new models, shall be carried out in a foreign subsidiary; or, in some cases, by an overseas subsidiary jointly owned and run with a local partner. Both between two corporations in different industrialized countries and between one in an industrialized and one in a developing country, corporate partnerships or co-operation agreements are becoming more and more common. This is especially so in the more advanced technology sectors where the research and development, or R & D, costs are high.

This is one of the many facts about the internationalization of production that have confounded the theorists of both right and left, both the liberals and the Marxists, American and European. The dominant theory for more than a decade since Raymond Vernon wrote *Sovereignty at Bay* has been that of the 'product cycle' (Vernon, 1971). This adapted conventional Ricardian notions of rent to the spread of business abroad. It explained how a company could extract a rent (i.e. a higher price than warranted by its costs of production, including interest on capital and normal profit under competitive conditions) by exploiting its monopoly of a new product. As competition at home grew, it first exported the product, then produced it abroad, extracting at each point of the cycle another kind of rent. The cycle was completed when the accumulated rents invested in innovative R & D produced another new product to start all over again.[10]

This was elegant and parsimonious, but failed to explain why the oil companies, whose product was hardly new, still dominated the league table of big international business and did so even after their cartel, known as the Seven Sisters, was broken by nationalization and the OPEC organization of governments. Nor did it explain the reverse flow of European (and Japanese) companies into the United States after the US companies had 'invaded' Europe in the 1950s (Franko, 1976; Savary, 1984; Lall, 1983). Nor did it explain satisfactorily why, after the oil companies, the businesses that 'went international' were so often not manufacturing a product at all but only selling a service — not only the banks and insurance (and reinsurance) companies but advertising enterprises like J. Walter Thompson, accountants like Arthur Anderson, art dealers like Sothebys, consultants like McKinsey, databank services like Lockheed Dialog. In the 1980s, the internationalization of service businesses was proceeding faster than anything else.

This was one of the many facts that Marxists and dependency theorists found hard to explain. Their presumption was that the tendency in the capitalist system was for the rate of profit to fall, making it necessary to find new ways of making workers work harder — Fordism and the stopwatch on the assembly line — or to find new, cheaper, foreign workers to exploit. This notion is confounded firstly by the obvious fact that in modern industry the labour cost element is relatively insignificant, the worker's productivity being determined far more by the capital, energy and technology invested in the production process, and, secondly, by the fact that in many international service industries the workers are often paid rather well and that those who are badly paid (in hotels, fast-food franchised business and so forth) are no worse off than the employees of their local competitors.

Most confounding still, especially to the dependency theorists, is the fact that so many of the developing country governments who have been most vociferous about the exploitation by the foreign multinationals have changed their attitudes under the pressures of debt and a shortage of foreign exchange and foreign credit. While bargaining quite toughly over such questions as how much the company would contribute to the national balance of payments in exports, or how much it would contribute to economic development by training local workers and managers, the LDCs have in fact become rather keen to attract foreign companies. Not only that, but enough is known about the extent of internationalization of business to the Thirld World to show that all the UN and other statistical figures entirely fail to catch the great number of small and medium-sized private companies, often family-owned and mostly Indian, Chinese or Levantine, that have been quietly expanding their international business.

As John Dunning has argued, even though none of the available theories are wholly satisfactory, each of them may contain some useful element of truth about internationalization of production (Dunning, 1985). It may therefore be necessary to collect bits from each of them, adopting what he has called an eclectic approach. A major contribution to such an eclectic approach, it seems to me, came from Fred Meyer, who explained that the accelerating rate of technological change plus the escalating costs of replacing obsolete plant with new plant incorporating new technology meant that firms had less time in which to recoup the ever-increasing cost of their past capital investment (Meyer, 1978). The profits to be made from selling on a national market were just not sufficient to keep the firm in business; it was forced, therefore, to adopt a global sales strategy and hence, because of the preferences in state policies for local production over imported products, a global production policy.

Neither Meyer nor the other economists ever claimed that technology, or corporate profit-making, was the whole story. A necessary condition for so rapid a spread of international production was the political acquiescence of other industrialized countries with the open world economy objective so actively pursued and promoted by the United States. Opinions differ as to the guiding motive behind American post-war policy in economic matters. On the left, the wish to make the world economy safe and welcoming for American capital is stressed (Block, 1977). On the right, it is the American conviction that political liberalism and economic liberalism go together so that freer trade and freer movement of capital are not just an end in themselves but a means to building a free (i.e. non-communist) world (Kindleberger, 1987; Diebold, 1980; Maddison, 1982).

Nor should domestic politics be forgotten. Ralph Nader was one writer who justifiably pointed out that the American lead in the internationalization of business could never have come about but for a radical change in US policy in the course of the nineteenth century.[11] Early American law insisted on open accounting, stockholders' rights and federal chartering of companies. By the 1890s there had started a Dutch auction of minimal state chartering, especially by small, poor states like Delaware and Rhode Island. From then on, managerial control was paramount. A secretive, obfuscating system of corporate accounting was developed which kept stockholders in virtual ignorance of corporate strategy but which also sometimes consoled them with capital gains and bonus issues.

At the same time that state chartering was enhancing the power of managers over investors, the US Congress was reacting against the over-weening economic power of Carnegie in steel, Rockefeller in oil, Dupont in chemicals. The first of several anti-trust laws, the Sherman Act, was passed in 1890. These laws have also had a big influence on the subsequent development of American international business, for the essential anti-trust rule said that bigness in itself was no crime but that there must be competition. It was contrary to US anti-trust laws for companies to act together in restraint of competition within the United States. What they did outside the United States, however, and provided it had no effect on the US market, was their own business. The need to observe this fine distinction and to steer clear of anti-trust suits brought against them by the anti-trust division of the US Department of Justice — especially active in the New Deal days — was one strong reason why US corporations have preferred until quite recently to keep 100 per cent ownership over their foreign subsidiaries. There is little doubt that this preference, excluding local participation, greatly added to the resent-ment and suspicion of the foreign 'multinational', especially in Latin America, where US corporations dominated the local scene.

More recently, there have been other ways in which state policy has had a significant influence on the evolution of international business. One such was the US government's Interest Equalization Tax of 1963, reinforcing other banking regulations operative only within the United States. These powerfully motivated American banks to follow their corporate clients to Europe and to deal not in dollars in New York but in Eurodollars in London and other financial centres. (Bank of America is credited with starting up the 'Asian' dollar market in Singapore.) The exodus overseas was reinforced by the Johnson Administration's discouragement — in defence of the US balance of payments — of capital outflows by big American corporations. Instead of issuing stock for use abroad on Wall Street, they raised money by Eurodollar issues in London (Strange, 1986).

The role of the state, working through financial and industrial policies, is something that the literature from business schools, with their eyes focused on the corporation at the receiving end of policy, has sometimes underplayed. The whole question indeed does not lend itself as easily to theorizing as do some other branches of social science. For the corporation is both the partner, and sometimes the national cham-pion, of governments; and sometimes their adversary. It is both the suppliant of the state when it wants protection or subsidy from govern-ment, and at the same time the quarry of the government inspector, the tax-collector and the regulator.

The ambivalence of the state towards the corporation has been well illustrated recently in the attitudes of European politicians to Reagan's Strategic Defence Initiative (SDI) programme. While opposed to it politically both on the grounds of its potentially inflationary expense and on its potentially destabilizing effects on the balance of power and mutual assured destruction (MAD) between the superpowers, both the French and German governments came to realize that for the national economy to keep in the forefront of certain advanced technologies — an obvious national interest — French or German companies could benefit by getting SDI contracts from the US government. On balance, the national interest might be better served if they co-operated with the United States than if they did not.

To sum all this up, we may say that the nature of the global production structure has become increasingly dominated by international business but that this cannot be adequately explained by reference to any single factor or aspect. It is the combined result of state policies *and* of market trends, of management strategies *and* changing technology. It reflects both domestic decisions taken according to political preferences within the leading national economy, that of the United States, and the acceptance of multilateral agreements on trade and money by enough other industrialized countries to make sure that not even its rejection by the Soviet bloc and China could stop the emergence of an increasingly open world economy.

Assessing production

Weighed against the four basic values of political economy, the dominant production structure scores highly on its efficiency in producing wealth; moderately on the autonomy it permits to states; moderately or poorly according to different opinions on its basic order or stability. Its score on the fourth value or criterion of justice is the most open to question. It depends, firstly, on the subjective notion of what is fair or equitable; secondly, on whether we are talking about justice between nations organized as states, about classes or other economic groups, or about individuals. It also depends on whether we score justice against some absolute standard, or just relatively, in which case we should compare the justice of a market-oriented production structure with earlier feudal, theocratic or tribal production structures or with contemporary command-based production structures.

Compared with either of these, there is little doubt on the score of efficiency. The increase in the production of food, raw materials, manufactures and services in the last hundred years is phenomenal and unprecedented. That so much of the wealth produced is devoted to armaments and defence is a result of the security structure. That structure has also been one of the major causes of the instability and disorder that has marked the production structure. Interruption by war has always set production back in the regions that are theatres of war, while boosting it in others. The other cause of instability and disorder in the production structure has been the interruption or collapse of the global credit mechanisms, cutting off the capital needed for investment and thus arresting the growth of production. The instability of the production structure in recent times has been unevenly felt in peace, as in war, the burden of what is euphemistically called 'adjustment' falling much more heavily on the developing than the industrialized countries.

This leads us back again to the debated question of justice. It perhaps merits some comment before we consider the other debated question of autonomy, of whether and how the production structure may be weakening or undermining the power of states.

There is no doubt in my mind that the great expansion of the production structure has shifted the pack of cards and dealt them out differently both to states as players and to social groups as players. It is true that the way the cards are played, by states, and by ruling elites, by managers of enterprises, leaders of political parties or labour organizations will affect outcomes. In any game, some hands of cards will be well played, others badly. A book like Mancur Olson's *The Rise and Decline of Nations* suggests some of the factors that cause hands of cards to be well or badly played, that explain why some societies adjust successfully to external changes and others poorly or, as he puts it, sclerotically (Olson, 1982). It is a question with which economic historians — Angus Maddison or Al Hirschman, for example — have wrestled with for years, or if you think back to Gibson, Spengler or Weber, for many decades, even centuries. But I do not think who-gets-what out of the production system can entirely be reduced to how good or bad national responses have been to economic opportunities.

In the first place, the aces and deuces in any hand of cards are randomly distributed by nature and the market. Some countries have large cheap oilfields, others none. Some produce ostrich feathers or whalebones for corsets which no one wants any more. And, in the second place, as the world economy has become more integrated and the production structure has become global instead of national, it is obvious that the firstcomers, in producing for and selling to this market, have had tremendous and partly fortuitous advantages over the latecomers. This point comes back to the question of population mentioned earlier in the explanation of European success in industrialization compared with that of China. It concerns the difficult transition from a demographic profile characteristic of a primitive subsistence society, through that characteristic of a developing country in which high birth-rates produce a large base of young age-groups in the profile so that it resembles an elongated cone like a plastic traffic marker, to that of an industrialized society in which birth-rates have fallen and the profile looks more like the top half of an onion. The transition was eased for the European and American firstcomers and has been progressively more difficult for those that followed. Last in the

Table 4.1 World Population by Areas, 1950–1984 (millions)

	1950	1960	1970	1980	1984	Average Annual % Increase 1965–70	Average Annual % Increase 1980–85
Total	2,504	3,014	3,683	4,453	4,763	1.9	1.7
Africa	222	278	357	476	573	2.7	3.0
North America	166	199	227	252	261	1.0	0.9
Latin America	165	217	284	362	397	2.7	2.3
East Asia	671	801	984	1,183	1,239	1.6	1.1
South Asia	695	864	1,111	1,408	1,539	2.6	2.2
Europe	392	425	459	484	490	0.6	0.3
Oceania	13	16	19	23	25	2.0	1.5
USSR	180	214	242	265	276	1.0	1.0

Source: United Nations

progression comes Africa, where numbers are still multiplying faster than output and the production structure is therefore called upon to work harder to produce enough per head of population than it is in regions more advanced, not just in the ability to produce but in the demographic transition from the traffic marker pattern to the onion pattern. World population rose rapidly from 2.5 billion in 1950 to over 4.5 billion in 1984 (topping 5 billion by 1987), as compared with an earlier period from 1850 to 1950 when it took a hundred years for world population to grow by 1.5 billion. Numbers have increased most dramatically in the three 'developing' regions of Latin America, South Asia and Africa, in all of which numbers have more or less doubled since 1950. By contrast, numbers both in North America and the Soviet Union have been stable. The other striking fact is that average annual growth-rates have slowed quite markedly even in the same developing regions of Latin America and South Asia — but not yet in Africa. Some of the predictions made in the 1970s that world population would double in less than thirty years and that by the year 2000 there would be a crisis of inadequate production, have been proved wrong. They assumed unchanged average annual growth-rates. The problem for coming decades is much more one of managing a demographic transition in the latecomer regions like Africa than of coping with an inexorable and continuing growth in numbers. In 1973, according to the UN, food output overtook population growth for the whole world, and by 1975 had overtaken it even in the developing countries.

In some ways it is arguable that the reshuffling of the pack in the production structure has affected class relations more directly than it has affected international relations. Internationalization of production, sometimes referred to as world-wide sourcing, has certainly had a major impact on labour–management relations. The fact that in many industries a transnational company can move its plant, or expand elsewhere, while the worker cannot move to another country has robbed labour unions in industrialized countries of some of their power to win concessions from management by the threat to strike. If there are too many strikes — as at the Ford plant in Dagenham in England in the 1960s — the management will decide to close or to contract the plant and produce in Spain or Germany instead. The labour movement has searched in vain for a way to organize transnationally to match the new global mobility of employers. Solidarity associations like Charles Levinson's International Metalworkers Federation in Geneva tried hard to get workers to support with money or industrial action the strikes called in poorer countries. The International Trade Secretariats organized on a sectoral basis tried hard to get information about the profits made by TNCs in countries where workers were asking for higher wages. But the obstinate fact remained that change in the production structure plus the same immigration laws supported even by left-wing parties and voters had destroyed for ever the idea that there was a common class interest for workers in every country. On this issue it would take more than singing 'the Internationale' to unite the human race. Brazilian and German car workers in Europe or America are competing for the same share of the cake. Textile workers in Singapore or Taiwan feel very little solidarity with textile workers in Europe or America when the latter campaign for a yet more restrictive Multifibre Agreement. Seamen in Britain campaign against flag-of-convenience ships because they employ non-union sailors, while seamen in the Gulf states or the Pacific islands are all in favour of the chance such ships offer to get a job at sea. As the distinguished Cambridge economist Joan Robinson once observed, 'There's only one thing worse than being exploited, and that's not being exploited!'

Some workers have found that bargaining with management to raise their standard of living is self-defeating; they must bargain with government instead, using demonstration, disruption and vote-switching to influence policy on wages and on welfare systems. Other workers meanwhile find that the transnational corporation, by making a co-operation agreement with a local partner, has opened new job and training opportunities that the local partner alone could never have afforded.

It is true that the corporate managers often live and behave like a privileged ruling elite. And it is arguable that one of the consequences of recent change in production has been to enlarge the gap between the worlds of big business and of small business. Here again there is more inequality, whether we look at the power of business to move and protect markets, to generate and choose new technology, to pick the location for new plant and employment, to bargain with governments and with banks to get access to credit. Yet the concentration of economic power is not inexorable. There are also contrary, centrifugal forces at work. Big businesses lose their specialists and experts who set up on their own in some niche of the market they have made or discovered under the wing of the big company. Big companies, like big empires, are obliged to decentralize, to give local bosses more freedom to respond to local conditions and local pressures. The 'loyalty' of the TNC itself to the government of the home state is no longer something the latter can take for granted.

The disparity between economic groups does not only concern managers and industrial workers, big business and small business. Primary producers, and especially farmers, have benefited unequally compared with industrial producers from the expansion of world GNP, even where, as in Japan, the United States or the European Community, they have been protected, subsidized and supported by the intervention of the state to ameliorate the vagaries of the market and their weak bargaining position *vis-à-vis* the brokers and buyers. The net result has still been a widening gap between average incomes in agriculture and average incomes in industry (Gale Johnson, 1973).

The justice or injustice of the distributional effects of change in the production structure in short have been uneven, complex and subjective. Some wider issues concerning the system in general remain to be considered. Among these, there are three, of which the first — whether states have the power to control the transnational corporations — is familiar to most people and has been much discussed. Less familiar but no less important are the other two: whether the fiscal problems of the state have been complicated by the internationalization of production; and whether the state's function in relation to risk — that inherent characteristic of market-based systems — has undergone significant change.

States have tried to assert control over transnational corporations in two ways — nationally and by multilateral agreement. The latter has been the least successful. After a decade or more of experience in various international organizations, it seems that the minimalist approach of the OECD countries has proved more realistic than the maximalist approach favoured by the 'Group of 77' developing countries at the United Nations. The OECD Guidelines for multinationals were issued in 1976, rather hurriedly to pre-empt the parallel efforts of the United Nations. These guidelines were intended to encourage rather than to enforce good behaviour by corporations operating away from home. 'Good' is taken to mean behaviour that is socially and politically acceptable to the political authorities — which may be religious as well as secular — of the host states. For instance, oil companies operating in strict Muslim countries like Saudi Arabia would find in the Guidelines a legitimate justification for making rules to limit their employees' use of alcohol in such countries. To that extent, the guidelines would reinforce the political authority of the company over its employees. Where and how they hold a party and how they spend their time off, after all, has nothing to do with the economic, profit-maximizing role of the corporation; it is therefore an essentially political intervention. Such an intervention could affect its relations, for good or ill, with the host government as another kind of political authority — and in turn with the government's relation with the political authority or religious leaders.

The UN draft Code of Conduct for Transnational Corporations by contrast has had little or no effect on the behaviour of either states or corporations, since the drafting group in new York was unable, after ten years of trying, to reach an agreed form of words. The text is therefore peppered with square brackets adding '[shall]' after '[should]' and vice versa. If the disagreement is ever resolved it will only be done by resorting to ambiguity.

At the national level, the developing states that wanted to have the mandatory 'shall' instead of the advisory 'should' put into a UN Code were meanwhile seeking to use national political power against the foreign corporations. They began by nationalizing them, first the mineral and oil companies and then banks, insurance, breweries and other enterprises. Their right to do so — since industrialized countries had often done the same — was unchallenged provided only that they observed the rule of customary international law that compensation should be made promptly, in full and equitably. Yet the developing-country governments very often found that they had won an empty victory, and too often at a high price. They had the mines, or the oilwells, but not the same power to exploit the market. Whether it was Chilean copper or the Guinness brewery in Nigeria, the displaced companies kept control over market access, by making long-term contracts with the customers, for instance. They also had command of the technology necessary to remain competitive in world markets.

Similarly, even the more developed countries like Canada, which in the 1970s set up watchdog agencies like the Foreign Investment Review Agency (FIRA) to protect the country against domination by foreign (i.e. US) corporations, discovered in the 1980s that it was impossible to draw up clear, uniform rules about which US corporations should be allowed to operate in Canada and which should be refused. The question, in practical politics, was rather how many concessions the government could get out of the corporation as the price for its right to enter the Canadian economy.

Developing countries came increasingly to the same conclusion. Bargaining with corporations that could be made to help national economic development by earning foreign exchange, by exporting petroleum products or chemicals or cars looked to be a more rational choice than throwing them out. Other conditions, such as appointing local managers or training skilled workers, providing medical services or even conducting industrial research in the country, could be added if the corporation could be persuaded that the new symbiotic relationship with the government was worth its while. Whether it could or not was apt to vary a good deal from state to state. Some states were too small, too poor, too unstable for the corporate managers to be convinced that it was worthwhile making such deals in order to gain a place in the national economy. So, whereas in the old nationalization strategy, all states had equal power to nationalize, in the new strategy of production co-operation the inequality of states in bargaining power was very marked. Asian and Latin American governments usually got better deals than African ones, for instance. States acting as gatekeepers had reasserted their power over corporations but were able to do so very unequally. Those with most social cohesion, political stability and economic growth potential were able to use the power of the foreign corporations to reinforce that of the state; while other states which lacked these three desirable qualities found the corporations less willing to help and consequently more apt to look like adversaries still and not partners.

Tax issues

The fiscal question in a nutshell is whether the transnational corporations have been poaching on the state's right to tax. The monopoly over the right to raise revenue by taxation has been one of the basic rights attributed to statehood, comparable to the state's exclusive right to the monopoly of violence and the use of force by the police or the army to carry out its decisions. The state might subcontract the function to tax farmers, or allocate, as to provincial or city authorities, part or all of its right to tax, just as it might permit private individuals to bear arms. But it could always withdraw such concessions if it so wanted.

The question now is whether this traditionally exclusive power claimed by all states alike is being eroded by large corporations through their control over the production structure. Not only are they able to evade the taxing power of the state, but they themselves are able to raise 'revenue' in the shape of costs treated as tax-allowable expenses from their own operations. This is revenue that they can then dispose of for purposes that are no less self-regarding than those of the state and which in some ways they rather resemble. Just as states apply national revenue to defence, so corporations spend money on industrial espionage, on plant security or on advertisement to protect their property, their status and their market shares. Just as states spend on research and training, so do companies. Just as rulers have often allocated a good share of state revenues to indulging their own tastes for luxury, self-glorification or patronage of the arts or sport, so too nowadays do the chief executives of large corporations indulge themselves.[12]

Nor are the TNCs the first authorities to act alongside states as tax gatherers. Religious institutions have always done so, using as a lever their power over a person's security after death instead of the political power over his or her security before it. There, too, revenue was often spent on lavish temple buildings, on long-term investments in education or research and even on personal adornment and aggrandisement.

Thanks to the sophistication of accountants — especially since inflation in the 1970s gave rise to what is euphemistically called 'creative' accounting — a corporation's tax revenue is only deductible by inference from the ways in which it spends money or (when it discloses it) from the build-up of reserve funds of one kind or another. What is fairly clear is that some enterprises in certain sectors of the world's production structure have been very successful in escaping the tax power of the state. Large oil companies and large international banks both made vast profits in the 1970s and 1980s. In both cases most of these profits were generated outside the United States, whose Internal Revenue Service — significantly named — was inhibited about applying the same rules that they would have applied to profits made within the territorial United States. Other governments have followed, by and large, the American lead, and perhaps because both oil companies and large banks, supplying energy and credits respectively, are such important cogs in the production structure, few politicians in any industrialized country have questioned the exceptional, preferential tax treatment given to them.

About the only serious attempt by any political authority to challenge the transnational corporations (and by so doing to reverse the process of erosion of state power in taxation) was made in California where the state legislature introduced what were called unitary tax laws. These declared the State of California's right to tax a corporation operating in the state on the basis of its world-wide operations and the proportion of these that it estimated to be attributable to its local operations. This declaration seemed fair enough in view of the spreading practice by large corporations of setting up holding companies in tax havens, large or small, so as to make sure that their profits were always declared where the taxes were lowest. After a few years, however, so many large TNCs had started to leave California, or to reduce their operations there to a minimum, that the unitary tax idea has more or less been abandoned. The state, it seems, is unable or unwilling to raise its revenue from the largest and richest enterprises at work on its territory because it is in competition with other states.

Whether or not we think that corporate tax 'management' is deceptive and corrupt and that much extravagant executive consumption has no real 'economic' justification, the tax issue is a basic one of international political economy on which much more research is needed. For the leniency accorded to the corporations increases their power to shape the production structure of the world in the future — a structure within which not only they and their successor-managers but also states and individual people will have to live (O'Connor, 1973).

The third set of issues concerns risk. All production structures incur risk — risks to life, to health, to other people's property or to future prospects for prosperity. The ploughing-up of the prairies incurred the risk of creating dustbowls. The mining of salt incurred the risk of subsidence, the mining of coal the risks of lung disease, firedamp and burial alive. Today, risks result from the production and use of asbestos and pesticides, and from the carriage of oil and LNG by supertankers.

An important and also under-researched question is whether the global production structure created and operated in large part by the TNCs is significantly adding to the risks incurred by and for world society. A secondary but still important question concerns the subsequent management of risk: who is held by political authority to be responsible for the consequences of various kinds of risk?

In modern times this has always been an important political issue in capitalist societies. The chosen solution explains why, in most large cities today, some of the largest, most lavish buildings are not temples or cathedrals but the headquarters of large insurance companies. For, if large risks are run by small people, or small, poor enterprises, insurance is the obvious answer. That is why, in many states, it is illegal to go to work without contributing, directly or indirectly, to insurance against injury at work; and why in many countries it is illegal to drive a car without insuring against the risk that it may cause damage or injury to someone. In the United States, product liability has been built into the industrial structure. Since the lawyers who bring successful suits against firms who have sold faulty or dangerous products also get a percentage of the damages awarded to the plaintiff for themselves, it has had the active support of the legal profession. Indeed, the same principle has been extended to doctors and to the lawyers themselves. This has meant that part of the 'price' of medical or legal services represents the insurance costs necessary for the protection of doctors and lawyers against the unintended consequences of their professional conduct.

These changes, part technical, part regulatory, have also had an impact on international relations. When, for example, a Swiss chemical company inadvertently spilt toxic waste into the Rhine, it was the Swiss government to whom the French, German and Dutch governments complained. International law on such issues is still far from clear. It is likely to remain so as long as the more powerful states refuse to accept their own liability for environmental and other damage. Canada, for example, has been powerless to stop the United States allowing its industries to generate acid rain which falls on Canadian forests — just as the Scandinavians have been unable to get Britain to stop doing the same to their forests.

But while it is states which have the policy-making problems of pacifying and compensating victims, of limiting and clearing up damage, and of regulating to minimize risks, it is not usually governments *per se* that create the problem. The fact is that the state is unlike the rash and dangerous driver who can be deterred but cannot be stopped from imposing risk on others, but who can be made to insure his own ability to pay damages. The state cannot be obliged by international law to regulate industry strictly and prudently, nor can it be obliged to take out insurance against industrial catastrophes like the Union Carbide disaster at Bhopal in 1985 or the Soviet Union's nuclear power plant fire at Chernobyl in 1986. If the ability to pose difficult problems for others is one of the attributes of power, then it would seem that large economic enterprises, whether private or state-owned, are in the process of filching power from the state.

These are by no means the only issues to arise from the tremendous dynamism of the global production structure. But they are sufficient to show how radically the questions for political economists are apt to change when the production structure of each national economy is no longer so firmly under the predominant authority of each respective national government. Change in the production structure changes the very nature of the state. Its capabilities are changed and so are its responsibilities. And the familiar categories of international relations, including international economic relations — the Atlantic alliance, the Soviet bloc, the Third World — come to lose the homogeneity that they once seemed to have.

Change in the production structure deals out a new hand of cards from a reshuffled pack. Governments — of developed as well as developing countries — corporations, banks, labour unions, farmers and many other groups in society, including political parties, face new and difficult problems in deciding how best to play the hand.

Chapter 5

The Financial Structure

In the international political economy, power is held by those who can offer or deny security, and by those who manage the creation of wealth by production. But besides the security structure and the production structure described in previous chapters — and no less important than either — is the financial structure. The power to create credit implies the power to allow or to deny other people the possibility of spending today and paying back tomorrow, the power to let them exercise purchasing power and thus influence markets for production, and also the power to manage or mismanage the currency in which credit is denominated, thus affecting rates of exchange with credit denominated in other currencies.

Thus, the financial structure really has two inseparable aspects. It comprises not just the structures of the political economy through which credit is created but also the monetary system or systems which determine the relative values of the different moneys in which credit is denominated; in the first the power to create credit is shared by governments and banks (and much will depend therefore on the political and regulatory relation of the one to the other). In the second, the exchange rates between the different moneys, or currencies, are determined by the policies of governments and by markets (and again much will depend on how much freedom governments allow to markets). A financial structure, therefore, can be defined as the sum of all the arrangements governing the availability of credit plus all the factors determining the terms on which currencies are exchanged for one another.

To a large extent the financial structure of the international political economy can be visualized as a half-way house, a hybrid that is partly a truly global system, and partly still a series of national financial and monetary systems, even though all of these are increasingly susceptible to influence and pressure from the world outside the frontiers of the state. It is global in that all the major capital markets of the world are so closely linked together that in many respects they function as if they were one system. They react promptly and visibly to developments elsewhere in the system. The bankers and dealers in securities operate as though time zones were more significant than political frontiers. They often work in syndicates, supporting each other while at the same time competing for business. The big operators have branches or offices in all the major financial centres; and their customers who deposit money are seldom content to put it all in one national basket.

But at the same time the continued co-existence of national currencies shows that frontiers do still count. Within those frontiers, it is the government of the state that is held responsible politically — however unfair this may sometimes be — for the weakness or strength of the national currency. It is the state that acknowledges this responsibility and does what it can to manage the value of money denominated in the national currency — in dollars or yen, marks or francs — so that it serves what it perceives as the national interest. Governments do not always succeed in achieving the goals they set themselves. But they have not yet abdicated their role as monetary managers. The role that they allow international organizations to take over from them is still very limited. And despite the fact that some assets are now denominated in a basket of European currencies called the ECU (European Currency Unit) and that some contracts are written in another basket called the SDR (Special Drawing Rights), which includes — as the ECU does not — the US dollar, it is still true that most transactions in global financial markets and most credit instruments traded in them are still denominated in one or other national currency.[1] In a nutshell, one may say that the markets are predominantly global, while the authorities are predominantly national.

Socialist and market systems

At this point, if we are to attempt an analysis of the international political economy that embraces and applies to the whole world, we have to immediately qualify that statement by pointing out that, within China, the Soviet Union and the other socialist countries, the state operates a credit system in which markets play very little part. There *is* still credit — for traders, farms and factories and even for some purposes for individuals — but it is allocated according to a state plan and not according to the perceptions of profit and risk by banks and institutions operating in a competitive market. It is therefore still possible to say that no advanced economy can exist without credit. Even in socialist economies, credit is far more important, and there is much more of it, than the cash that people carry round in their pockets or the funds they save and deposit in banks. This has been so ever since the nineteenth century, when banks became crucial to every industrializing country for the financing of productive investment. The banks lent to entrepreneurs at home and some of them lent, or managed to raise money by issuing bonds for, entrepreneurs or governments in other countries. Every materialist society, whether it is capitalist or socialist or a mixture of both, has to have a system for creating credit. Credit is literally the lifeblood of a developed economy. Like blood in the human anatomy, money in the predominant form of credit has to reach and renew every part of the economy. It has to circulate regularly and reliably. It has to stay healthy and stable or the society suffers, just as the body suffers if there is disorder in the blood or too much or too little of it. It follows that, in all materialist societies, the power to create credit is politically very important. (Of course, there have been some rare societies devoted almost entirely to the pursuit of spiritual or non-material goals. In such societies there is little power to be derived from the creation of credit. But today such societies are rarer than ever and socialist, capitalist and mixed-economy societies all aspire to more wealth and better living standards, however these may be defined.)

Broadly speaking, the difference between the capitalist or market economies and the socialist or planned economies is simply that in the former the power to create credit is shared between the state and the private banks, while in the latter the state merely delegates its credit-creating powers to the state banks. It is they who carry out, not the dictates of the market as they perceive it, but the commands of the state planners. There can be little doubt that the socialist system is less efficient than the market system at creating wealth. There is every reason for state banks to play safe and avoid risks; there is little incentive for them to take a chance and give credit for untried ventures or for small, unknown entrepreneurs instead of for large, established state enterprises. The whole concept of venture capital is alien to socialist thinking. Only when the security of the state requires that the defence forces should be equipped with the most advanced technology or when there is some major change of development strategy — as when Krushchev called for the modernization and expansion of Soviet agriculture — is capital on a large scale created by the state banks for new borrowers. The interests of the consumer, the man and woman in the street who has to line up to buy toilet paper or fresh vegetables, come last in the system. A certain sclerosis characterizes the economy, mainly because of the limited access to credit. It has been the recognition that this sclerosis was slowing down economic growth and handicapping the whole society that explains the recent push for economic reform in both the Soviet Union and China.

Both governments can see, however, that the price of greater efficiency through liberalizing the system of credit creation carries the risk of greater instability. The market system may be more efficient and flexible and better adapted to change and innovation; but it is also more unstable. It suffers bankruptcies and bank failures. It experiences financial crises both national and international. There is unemployment and idle resources when the bankers lose confidence in the financial prospects of trade, industry and agriculture. Financial boom times are apt to be followed by financial slumps when governments find it hard to get growth going again. In all the market economies, as President Hoover remarked wryly sometime in the 1930s, money is apt to be like a cannon aboard an old-fashioned sailing ship: it is a source of strength and power when kept under control but lethally destructive when it breaks loose.

Not only is the market-based financial structure more unstable; it necessarily increases inequality. Just because it offers such opportunities to financial institutions and their managers and employees to make large amounts of money very fast, so it tends to widen the gap between rich and poor. Bankers and financiers are then apt to be resented, not only because they are wealthy but because they have become so without being productive; they have made money out of money.

In the monetary relations between socialist states as compared with those between market economy states, the same balance of advantage and disadvantage can be seen as in their respective credit systems. The market-based system is more efficient, and by creating new opportunities, it enlarges freedoms and increases international trade and consequently wealth. But the benefits are distributed evenly and the system is susceptible to financial crises and conflicts as states differ from the markets in their view of what is a desirable exchange rate. In the socialist bloc of East European states, a striking difference between them and the Western bloc has been their total failure ever since the early 1950s to develop an effective system of multilateral payments. This means that exchange rates are stable but irrelevant; each economy is reduced to bartering, in effect, with its socialist neighbours. Moving beyond a bilateral payments system risked undermining the control of the government over the economy and the Party over the government. Nor were the more successful and efficient socialist states prepared to finance the deficits of the less successful and less efficient ones. The result was that setting up a Comecon clearing system or introducing a transferable rouble for intra-Comecon settlements never had more than a marginal effect on the system. And the frustrations of the Comecon system have inevitably enhanced the attractions for the East Europeans of earning hard Western currencies by exporting outside the system and of borrowing hard Western currency whenever the Western banks were prepared to lend to them. The consequence is that, while it might have made sense ten or fifteen years ago to analyse the financial and monetary structures of the socialist states in isolation from those of the world market economy, this division between them is much less clear today. For better or worse, the socialist economies are becoming increasingly integrated and involved with the global financial structure dominated by the major market economies. While the Western market economies and the developing countries are very little affected by what happens to the financial structure of the socialist countries, the converse is no longer true. Although still somewhat protected by managed trade and managed borrowing and a strict set of controls over access to foreign exchange, the socialist countries are no longer as insulated as they once were. As they make increasing use of Western credit for trade and investment, as they become increasingly involved with Western (including Japanese) banks, so they become more and more vulnerable if the system behaves in an unstable way.

Primitive and developed financial structures

It is these political and social effects of the highly complex and developed financial structures of the world market economy that have to be analysed. As with the other basic structures, it is not enough just to describe them or to explain the functions of the institutions that operate within the structures. The international political economist has to ask questions about the political and social consequences, the who-gets-what in terms of benefits and costs, risks and opportunities; and to consider the mix of values that this produces for society and therefore the political issues that it presents.

One simple way to do this, which cuts through a lot of the arcane technicalities of money markets and banking practice, is to look for the political and social differences between a primitive and a developed monetary system, including in that term both the financial structure of credit creation and the monetary relations of societies with different currencies or forms of money.

A primitive economy, to begin with, makes very little use of money. A good deal of production is for the producers' own use. Money is only needed for the 'extras' that people cannot produce for themselves or cannot exchange by bartering with their neighbours. The money economy is only a small part of the real economy. And when people do use money it is used mostly for current transactions — as a medium of exchange for goods or services. Because the primitive economy is apt to be rather poor, there is little use of money as a store of value or as a unit of account — the other two functions of money distinguished by the economists. Nor are there great problems of foreign exchange since contact with the outside world is limited and trade is mostly by barter. Money moreover tends to be in a form that can be seen and touched — asset money as the economists would say — not fiat or credit money. So it is apt to be some reasonably portable but scarce commodity — metal or shells or beads — over whose supply the ruler has little control.

At intermediate stages in semi-developed monetary systems, the money economy begins to penetrate more of the real economy. Physical asset money becomes more sophisticated. Money is made into coins. Rulers are no longer content to exact taxes in goods or labour. They insist that taxes are paid in their own coins, usually stamped with their own head. At this point the rulers discover an easier way of extracting resources from the society — they debase the coinage. Cleopatra and the

Roman Emperor Nero were among the first to do so. By their time, the art of foreign exchange dealing had been discovered as traders and travellers needed to change one kind of coin for another. The practice grew of borrowing money and recording debts and of charging interest for loans. Croesus was a Roman landowner and senator who did this and the expression 'as rich as Croesus' shows that the chance to make money out of money is no new thing.

Next, banks appear. To begin with, they accept money or valuables for safe-keeping, give the depositor a receipt and allow him to draw on his deposit and to settle accounts with third parties through the bank. Finding from experience that all the depositors will not want to draw money out at the same time, the banks lend, at a price, to others. The borrowers draw on their bank loans. Credit has been created. Pretty soon, the banks start printing 'promises to pay' beyond their liabilities to depositors and borrowers. These paper bank-notes circulate throughout the economy, adding to the supply of money in the form of coin. As the number of banks and other specialized financial enterprises grow, the variety of forms of credit money — what the bankers call 'credit instruments' — multiplies. Financial markets proliferate. Meanwhile, the rulers have found in the bankers a new way to pay their debts — by borrowing. Sometimes, as in medieval France or England, they borrow so much that they are tempted to expel, disband or even kill their creditors to get out of having to repay their debts. By the eighteenth century, in Britain, in France and in the American colonies as they then were, governments had learned by bitter experience that while banks and credit money offer new ways of financing the state, there are heavy risks to the economy and civil society if they allow so much credit money to be created that people lose confidence in the ability of the bank or the government to honour its debts and start refusing to accept it. At this point, Gresham's Law operates: bad money drives out good. The good (usually specie — i.e. gold or silver) money is hoarded and the paper kind becomes worthless. This happened in the American War of Independence when the phrase 'not worth a continental!' — referring to dollars issued by the Continental Congress — entered into the language. Governments then discover, usually by bitter experience, that the power both of banks to create credit and of governments to create credit for themselves by printing paper money has to be controlled in some way if the economy (and possibly the political system too) is not to suffer. For the 'death of money', whether it comes about by inflation or by a political revolution sweeping away the government, inevitably brings trade, investment and economic life generally to a standstill.

The political consequences of this economic transformation from a primitive to a developed financial structure can be, and usually are, both good and bad. Governments accumulate more responsibility for managing the system and making rules for the banks and for the conduct of financial business and financial markets. They are correspondingly tempted to exploit this new source of power in the direct self-interest of the ruling groups or classes and the state bureaucracy and at the possible expense of the economy as a whole.

But they are also able to use the system through borrowing as well as taxation to provide public goods in the form of roads, power plants, weapons systems for greater security, and welfare services. This last point is important. In political terms, money is a substitute for force as a means to economic growth and as an instrument to provide collective goods. The Incas and the Pharaohs could organize great public works programmes (chosen by themselves, naturally) without money. But political systems where power was more dispersed or more constricted were unable to invest (and thus to increase wealth) until they developed their monetary systems. Money is thus a necessary adjunct to liberty if a society wishes to enjoy *both* freedom *and* wealth.

A society that wishes seriously to improve its living standards and therefore to pursue economic growth, but still wants to preserve its political freedoms, can do so by developing its monetary system and assuring the economic freedoms that money allows. Development of a monetary system therefore usually goes with some dispersion of political power through the dispersion of the economic power which the accumulation of capital confers. Conversely, the planned authoritarian economies of the Soviet bloc or China, although they have pursued wealth through economic growth, have not pursued freedom and so did not need to develop their monetary systems.

Developed monetary systems do tend, however, to increase inequality. If some people can accumulate capital, they can also use it, through the increased bargaining power it confers, to exploit the labour or other resources of others. By this means they widen the gap between rich and poor.

Depending on the political structure, this inequality will sooner or later give rise to corresponding demands for a more developed welfare structure to complement and make good the perceived deficiencies brought about by monetary development. The more power in the political structure is dispersed, the sooner the demand for increased welfare provisions to redress the inequalities of wealth and of risks; the more concentrated and centralized the political power, the longer such demands can be held in check. The Romans, for example, combined a relatively authoritarian oligopolistic political structure with a relatively developed monetary system in which many transactions used liability money, in which credit was available for investment at variable rates of interest and foreign exchange dealing was common. Great fortunes were amassed and the gap between rich and poor widened. But although a repressive political system kept control of the slaves — on whose labour the economy was based — the property-owning oligopoly still found it had to accede to the demands of the artisans of Rome for a welfare system, in the form of free corn and lavish circuses.

Developed financial systems also tend to increase instability and to do so in a number of ways. There is a tendency, inevitable in a system dependent on the activity of banking institutions, to 'overbanking' — that is, to the imprudent expansion of credit with increased profits to the banks but increased risk to the system of financial panic and collapse. Regulation of banking to avert this threat is therefore desirable (but not always forthcoming until after the experience of catastrophe).

There is also a tendency to instability, arising either out of the over-expansion of credit in the private sector (as above) or out of the irresistible temptation which a developed monetary system always offers to the government or other political authority to exploit it for its own purposes; in short, to indulge in taxation of the economy through inflation. It follows that the political economy has to suffer either the social shocks of unchecked inflation or else the pains of checking inflation, which may involve a measure of brutal deceleration in growth and the experience of unused productive resources (including unemployment).

One final observation about developed monetary systems is perhaps worth adding. It is that disadvantaged groups in monetary systems usually behave somewhat differently to disadvantaged groups in political systems. In the latter, dissidents can readily be found who are dedicated to the total overthrow of the system, revolutionaries who want to preserve little or nothing of a system they find grossly unjust or economically inefficient. But the dissidents in a monetary system are usually well aware that its development has been a slow process, requiring the gradual building-up of confidence, and that once confidence is shaken and the system destroyed it is not easy to restore the one or rebuild the other. Their opposition tends therefore to be inhibited; punches are pulled, no matter how deep their criticism of the system's social and political consequences. Neither the British Labour Party, when it came to power in 1945 nor any other European social democratic parties – not even the Italian Communists — propose radical overthrow of the national monetary systems developed under capitalism. Similarly, it can be argued that none of the 'opposition groups' in the international monetary system — neither the French in the inter-war period or under General de Gaulle in the 1960s, nor the newly-rich OPEC oil states in the 1970s — have carried their criticism and opposition to the point of wilfully disrupting the system of which they, too are a part. The point is only worth making because their inhibition in this respect can easily be misinterpreted as acquiescence or even approval.

The consequences of monetary development can thus be quickly summarized as follows:

— It accelerates economic growth, by facilitating economic exchange (trade) and by encouraging production through investment. Time transactions allow the 'storage' of purchasing power and the accumulation of capital and its application for expensive productive enterprise.
— It confers power on those able to accumulate capital or with access to credit. The more open the system and the more widespread the capacity for capital accumulation, the greater the dispersion of power in the system.
— It increases economic inequality and thus stimulates, sooner or later, demands for an improved welfare system to redress inequalities of wealth and inequalities of risk.
— It increases the economic instability of the system through tendencies to inflation, to overbanking and to cyclical variations in economic activity.
— It increases the demands made on political authority both for the provision of welfare and for the imposition of complex and precise rules to govern the operation of credit institutions and money markets.
— It makes it easier for political authority to provide public goods for the safeguarding of political security, for the further development of the economy, or for the maintenance of social stability through the welfare system.
— It also, however, increases the opportunities open to authority to exploit the system for political purposes, particularly because opposition groups will perceive the benefits they derive from the system and the risks they too run from its destruction and will consequently be inhibited in pressing their objections and criticisms.

An orderly, developed monetary system would thus be characterized by steady (and not too jerky) growth; by increasing controls over the credit structures, its markets and its operators; by increasing allocation of financial resources to the welfare system and further provision of public goods.

A disorderly system, contrariwise, could be characterized by growth interrupted by periods of failing confidence and unused, idle productive resources; by the threat of inflation due to the creation of credit-money by governments or banks, or by both; by the threat of financial crisis and collapse; and by exploitation of the system by political authority for its own particular ends rather than for the general welfare.

The puzzle of the nineteenth century

When we look at the world's financial structure in the long perspective of history it seems as though it has alternated, ever since it emerged as a developed system of credit money, between periods of disorder and instability and periods of calm and order. In that way, it has been much more like the world security structure and less like the production structure. The production structure looks in retrospect to have progressed much more steadily. Economic growth has been slower at times than others and there have been slumps as well as booms. But it has only occasionally actually regressed and produced less and the change of pace was often the result of forces external to it — the booms often being associated with war in the security structure and the slumps with trouble in the financial structure.

By contrast, in both the security structure and the financial structure, the nineteenth century — or to be more precise the century between 1815 and 1914 — looks very like an island of relative order and stability sandwiched between an earlier and a later century, both characterized by relative disorder and instability. For England and France the eighteenth century started with some terrible experiences of financial excess and disorder. In France, the Regent who succeeded the spendthrift Louis XIV was misled by the Scottish adventurer John Law into letting the Banque Royale and then the ill-fated and fraudulent Compagnie de l'Occident to issue paper money so recklessly that the bubble burst, which instigated the French people's deep distrust of paper money. In England, another Scot, William Paterson, persuaded the government of the financial attractions of setting up a Bank of England with monopoly powers over government debt. There, too, paper money was printed recklessly and the British government was only saved by the accident that the South Sea Company outbid the Bank of England for the handling of these government promises to pay. This was lucky because, when the South Sea bubble eventually burst, the government could deny its responsibility. Of the two countries, the English learnt their lesson best.[2] Even so, they did not notice until it was too late that the American colonies were also finding how much easier it was to print debt than to collect taxes. And of course the financial controls that London put on the thirteen colonies were among the first restrictions to be torn up when the Americans declared their independence in 1776. The American Revolution, like the later French Revolution, led to a 'death of money' through inflation. Like Louis XIV, Napoleon too left France in a state of bankruptcy — the reserves all gone in the pursuit of military glory.

So what was the secret of financial order in the century after Waterloo? Never since then has there been so long a period of financial stability, both in the credit system and in the relations of major trading currencies. The main reason was that the leading trading country, Britain, had a stable currency and that so much international trade and investment was conducted in sterling that the effects of national financial stability spread outwards to the expanding world economy. (True, the periphery was not nearly as financially stable as the centre, but then it was not as important for the system — only for those who happened to live there.) The price of gold in pounds sterling (and conversely the value of sterling in terms of gold) did not change throughout the period. Once the restrictions imposed during the long war with France had been lifted, any Bank of England note was freely convertible into gold and there was nothing to stop people hoarding gold or selling it abroad if they wanted to.

It was no accident that sterling was stable, despite the new supplies of gold coming unexpectedly on to the market from the 'gold rushes' of Australia, California and the Yukon. A democratic Parliament, convinced by argument and experience of the value of stable money and the danger of unchecked government borrowing, passed in 1844 a Bank Charter Act defining the special powers of the Bank of England — but also laying down limits on the power of any British government to expand the money supply without asking the permission of Parliament. Before 1914 such permission was asked only once, when the Bank of England allowed a rash and unlucky bank called Overend, Gurney to go bankrupt. This made the rest of the City of London so nervous that, as the lender of last resort, the Bank of England needed to have extra funds to lend them, thus stopping the panic before it did damage to the real economy. And the example certainly reinforced the authority of the Bank of England over the City. Thereafter, the 'Old Lady of Threadneedle Street' had only to purse her lips and frown and the banks obediently took the hint and curbed their lending. It is worth noting that no US Administration has ever had so strict a curb put on its monetary policies by the US Congress.

Another important factor was the deliberate hands-off policy of British governments towards the business of foreign investment. The dangers of lending British funds abroad had been recognized early on by Palmerston in the early years of Victoria's reign. A Memorandum of 1848 had warned the foreign borrowers that the British government might intervene if a debtor defaulted on bonds issued for it in London. But it also warned the British finance houses that it *might not*, and that they themselves might have to bear the consequences of having lent imprudently abroad. This uncertainty over how the state would behave to foreign defaulters helped make the banks careful. And it could be sustained all the better because, unlike the French or German governments, the British government did not habitually use its influence over the City as a tool of diplomacy, insisting as Bismarck did that the banks lend to this ally instead of that, whether or not it looked like being able to service the debt.[3] A hands-off policy on foreign lending distanced the state from the private banks and made them doubly cautious. US banks have had a quite different experience. Firstly, there were the Caribbean customs-house takeovers by the US Marines in the early years of the twentieth century. Then, under Franklin Roosevelt, the US government again intervened with stabilization funds for Latin American countries in trouble in the 1930s. And finally the US government came to the aid of US banks over-extended in Mexico and Brazil in the 1980s. The rescue of Continental Illinois in 1984 only confirmed their belief that in the last resort the government would never let the big banks fail for fear of the effects on the US economy.

Two other differences are worth noting. In the nineteenth century, most of the finance provided by the City to the world economy was in the form of trade bills, not bonds. It was actually tied to a real exchange of goods, whereas much of the finance lent to developing countries by US banks in the 1970s and early 1980s was in open-ended loans which could be used to maintain an overvalued currency or spent in totally unproductive ways. Even when they issued bonds, moreover, the British banks were not themselves carrying the risk of default by the borrowers. If the bonds lost value, and even if they became quite worthless, it was the unfortunate bondholder — often a gullible small investor lured by higher returns on his or her savings — that stood to lose. One further factor insulating the domestic British economy from the risks involved in lending abroad was the separation of the domestic and the overseas banking systems. Domestic commercial or high Street banks were forbidden to dabble in foreign securities. There were also limits on the securities that legal trustees and executors could buy, which had the same effect.

And there was one final factor that allowed the steady outflow of British capital before 1914 to help the world economy to grow reasonably steadily. It was India.[4] Trade deficits elsewhere in the world economy were matched by a persistent trade surplus from India. But Britain's political control over India allowed London to extract annual shipments of gold in respect of Home Charges and to use its control over the sterling–rupee exchange rate and other devices to stop the gold seeping back to the Indian economy. Well might the governess in Oscar Wilde's lighthearted play *The Importance of Being Ernest* tell her young charge to get on and read her book on Political Economy — but add, 'The chapter on the fall of the Rupee, you may omit. It is somewhat too sensational for a young girl!'

What all these factors add up to is just this. It was not some mechanical, automatic system called the gold standard that accounted for the relative stability of the developing global financial structure before 1914 and for the relative orderliness of the major exchange rates affecting world trade. It was a series of politically effective arrangements imposed for a variety of reasons, most of them domestic, by one particular government on its financial institutions and financial markets. Because these institutions were the main channel through which credit was passed to the rest of the world, their effects were widespread.

Karl Polanyi, justly respected as one of the pioneers of modern international political economy, argued that the two sustaining structures of order in pre-1914 international society were the gold standard and the balance of power between the major states in Europe (Polanyi, 1957). Both served to restore equilibrium when threatened by destabilizing change. But the 'gold standard' in his book was a kind of shorthand for the arrangements governing both the creation of credit and the management of exchange rates. He did not argue that economic stability was maintained (so far as it was) because countries kept to the rules of the game as laid down by theorists who, influenced by the theoretical model developed by David Ricardo, thought that exchange rates would change in response to inflows and outflows of gold, and that these would automatically lead governments to expand or to restrict the supply of credit, thus influencing price levels in the national economy. Economic historians agree that governments did not keep to the rules of the game; that (like Austria or Russia) they often devalued to maintain incomes from exports; that reserves of foreign exchange were used in the adjustment process just as much as gold movements, and that it was, in fact and as Polanyi also said, a sterling–gold system that preserved monetary order. Britain, too, was ready and able to act as shock-absorber to the system when, every ten years or so, some 'exogenous shock' as the economists would say today, threatened to upset the balance.[5]

Polanyi's purpose — he himself was a Hungarian refugee in the 1930s — was to find an explanation for the rise of Fascism in Europe. He saw World War I as the consequence of a gradual erosion or decline in the effectiveness of the balance of power in politics and of the 'gold standard' in economics. To my mind the thesis is arguable rather than totally convincing. What *is* incontestable is that World War I not only led to the break-up of three empires — Austria, Russia and Turkey — and extensive default on foreign debts but also brought upon national economies such very different inflation rates that it totally destroyed the pre-war network of exchange rates between them. It also led Britain to suspend gold convertibility along with the restrictions of government borrowing, so that at the end of the war Britain was burdened with war debts to America and unable to resume her pivotal role in the financial structure.

Too rapidly perhaps, the war had transformed the United States from one of the main debtor countries in the system to the system's main creditor. And as Charles P. Kindleberger first argued (and many others have echoed), the United States in the inter-war period was psychologically unready and politically unwilling — as Britain was unable — to assume the responsibilities of hegemon, or leader, in the financial structure, supplying credit, an open market and the facilities of a lender of last resort at times of uncertainty and crisis. Yet what was striking was that both countries' central bankers at the time perceived clearly the desirability — for the stability of the whole system as well as for their respective economies — of maintaining a stable balance, of having a set of rules or guidelines and of maintaining the confidence of financial markets. Montagu Norman for the Bank of England and Benjamin Strong for the Federal Reserve Bank of New York — which was the 'foreign ministry' so to speak for the Federal Reserve System in Washington — did their best to co-operate and to co-ordinate policy even while the politicians in Washington rejected the League of Nations and retreated into isolationism. But two big obstacles — both political — stood in their way. One was the emotive and knotty question of war debts and reparations. The Genoa Conference of 1922, which might have been the Bretton Woods of the inter-war period, failed to reach agreement because France insisted that the reparations questions had to be settled first and neither Britain nor the United States by then thought this was a matter of the first importance. The second obstacle was the 'domesticism' of US monetary policy, to use a phrase that Henry Nau has used of US policy in the 1980s (Bergsten and Nau, 1985). Strong always insisted with admirable frankness to Norman that the co-operation of the United States with Britain on monetary and financial matters (like interest rates or exchange rates) was only possible if it did not conflict with US domestic economic management. That would always have to come first.

And so it was that a change in US interest rates, undertaken in 1928 for domestic political reasons, started a chain reaction that not only led to a stock market boom and crash at home — with reverberations throughout the world — but also to the sudden interruption of a flow of short-term US capital to Europe that exacerbated banking difficulties and ended tragically in the collapse of the Kreditanstalt Bank in 1931 and the big devaluation of sterling when it 'came off gold' (i.e. suspended convertibility of pound notes into gold) in the same year. The result, as everyone knows, was that debtor countries could no longer raise money in New York or in London. Credit creation by banks and governments in the world economy virtually ceased and many debtors defaulted. Too late to have much effect on the general loss of market confidence in the economic future, the United States, Britain and France agreed in the Tripartite Agreement of 1936 to a mutual support arrangement which restored some stability to their exchange rates.

The golden years?

In most books on the international economy after World War II, the Bretton Woods system — the International Monetary Fund in conjunction with the General Agreement on Tariffs and Trade (GATT) — plays a leading role in the story. The open, liberal economic order, so conventional wisdom has it, can take credit for the successful post-war recovery and subsequent growth and expansion of the world market economy. A 'regime' imposed by United States hegemony on the lukewarm Europeans and the quiescent Third World provided rules for the liberalization of trade and the management of exchange rates between currencies. The forces of the market so sustained and liberated from the shackles of state intervention did the rest.

According to this version of modern economic history, all went well until European — especially West German — and Japanese economic recovery put the system under stress. As a result, American hegemonic power and with it the Bretton Woods regime declined. The system became even more unmanageable when the oil producers imposed a sharp increase in the price of oil, throwing the network of exchange rates into confusion and bringing about a combination of inflation and slow economic growth against which governments, including that of the United States, were impotent.

To my mind, this version overrates the importance both of the so-called Bretton Woods system and of the extent of American hegemonic decline. It is the financial structure — the credit-creating mechanisms — that should take the main credit for the 'golden years' of the 1950s and 1960s; and it was not the decline of American hegemonic power in the 1970s and 1980s so much as its misuse, exploiting the system rather than managing it, giving too much freedom and responsibility for credit creation to the banks, that was at the root of subsequent troubles. It was the pursuit of short-term instead of long-term national interest that sowed the seeds of monetary disorder and financial instability.

The rapidity and success of European economic recovery and reconstruction after the war could only have been achieved with the help of credit created by the US government, mainly through the Marshall Plan. From 1946 to 1958, US aid and government loans to Europe amounted net to $25 billion. All this American aid would probably not have been approved by the Congress had it not been for the creeping consolidation of Soviet power over the political systems of Eastern Europe, and the fear that if the United States did not help the governments of Western Europe, and especially of France and Italy where Stalinist communist parties were strong in the labour unions, the whole of Europe would have escaped Nazi domination only to fall prey to Soviet domination. But whatever the motivation, the credit extended to the sixteen countries of Western Europe came in the nick of time, just as their own resources were reaching exhaustion.[6] This capital flow, the economic historians agree, not only had a pump-priming effect on infrastructural and industrial investment in Europe, its psychological effects on business decisions were crucial. The result was that in the 1950s the European countries devoted a higher proportion of their GNP to investment than in any previous recorded period.[7] And when the four-year European Recovery Programme ended in 1952, the United States continued to send economic as well as military aid to Europe under the Mutual Aid agreements that sustained the NATO alliance. Moreover, the United States used its credit to push the Europeans much further and faster than they would otherwise have gone towards liberalization: by returning trade from state-controlled to private decision-making; by taking off tariffs and quota restrictions on intra-European trade even when this meant discrimination against dollar imports; and by developing through the European Payments Union (EPU) a functioning multilateral payments system that was a major factor in the continent's economic growth. Only with the EPU, moreover, was it possible to manage so smoothly the transition to convertibility of European currencies at stable exchange rates as provided under Article 8 of the Bretton Woods agreement.

For, until December 1958, the so-called 'Bretton Woods system' had existed only on paper. By an American decision endorsed by the IMF's Executive Board, no country receiving Marshall Aid from the United States was eligible to draw on the IMF. For all practical purposes therefore the system was put in cold storage until the European countries were confident that they could maintain fixed parities for their currencies in the market. The only significant drawings made on the IMF before 1958 were those necessitated by the flight from sterling after the ill-conceived Anglo–French intervention in Suez in 1956.

As a system of rules governing the relations of national currencies, Bretton Woods only really worked for one short decade, from the end of 1958 to March 1968. That was when, with the introduction of the two-tier gold price, the first break was made in the anchoring of exchange rates to the price of gold (via the convertibility of dollar reserves in other central banks into gold). It was then, too, that the US Treasury effectively stopped allowing the Germans, the Canadians and others to draw on US gold reserves (see Strange, 1976). By 1971, the system was thrown into total disarray by President Nixon and was finally abandoned when the dollar was floated and exchange rates were left to market forces in 1973.

Even during that decade, the Bretton Woods rulebook was not only substantially rewritten, but was only made workable at all by two things.[8] One was the series of supporting measures taken by governments of the major trading countries to support the fixed rates of both the pound sterling and the dollar, despite the visible vulnerability of the one and the mounting payments deficit of the other. These included the Gold Pool, the extra, reinforcing funds for the IMF made available through the 1962 General Arrangement to Borrow, the swap network by which central banks could automatically borrow foreign exchange from their fellows, and the American Interest Equalization Tax of 1963 which effectively deterred foreign borrowers from borrowing on American capital markets.

The other thing that made Bretton Woods workable in the 1960s was the outflow of American public funds and private capital into the world economy, which carried on the job of keeping up real investment in trade and industry and thus sustaining Western economic growth. So long as there was growth, no one was going to worry too much that the rules were being broken or that the US deficit and therefore the growth could not go on forever.

As Robert Triffin kept insisting from 1959 on, simple logic showed that a system that kept exchange rates stable only as long as other countries were content to hold gold-convertible dollars in reserve was doomed. Sooner or later, the volume of dollar IOUs in foreign hands would be so much greater than the US gold reserves that the 'overhang' would destroy confidence in the US ability to honour the IOUs. Then, either the price of gold would have to be raised and a new set of rules agreed, or the dollar would have to be devalued.

Meanwhile, there were two non-trade items in the US balance of payments from the 1950s even into the 1970s that kept the country in deficit on its balance of payments but at the same time kept the credit-creating financial structure expanding. One stemmed from the security structure and was the continued US government spending on keeping its armed forces abroad in Germany and Europe and then in Japan and Vietnam fed and armed. And the other stemmed from the production structure and was the competition among US corporations for larger shares of the growing European and world markets for manufactures. The incentives for them to buy up European companies with dollars or to spend dollars setting up subsidiaries in Europe, were increased when in 1958 the Treaty of Rome setting up the European Economic Community put a common external tariff around the six member countries (France, West Germany, Italy, Belgium, the Netherlands and Luxemburg), thus creating a protected common market in which it was obviously better to be a manufacturing insider than an exporting outsider.

The move of US companies into Europe was a big factor in the phenomenal expansion in the 1960s and 1970s of the Eurocurrency markets. No analysis of the global financial system that leaves these out can be complete. For the introduction of the Eurodollar — a quite new phenomenon in international finance — not only developed into a major engine of credit creation for the real world economy but eventually also put such tremendous pressures on the exchange rate system that by 1973 it seemed far easier to give way to the forces of the foreign exchange market and to abandon fixed rates than to restrict it and make the necessary policy changes.

Briefly, the Eurodollar market (and later markets for Eurosterling, Euromarks, Euroyen, etc.) developed because of two inviting gaps in government controls over the power of banks to create credit. The American regulatory system installed during the 1930s had tried to prevent short-term funds being too large or too mobile by making it illegal for banks in the United States to pay more than minimal interest on short-term deposits. But the rules did not apply to interest paid on dollar deposits with US banks' branches in London. The Bank of England, meanwhile, even after 1958, still kept strict controls over British foreign investment and over financial transactions *in sterling*, other than payments for trade transactions. But it decided that it was safe to allow British and foreign banks in London to raise and lend money and conduct all forms of financial business, not in sterling, but *in dollars*, because it could not jeopardize the British balance of payments. Thus the Eurodollar loan became a new unregulated growth point in the international financial system; and the faster US corporations moved to Europe, the faster their bankers followed them to London, and later to other European cities. The business was highly profitable to the banks and attractive to the corporations and to anyone else dealing in dollars because any dollars deposited in London, even for a very short time, earned good interest and could easily be used as dollars in the United States or converted into other currencies. The Eurocurrency market grew from $3 billion in 1960 to $75 billion in 1970. After 1973, when the oil producing countries succeeded in quadrupling the price of oil and deposited the proceeds in the Euromarkets, mainly in dollars, the growth accelerated, rising to over $1 trillion ($1,000 billion) by 1984. Its appeal for the oil states was that it was apparently beyond the reach of the US government; it was movable; it was secret; and it paid a handsome and floating rate of interest.

In sum, the 'golden years' of growth in the 1950s and 1960s are better explained by the steady expansion of credit — public and then private — in the world economy than by the reduction in the barriers to trade (see below, Chapter 9) or the observance of rules regarding exchange rates. Yet there was also a dark side to those golden years. This was the time when the seeds were sown, and started to grow, of the inflation of the 1970s, and thus of the subsequent corrective deflation of the 1980s; and when the international banking business began to outgrow national systems of regulation and control. Contrary to all the assurances of free-market economists, the abdication of governments to the foreign exchange markets as the arbiters of exchange rates led not to less volatility and fewer financial crises but to more.

The paper dollar standard

The most important result of the 'breakdown' of Bretton Woods was political. (It was not in fact a 'breakdown' in the sense of mechanical or structural failure but a deliberate decision *not* to make all the difficult adjustments necessary to keep to a fixed-rate system, as I have argued elsewhere (Strange, 1986, Chapter 2). This result was the removal of even the tenuous discipline which the gold exchange system had imposed on US governments in the management of the dollar. As Triffin observed, instead of what General de Gaulle had called the 'exorbitant privilege' of being able to print IOUs to finance its deficits, the United States could now print dollar IOUs that could not be changed for gold and either had to be held idle in reserve or spent on buying US goods and services. In short, it had introduced a paper dollar standard. And as the currency in which three-quarters of all Eurocurrency deals were done, in which oil was priced and most international trade was invoiced, the volatility of other currencies was less important to Americans than the volatility of the dollar was to the Germans, the Japanese and the OPEC and the NOPEC (non-oil producing developing) countries. The size of the US economy helped too.

It meant that the US government by easing credit terms at home or by lowering taxes could generate some economic growth even though it might be shortlived. President Ford did this in 1974/5 and Reagan did it again in 1983/4. And through the Eurocurrency market US corporations could continue to raise and send money outside the United States, so that the US national inflation rate did not necessarily correspond to the rate of credit creation in dollars.

Other currencies, moreover, tended to be made more volatile in relation to each other — as the Europeans soon found out. They tended to be polarized into strong and weak currencies. The foreign exchange markets were more impressed with a country's prospective success (on the basis of its past record and current policies) in fighting inflation than with the surplus or deficit on its current account. But as a currency judged to be weak depreciated on the foreign exchanges its imports became dearer and its fight against inflation all the harder. Conversely, currencies considered 'strong' — even when as with both Germany and Japan they were faced with large oil bills — tended to rise in value so that their imports got cheaper and it was easier for them to keep inflation under control. This polarization of European currencies frustrated attempts in the European Community from 1970 to 1978 to keep their exchange rates close together and thus to insulate themselves from the volatilities of the floating rate system. Under such circumstances, it became clear that competitiveness in trade no longer determined the value of a country's currency, as the economic textbooks had said. It was monetary movements on a short-term international market that had the last say.

At the same time as the markets almost entirely took over from governments the determination of exchange rates, the banks took over almost entirely the financing of Third World deficits, many dramatically increased by the higher price of imported fuel. Worried at first by what the OPEC countries might do with their new wealth — it was forecast, wrongly as it turned out, that the oil surplus in 1974 would amount to $85-100 billion — the Western world was generally much relieved when the oil states decided to put it with their banks into Eurodollars, and even more so when the banks promptly turned the funds over and 'recycled' the petrodollars into floating rate loans to the NOPECs. The floating interest rates on their loans meant, however, that the LDCs took on the risk that they would have to pay more in future to service past debt. This would happen if ever inflation was checked in the major industrialized countries so that real interest rates (as distinct from nominal ones), instead of being very low (or even, as in 1975 and 1979, actually in some cases below zero), went up to 5 per cent or more. On a debt that was counted in billions of dollars the difference would be substantial.

This was precisely what happened when, after some hesitation under President Carter, the United States finally decided that it was time to check inflation and the ominous fall in the value of the dollar. This had got so bad by 1978 that even the National Security Council — not a body that normally concerned itself much with financial matters — began to fear the consequences for US foreign policy and defence. With Paul Volcker at the Federal Reserve Board, in 1980 President Reagan sponsored a radical change in US monetary policy at home that had tremendous reverberations throughout the world economy. Shorn of the technicalities, this was a deflationary policy that, by restricting the money supply, checked the creation of credit and let competing demands for it push up the price of borrowing money from the banks.

One immediate effect was to make holding stocks of commodities very expensive. Reducing inventories started an avalanche of falling commodity prices which hit the developing countries in 1981/2 just as the price of new Euroloans to cover their deficits — often swollen by the second oil price rise of 1979/80 had begun to pinch. Vaguely aware of the mounting difficulties of Third World debtor countries, the banks did not stop lending to them but tended (as in the case of Mexico) to lend at shorter and shorter terms. This meant that the peak of repayments falling due bunched closer and closer so that the inevitable moment came when the country could no longer find the dollars to pay.

By contrast, the US change of policy made it easier for the Europeans, fed up by 1978 with the polarizing splits between their respective currencies and determined to create a 'zone of monetary stability' in Europe, to launch the European Monetary System. A weak dollar had pulled them apart; now a strengthening dollar pulled them together.

To sum up, the financial structure under the paper dollar standard in the decade 1973 to 1983 was beset by uncertainty and violent change. There were losers and winners but it seemed to be a matter of blind chance more than purposive political action that decided who was going to win and who lose, which countries, which social groups and even which individuals would have their plans set adrift, their hopes dashed and their world turned upside down. Volatility, far greater than had been experienced in the previous decades, characterized all the main variables: exchange rates, interest rates, inflation rates, oil prices and commodity prices — even freight rates for shipping, which suffered the worst slump since the 1930s.

Under such conditions of uncertainty, countries, corporations and banks all did what they could to reduce their vulnerability. They hedged their bets, as the gamblers would say. They bought or sold foreign exchange forward, dealt in commodity futures and then in financial futures. The one group that profited — with the rare exceptions of the few that went bust — were the financial operators. Banks (and oil companies) made profits as never before. Financial business boomed and created new jobs and new opportunities for tipsters, researchers, commentators and others catering for the growing demand for information and advice. Competition between the banks accelerated the process of financial innovation. By this is meant the invention of all kinds of new devices, first to reduce vulnerability to inflation, or to government tax or regulation, and then to hedge against uncertainty. A whole new language had to be invented to describe these devices — money market mutual funds, swaps, options, NOW accounts, zero-coupon bonds, off balance-sheet financing, and so on.[9]

Instead of responding to this expansion and increased sophistication, which was greatly aided, of course, by advanced technology in computers and communications systems, with more supervision and control, the Unites States from the mid-1970s led the way to more deregulation of money markets and financial operators. Other governments, like Britain or even Australia and Japan, were obliged to follow or to let US banks enjoy a competitive advantage over their own and see the financial business move away to New York or Chicago. Deregulation was in fact started in the Carter Administration on the false assumption that banks were like trucking operators or airlines and could be made to compete more efficiently if they were subject to less government control.

The assumption was false because, while firms in the real economy compete by reducing costs, increasing productivity or cutting costs, banks sell very similar services and their main 'raw material' is money, borrowed (in the Euromarkets, from other banks) at the same price. They can best compete by taking risks, but it will be some time before the penalties for taking on too much risk have to be paid for in written-off debt. The most profitable (i.e. successful) competitors in banking business, therefore, tend to be the biggest risk-takers. Thus it is that 'risk-based competition propels the entire system towards excessive levels of indebtedness.'[10] At the same time it has to be noted that under the paper dollar standard the structural power of the United States made it safer for the US banks than for, say, German banks in the foreign debt business to run risks in the first place and to pay the penalties of their bad decisions. The US government, when Mexico was unable to keep up its payments to the creditor banks, came to the rescue and not only itself provided funds 'up front' as the bankers say but also used its influence with the IMF and other central banks to provide new money to keep Mexico solvent. Whereas, when Poland got into the same difficulty — exacerbated this time by US sanctions against the imposition of martial law by Jaruzelski — the German government was unable to come to the rescue and the German banks had to write off their debt and absorb their losses.[11]

Issues in the 1980s

The rapid changes briefly sketched above in the banking or credit creating structure and in the nature of international monetary relations between states present a picture of a system busily creating more problems than it appears able to solve. In fact, with some of the problems, even the experts are beginning to admit that they do not know what the solution is. The problems concern both the relationship between states, as the authorities responsible for currencies and for the control over 'their' banking system; and the relationship between the states involved in the world market economy and the financial markets which, now, both serve that economy and threaten to jeopardize its future.

These problems can be summarized under four broad headings:

— the management of sovereign debt;
— the supervision and prudential control of banks;
— the restoration of stability and credibility to the US dollar;
— the bankruptcy of economic thought in a global financial structure.

1. The sovereign debt problem arises basically because, in a political structure in which authority is divided according to territory among the governments of sovereign states, states (unlike firms) can borrow but cannot be forced by their creditors into bankruptcy or dissolution. It is not a new problem but it has now arisen in a different form than in the nineteenth century because the risks of capital loss, as explained earlier, are left with the banks and not the bondholders and the risk of higher interest rates is left with the borrowers. It is also a bit different in that some of the solutions used earlier, such as the customs-house takeover and the 'temporary' administration of the country or part of it (as in the case of Egypt) by the creditors, are politically unacceptable and therefore too costly in political terms.

This time, it arose because of the 'feast-or-famine' proclivities of the big US, European, Japanese and other (including Arab) banks. First, they lent far too much, too easily and thoughtlessly to the developing and to the East European countries, wantonly pressing loans on them even when they did not particularly want them (see Sampson, 1981; Moffitt, 1984; Delamaide, 1984; and Lever and Huhne, 1985). Then, from 1982 on, they got cold feet and stopped lending so that the volume of international bank lending which, starting at $2 billion in 1972, reached a peak of $90 billion in 1981 but fell to $50 billion in 1985. In the world political economy this has become primarily a problem of Third World debt. The Soviet Union, by coming to the aid of Poland when the clash between Solidarity and the Party had brought the economy almost to a standstill and the flow of foreign loans from a trickle to a stop, showed that it would not tolerate either East European default or Western intervention. From that point on, the two debt problems really had to be treated separately.

In the Third World, debt was a problem for the creditor countries because they did not really want to let the debtors default or 'decouple' (as some of them were inclined to propose doing) from the world market economy by not trading with or borrowing from it and by doing their best to be self-sufficient, autonomous and, as some argued, free. Anxiety to keep the debtors inside the financial structure despite their difficulties was all the greater if the debtor country was large, was a substantial importer of Western goods and was host to a large number of Western transnational corporations — none of whom were anxious to cope with a decoupled debtor country. Mexico and Brazil filled all these requirements.

Fortunately for the creditor countries, the International Monetary Fund was at hand, ready and willing to act as schoolmaster and government inspector, looking for Letters of Intent promising changes in economic policy of a generally deflationary, disciplinary, pro-market and anti-subsidy nature. From long practice with its missions to member countries' finance ministries and central banks — many of whose officials it had at one time trained or welcomed as delegates — the Fund was well equipped to send inspection teams to the debtor countries. These were accepted because they alone could issue the stamp of approval that would satisfy the private bankers that it was 'safe' to resume lending, even on a lower scale. Fortunately, too, the creditor countries had always, since the mid-1950s, dealt with debtor country debt on an *ad hoc* basis, one by one and pragmatically, avoiding general rules or standards. Thus it was that when any Third World country proposed a debtors' strike, a collective refusal to pay interest or repay capital, there were always a few important debtors who had just successfully negotiated help from the IMF, who were hoping private loans would soon follow and who therefore had a lot to lose if they joined the strike. For this reason, the debtors were weak collective

bargainers with the creditors. And thus it was on them that the adjustment costs mainly fell — the lower wages, cuts in food subsidies, ration-
ing of imports to bare necessities, the devaluations and the cuts in
government spending, even when this was for long-term development.

The question now and for the next few years is whether these reasons
for not defaulting will remain powerful enough to persuade politicians
to risk the unpopularity that conforming to IMF demands entails.
Aware that time might not be on the side of rescheduling solutions, in
1985 the United States came up with the Baker Plan to use official aid
increases as bait to get the banks to increase their lending to developing
countries. But, like the World Bank's efforts since 1983 to lure the
banks into co-financing deals, the Baker Plan remained a pious aspira-
tion. Perhaps the bait was not big enough. And perhaps the result will
be a long, miserable period of slow growth and painful adjustment for
the debtor countries, a slow-down which will also affect the export
industries of the rich countries.

As for the the who-gets-what of the debt question, it is clear that some
banks do well. Rescheduling and consulting for debtors can be very
profitable. Third World industries, protected by exchange controls, can
do well too if there is a market at home or abroad. Workers, including
some professional classes, often suffer cuts in their incomes. And poor,
least developed countries, who are the weakest bargainers of all, do
worst. The 'Third World' becomes more of a political and economic
fiction than ever before.

2. Like the debt question, the bank supervision problem is basically
political, not technical. For each of the major countries in the financial
structure, their banks are important earners of 'invisible' (i.e. service)
exports which can contribute substantially to the national balance of
payments. Hosts to financial markets also acquire prestige and income
from their foreign bankers who are like long-term visitors. Each state
is thus fearful of burdening its own banks and its own financial markets
with so heavy a handicap of banking regulation and restrictions that it
loses out in the competition for business. The result has been that
governments woke up belatedly to the dangers inherent in the
unregulated Eurocurrency and foreign exchange markets. They acted
after the Herstatt banking crisis of 1974 rocked confidence in the
viability of the system, but even then they did so with ambiguity and
hesitation. The first Basle Concordat of 1975 was an agreement among
the central bankers organized through the Bank for International
Settlements at Basle, Switzerland, that the 'host' country and the 'parent'
country would share responsibility for supervising the activities of the
foreign branch of a transnational bank. The host authorities would
make sure that its liquidity was sufficient and the parent that its

solvency was secure. The trouble was that the difference between liquidity (the ability to find the cash to settle unforeseen liabilities) and solvency (the possession of assets adequate to cover liabilities) is clear conceptually but fuzzy in practice, for a failure of liquidity can soon lead to a failure in solvency. Moreover, the Concordat was open to conflicting interpretations about which of the two authorities had primary responsibility. By 1983 a revised Concordat was agreed whose 'dual key' principle looks clearer on paper but which has yet to be seriously tested in practice. It does seem to extend the extra-territorial reach of US banking authorities not only over the branches of US banks abroad but also over foreign bank branches in the United States.

But the question of political responsibility in the US system is particularly confused because of the multiplicity of agencies involved. Besides the Office of the Comptroller of the Currency, which is only one branch among others of the US Treasury, there is the Federal Reserve Board, the Federal Reserve Bank of New York and the Securities and Exchange Commission responsible for security dealing and stock market operations — not to mention state banking agencies, between whose networks of regulation there are widening gaps for non-banks and others to creep into the business. Richard Dale concluded his study of the whole problem by saying that there were still serious internal contradictions in the supervisory system and that it was 'not an adequate substitute for a formal legal framework covering the regulation of multinational banking'.[12]

And, as pointed out earlier, while some experts and regulators in the United States are convinced that stricter rules are needed, there are others in government and in the Congress who are still convinced that deregulation would lead to more competition, more efficiency and a better banking system. Politics, and events, will no doubt decide who wins.[13]

3. Thirdly, we have the state of the US dollar, the most paradoxical and potentially dangerous aspect of the whole global financial structure. Here is the leading country of the world market economy, without whose say-so no reform or change has ever been made since 1943, acting in exactly the opposite way to that of a responsible hegemon, borrowing from the system instead of lending to it, so that it is actually now a bigger debtor than any of the developing countries, and consequently hooked on the horns of a dilemma of two deficits: its trade deficit and its budget deficit. To correct the trade deficit, especially with Japan, it has had to devalue the dollar in terms of the yen so that Japanese imports are made dearer and shrink and US exports are made cheaper and expand. But if it goes too far or too fast down that path, the Japanese banks and investors who have been buying US government stocks and US corporate securities may think that they are losing too

much in terms of yen values and may bring their money back. If the US government counters with higher interest rates to compensate them for the loss in capital values, it could, as happened in the 1960s when the British tried the same gambit, have a perverse effect, convincing the markets that the situation must really be bad if such desperate measures are necessary. Or, the high interest rate policy could work but at the cost of quenching economic enterprise, slowing growth and exacerbating the debt problem both for corporations, for the government and for the Third World.

The basic difficulty is that the Japanese are inveterate savers and the Americans are inveterate spenders; the ratio of savings to GNP is about 24 per cent in Japan and under 5 per cent in the United States. The US government has found it progressively more tempting to borrow from its booming banking system than to tax US corporations or even individual US taxpayers. For twenty-five years or more it has also sought to spend federal money both on an extravagant and largely unchecked defence programme and on education, health and welfare for its less privileged citizens. To change these long-standing political habits requires some fundamental changes in political ideas and attitudes.[14] Moreover, there is the further dilemma that, while the gravity of the situation calls for drastic action, drastic action might — to mix metaphors — rock the boat and upset the financial applecart.

4. More than anything else, perhaps, the financial structure that has evolved over the past four decades — often by a series of non-decisions and failures of political will more than by deliberate design — seems to lack both a political vision and, supporting it, an economic doctrine that is effectively convincing. There is a bankruptcy of ideas and theories in the profession of economics that is ominously reminiscent of the period 1929 to about 1934 or 1936. That was the year that Maynard Keynes published his *General Theory of Employment, Interest and Money*, at a time when other experts were either dumb with despair and confusion or were still mouthing ideas and advocating policies that were totally out of keeping with the times and the gravity of the problems. Then, as now, people and politicians looked in vain to the experts to show the way out of the mess.

The Keynesian prescription for government intervention to prime the pump and thereafter to use fiscal policies to regulate demand to take care of any surplus productive capacity worked well enough during the 1930s when the global credit-creating structure had virtually collapsed and the international capital markets were inactive. As soon as these revived and currencies became freely convertible, domestic economies became open to inflows and outflows of short-term money (as Britain's especially did, even in the 1960s), then demand management, wages and incomes policies and 'fine-tuning' using monetary as well as fiscal measures no longer worked. Moreover, the Keynesian doctrine, designed to get an economy out of recession, had no answer to inflation — nor in the 1980s did it have any answer at the purely national level to the subsequent global deflation in the context of an open world market economy. Applied to one economy, as the Mitterand government in France attempted during its first two years in office, Keynesian remedies proved a disaster, leading to inflation, a depreciating currency, capital flight and unsustainable foreign debt.

The opposite, monetarist camp has been equally bankrupt when its doctrines have been applied only at the national level. If Keynesian ideas had no answer to inflation, Friedmanite ones had none to depression. The Thatcher government in Britain, which followed Friedmanite dogma with more religious fidelity than Reagan did in the United States, succeeded in improving British productivity and the competitiveness of at least some British exports. But it did so at a very high social and economic cost, both in unemployed labour (and therefore high social welfare costs) and in neglect of the economic infrastructure of roads, drains and other public services.

The fact is that the vision of both Keynesian economists and monetary economists appears to be so myopic that theories stop short at the frontiers of the state, or the water's edge. Neither can see beyond. If either doctrine could be applied globally instead of just nationally, it might make some sense and produce some results. Keynesian ideas are still valid in times of depressed demand and idle resources. And if the subsequent recovery threatened to bring back inflation, monetarist ideas would also be valid — provided they were applied to the total credit-creating capacity of the global financial structure. To preserve a balance without swinging too violently from one to the other (or leaving it so late, as was done from 1977 to 1981, that the change had to be violent) would require political leadership and firm direction, and the close co-ordination of pump-priming policies in the main industrial countries. Ways would have to be found, for instance, to direct the Japanese surplus away from the United States and into the much more politically risky countries of the Third World, yet without imposing solely on the Japanese the cost of running those risks. Many economists, particularly in the United States, have been saying in the 1980s that the related problem of errant exchange rates can only be solved by monetary co-ordination between the leading national economies. It has become a parrot-cry with them. But this prescription often translates into the Germans and the Japanese doing as the United States bids, while the United States does as it pleases. No wonder the Germans and Japanese hesitate. The necessary and sufficient political conditions for the economic remedy to work have still, it seems, not been sought, let alone found.

Chapter 6

The Knowledge Structure

The power derived from the knowledge structure is the one that has been most overlooked and underrated. It is no less important than the other three sources of structural power in the international political economy but it is much less well understood. This is partly because it comprehends what is believed (and the moral conclusions and principles derived from those beliefs); what is known and perceived as understood; and the channels by which beliefs, ideas and knowledge are communicated — including some people and excluding others. These three levels or aspects of the knowledge structure have engaged the attention of very different people, from philosophers and social psychologists at one end to experts in advanced technology at the other. In between, there has been growing awareness by some economists and by some political scientists of the theoretical problems raised by asymmetries in networks of information and by divergences in perceptions, which result in 'discourses' in the social sciences so different (e.g. as between military strategists and developmentalists) that they can hardly communicate with one another. Disagreement about what the question is makes for a dialogue of the deaf when it comes to finding the answer. Analysis of the knowledge structure is therefore far less advanced, and has far more yawning gaps waiting to be filled, than analysis of other structures, even though they may be subject to less rapid and bewildering change. Ordinary people in their everyday wisdom have always recognized that 'knowledge is power'. But in a rapidly changing global knowledge structure such as we have today it is by no means clear to social scientists who has that power.

One trouble is that the power derived from the knowledge structure is often very diffused. And while the power derived from the other basic structures lies in the positive capacity to provide security, to organize production, to provide credit, the power in the knowledge structure often lies as much in the negative capacity to deny knowledge, to exclude others, rather than in the power to convey knowledge.

Power derived from the knowledge structure is also unquantifiable. The indicators that can be found are only the roughest of guides, for the authority accorded to people and institutions operating in the knowledge structure is necessarily much more subjective. Before we agree to recognize authority derived from knowledge, we have to be convinced not only that the knowledge 'they' have — whoever 'they' are — is important, but also that they do actually have it. This can only be a matter first of subjective value judgement, and then of subjective judgement of the possessors of knowledge.

Despite these difficulties, we still need to develop some analytical framework for assessing the consequences — for states, for social groups, and for the international system as a whole — of what look to be certain important current changes. Firstly, there are changes in the provision of and control over information and communication systems. Secondly, there are changes in the use of language and non-verbal channels of communication. And thirdly, there are changes in the fundamental perceptions of and beliefs about the human condition which influence value judgements and, through them, political and economic decisions and policies. Any study of the distribution of power and wealth in the international political economy will be incomplete that does not at least attempt to assess the consequences of all three kinds of change.

Readers will be aware that the so-called 'information revolution' has been the subject of a prodigious deluge in the mid-1980s of newspaper and journal articles (O'Brien, 1983; Stonier, 1983; Bell, 1974; Wriston 1986). Many of these have assured us of the importance to society of the combined effects of three fields of rapid technological change. One is the development of sophisticated computer systems and the widespread availability and use (at falling cost) of computers of all sizes and purposes. Another is the extension of systems of communication using orbital earth satellites, also on a scale that massively lowers cost and increases availability. The first has allowed an enormous expansion in the amount of data that can be cheaply accumulated, stored and retrieved by mechanical, or rather electronic, means; while the latter has made possible the cheap and rapid communication of information and decisions over long distances and in vast amounts. Time-honoured sayings like 'Out of sight, out of mind' lose their validity when firms selling such systems promise in their advertisements 'We'll always be with you'.[1] The third is the digitalization of language, opening new possibilities of the breakdown of one of the chief barriers dividing human groups from one another.

Yet much of the informed explanations of these technical changes, astonishing and almost miraculous as they seem, do not go beyond telling us what the technology is doing and how it is done. They assert that we are in the midst of a 'revolution' but do not explain in what ways this revolution is going to change the context of human relations, how it is going to shift power or redirect the efforts of human societies to new goals. Those three changes are surely the key tests of any real revolution. They are what the French Revolution did, or the Renaissance, or the Reformation. But since we are only as yet dimly perceiving the social consequences of these technological changes it is probably premature to talk of them as ushering in a revolution in the sense in which the term is commonly used in social science. At the moment, opinions differ. Some say that this is a revolution and that it is bringing about changes in human relations and in the organization of society and the locus of power and authority such that the changes may be compared with the change from a nomadic, hunting community to a settled agricultural one, or later, from a rural, agricultural society to an urban, industrialized one. Others insist that though these new technologies may have taken power away from some and given it to others, the system itself has not fundamentally changed. Authority is still derived predominantly from science: the real power still remains with the corporate enterprises as operators, and above them, as before, with governments of states as regulators and arbiters. The means by which states compete or co-operate and the weapons available to them may have changed, but the essential structure of power is much the same.

I do not claim to know for sure who is right. The question is certainly important. And clear thinking about it, whatever the conclusion reached, will be helped by using structural analysis in the ways suggested in this book. For the knowledge structure cannot be considered in isolation from the other three structures, with each of which it has close connections and mutual interactions. The basic questions, too, are still the same. *Cui bono?* Who gets the benefits and who pays? Who gets new opportunities to acquire wealth or power, security, or the freedom to choose? And who has imposed on them new risks of being denied these things? What effects do market mechanisms have on authority, including states, and what is the impact of authorities on markets and the operators in them? Such questions have the merit of getting beyond the state-centred approach which looks at the new technologies only as they affect the conventional forms of inter-state rivalry, or international relations in its narrow, traditional form.

Defining a knowledge structure

If a production structure determines what is produced, by what means, by whose efforts and on what terms, so a knowledge structure determines what knowledge is discovered, how it is stored, and who communicates it by what means to whom and on what terms. Just as power and authority are conferred on those occupying key decision-making positions in the production structure, so power and authority are conferred on those occupying key decision-making positions in the knowledge structure — on those who are acknowledged by society to be possessed of the 'right', desirable knowledge and engaged in the acquisition of more of it, and on those entrusted with its storage, and on those controlling in any way the channels by which knowledge, or information, is communicated (see Johnson, 1972; Carr-Saunders and Wilson, 1933).

One particular property of knowledge is that most of the knowledge that any of us lays claim to has not been acquired by our own individual efforts, but has been acquired by others — much of it by bygone generations. We have 'learned' it from them by communication systems — books, teachers, pictures, films and so forth. Knowledge, in short, is cumulative and communicable. More than the goods or services produced by the production structure, or the credit created in the financial structure, knowledge is — or rather, can be — by its nature, a public good. Its possession by any one person does not diminish the supply to any other. However, it is not truly a public good in the sense that the term is used by economists, for the value of the supply to those already holding the knowledge may well be diminished when it is communicated to others — hence the profits to be derived in financial markets from 'insider trading', which is no more than the exploitation of the possession of 'inside' knowledge or information not yet possessed by others.

There is a semantic question here which is puzzling but not really very important. Is there a difference between knowledge and information? For many purposes, the two terms are interchangeable. Knowledge is the broader term, since it comprises not just knowing facts, but understanding their causal and consequential relationships. It can also comprise practical knowledge, of how to make or do things. And it can be extended beyond the realm of material things to artistic, musical or spiritual knowledge. One would not normally use the term 'information' about these kinds of knowledge; they cannot easily be conveyed by simple systems of communication, whether by the spoken word or with a computer. Yet there is no very clear dividing line, no point at which one may say that the information to be communicated has become so sophisticated that whether it can be communicated or not depends on the ability of the receiver to understand and grasp it: when that is so, it must presumably be categorized as knowledge rather than as simple information.

Knowledge is also storable — or has been since the invention of clay and wax tablets in ancient history or of knotted string records in pre-Colombian America. Now it is spread in written or printed form and on film, tape and floppy discs.

More than other structures, the power derived from the knowledge structure comes less from coercive power and more from consent, authority being conferred voluntarily on the basis of shared belief systems and the acknowledgement of the importance to the individual and to society of the particular form taken by the knowledge — and therefore of the importance of the person having the knowledge and access or control over the means by which it is stored and communicated.

This is best explained by looking at one or more of the knowledge structures that operated in past times, of which, thanks to the systems of storing knowledge, we have some record and, thus in part at least, some understanding. We can consider, in turn, the power, authority and wealth conferred by the knowledge structures of medieval Christendom in Europe, of the secular state in the seventeenth, eighteenth and nineteenth centuries and of the knowledge structure in its transitional form that we have in the international political economy today.

Medieval Christendom

In the knowledge structure of medieval Christendom in Europe, beliefs placed a high value on the knowledge of how men and women might achieve eternal salvation. The belief in resurrection after death was strong enough and pervasive enough for legitimate power to be conferred upon those in the Church or the great religious orders whose claims to possession of this knowledge were generally acknowledged. Since the expectation of life in those days was so brief, and the knowledge of how to improve the conditions of material life and to guard against the hazards to the body of famine, plague and violence was so scanty, the alternative religious knowledge concerning the remission of sins and the acquisition of external salvation for the soul was highly valued. From this, and not in the last resort from military might or material wealth, the princes of the Church and their underlings derived power and authority over the laity. That power and authority was reinforced by control over the means of communication, in the form of sacred books and of literacy in a common sacred language, Latin. The sustaining assumption of the whole structure was that good men go to heaven and bad men go to hell; but also that all men were sinful and thus at risk, unless aided and absolved through the mediation of the Church.

Thus, the Church acquired authority over the rulers of states and over the merchants and craftsmen in the market. On both, the authority of the church was accepted as legitimate, and it was able to impose some constraints on behaviour. Kings and princes could be disciplined in extreme cases by excommunication, i.e. by vetoing their admission to heaven, if they disobeyed the rules of the Church. These concerned not only their personal behaviour, in marriage, for instance, but also their political conduct in peace and war. International relations, like other political relations, were therefore shaped in part by this knowledge structure, so that the behaviour of Christian rulers towards each other was supposed to be — and usually was — different in character from their behaviour towards infidels and heathens, as the history of the Crusades clearly shows.

If the security structure of the international political system was affected, so was the production structure of the economic system. The Church had views on the uses of money, including credit, and from time to time imposed effective control over the practice of usury. It supported the idea of a just price as well as a just war and tolerated the power of the guilds of merchants only if they administered the just prices. It even aspired to influence the consumption patterns of society, as when it passed sumptuary laws. It enjoined charity as a means to personal salvation and thus operated the only welfare and practically the only education system. On the basis of its authority in the knowledge structure it claimed certain rights and privileges for itself so that the accumulation of wealth in land and capital was largely reserved to itself and the major religious orders. The Knights Templar, for example, were the biggest and richest transnational enterprise of the Middle Ages.

The point that was mentioned earlier is worth repeating: power in the knowledge structure is more easily maintained if authority can limit access to it — and, as a corollary to that, if it can exercise a jealous defence of its monopoly position against any threat of competition. Rival authorities, in short, have to be eliminated or discredited. In this, it is closely paralleled by the jealousy with which political authorities in the security structure (lords and princes, for example) and managers in the production structure (guild members and, later, managers) defended their monopoly positions, resisting the encroachment of rivals, new or old.

Thus, in the knowledge structure of medieval Christendom, the Church claimed a monopoly of moral and spiritual knowledge. Its obsessive concern with heresy and witchcraft bore witness to its fear of rival claimants to the authority which it derived from the knowledge structure. Its two major potential rivals were Islam and the 'old religion', in all its variants, that survived from pre-Christian, pre-Roman Europe. Even after a thousand years of repression, as Shakespeare's plays repeatedly make clear, belief in witches, in magic and fairies, in sacred trees and supernatural creatures persisted. That is why it was in Spain, where Islam was most successful at gaining converts from Christianity, and in the rural peripheries of Roman and Church power where the old religions still had their strongest hold, that the Church behaved most brutally and violently in repressing every sign of opposition to its authority. This authority, paradoxically, was finally challenged and largely shattered from quite another direction — by the Enlightenment. What happened then was that the premium put on the sacred knowledge monopolized by the Church was bound to decline in value as the Protestant belief gained ground that the individual could communicate directly with God without the mediation of the Church. The Protestant idea of personal responsibility enhanced both the stature of the individual and the value of secular as distinct from sacred knowledge. The origins of the Enlightenment and of the authority of reason lay in the flowering of art and science in the Renaissance. It was then that the power of the Church to constrain either the political behaviour of rulers or the economic behaviour of merchants and traders began the long slow decline that culminated in the thinking of Voltaire and Rousseau and in the ideas of the French Revolution.

The scientific state

The political and economical changes brought about by the replacement of one knowledge structure by another had, however, begun to appear at least a century before the French Revolution. The Treaty of Westphalia of 1648 is familiar to all students of international relations as the benchmark of a new era in which the authority and sovereignty of the state would be unchallenged. By implication, it marked the virtual end of the constraints imposed on kings and princes by the Church. By the end of the seventeenth century, two of the leading states of Western Europe, England and France, had almost simultaneously recognized the importance of scientific inquiry and advance to the wealth and power of the state, by establishing respectively the Royal Society for the Advancement of Science and the Académie Francaise.

To the same end, the state took over from the Church responsibility for enlarging the education system, in universities as in schools. New patent laws secured monopoly rights for technical innovation through the institution of intellectual property rights. In the realm of ideas, Adam Smith completed the slow process of change by which the pursuit of profit, once a carnal weakness of the individual, began to be glorified as the surest safeguard of collective harmony and material progress.[2]

The new technology was also made to serve the interests of the state and to reinforce its power. Even though the technologies of telegraph, railroad and radio were initially developed to serve the interests of business and finance, the cumulative consequence of all three was to tighten the grip of government over the individual. It was owing to Marconi's radio that New York police were waiting for the English wife-murderer, Dr Crippen, when he tried to flee from justice to America. It was thanks to the telegraph and later the telephone that diplomats and generals lost their freedom of action to the central machinery of government. Aided by differences of language, national governments could use technology to keep control by censorship, by monopoly or by restrictive licensing over national systems of education, over national newspapers and broadcasting and even over the publication of books and periodicals.

Thus, in this new knowledge structure, the authority of the Church was displaced by the extended authority of the scientific state. For, whereas in the old structure, both the state and the market — the economy — had to some degree acknowledged the Church as master, in the new one it was the state — and beneath the state, the market economy — that were the masters. Science was the servant of both. Each of the major technical advances of the nineteenth century served both to expand the market and to enlarge the possibilities of enhanced power for the state. Each wave of technical innovation, it is now fashionable to think, acted as booster to another upswing in Kondratiev long waves of rising prosperity. Though some of these technical innovations — the telegraph, the steam railway engine and the steampowered ship — required some modification of state practice, usually by necessitating adaptive conformity to some agreed standards and system of management, none posed any fundamental challenge to the political authority of the state. Only indirectly, through the improvement in material living standards and through the demand of disadvantaged groups to share in that improvement, was the character of the state affected and the former ruling classes made to concede a wider sharing of formal political power.

What this scientific revolution did to the international political economy was, firstly, to consolidate state power over the individual, and secondly, to increase the disparity both of wealth and power between the rich and poor. This disparity applied to the classes and the states that were technically advanced, compared with those whose resources of men and weapons were no match for steel and explosives and the new systems of transport and communication. To take just two examples, Solzhenitsyn's *August 1914* tells in graphic detail how the Russian forces were fatally handicapped by the lack of a field telegraph system such as that used by the Germans. Unable to communicate with each other, they were unable to resist (Solzhenitsyn, 1972). And accounts of the battle of Omdurman tell how the British forces under General Kitchener, introducing the gunboat for the first time in modern history and equipped with rifles and artillery, wiped out the forces of the Mahdi despite the latter's great numerical superiority.

The enhanced ability to communicate over long distances, and the power to make privileged monopoly use of new techniques of communication were among the most important distinguishing marks of the modern scientific state. From Rome and ancient China onwards, empires had always recognized the importance of setting up swift and efficient lines of communication from the centre to the frontiers of empire. The possession of this new capability, no less than the capitalist drive for markets or raw materials, may explain the tendency of industrialized states in the nineteenth century to expand their empires in distant lands. William Melody has quoted Harold Innis, a Canadian economic historian, as saying that 'the subject of communication offers possibilities [for study] in that it occupies a crucial position in the organisation and administration of government and in the turn of empires and Western Civilisation' (Melody, 1985; Innis, 1950; see also Cherry, 1971).

In the change, however gradual or slow, from the knowledge structure dominated by the Church to the knowledge structure dominated by the scientific state, there were certain politically crucial changes. What is debatable today is whether comparable changes of a political character (i.e. affecting the who-gets-what and the locus of power and the allocation of values) are taking place as a result of what is loosely described as the 'information revolution'; or whether, after all, these changes are only technological, and therefore of the same order and moving in the same direction as those that have characterized the last two hundred years.

Belief systems

Structural analysis suggests that technological changes do not necessarily change power structures. They do so only if accompanied by changes in the basic belief systems which underpin or support the political and economic arrangements acceptable to society. This much is clear from a comparison of the medieval and early modern knowledge structures. In the first, the basic, shared belief that sustained authority in the knowledge structure was that 'Good men and women go to heaven and bad men and women go to hell' — or, to be more exact, 'Good men and women aided by the Church and bad men and women saved by the Church go to heaven, but men who reject the authority of the Church go to hell'. By the nineteenth century, the basic assumptions had changed. Instead, the basic beliefs were 'Material life is important. Science improves material life. Science also makes the nation-state more secure.' Out of the belief system came a new and different priority in the pursuit of values, both for the individual and for society. These shared values then conferred legitimate authority on markets and states. They legitimized a particular social structure of privileged groups and classes and a corresponding assignment of functions among classes. Thus, belief conferred authority.

But, once established, the authority of the state, legitimated by the knowledge structure, strove hard to maintain its monopoly position. The more its authority was threatened the more vigorously it was defended. The state, in many cases, asserted a unique right to judge what was acceptable and unacceptable conduct. The Church had asserted its legitimate authority to decide what constituted a 'state of grace' rather more than what constituted good conduct. The scientific state asserted its legitimate authority, derived from popular loyalty to and belief in the concept of the nation, to decide what was good conduct, who was loyal or disloyal, what constituted dissidence or treason to the state. In both knowledge structures, authority tended to exaggerate the power embodied in the knowledge structure — that of

God and of sacred knowledge monopolized by the Church, and that of science ('science can solve all problems') and the scientific knowledge nurtured (and sometimes monopolized) by the state.

In both knowledge structures, the violent repression of alternative knowledge structures tended to increase whenever the authority became weak or was subject to challenge. The challenge could come from an 'old religion', or from an entirely new belief system, or from a combination of the two. For example, the ideas contained in Fritz Schumacher's *Small is Beautiful* were explicitly derived from Buddhism.[3] The downfall of the Shah of Iran was effected by Islamic fundamentalists. There are times and circumstances when these old religions have sometimes been more serious opponents of the combined authority of science and the state than a cool, rational rejection of the omnipotent power of material scientific progress to solve the problems of material life, found in Fred Hirsch's *Social Limits to Growth* (1976).

At all events, the tide of support for an alternative knowledge structure such as characterized the latter periods of the Church's dominance may be seen today turning against the scientific state. In flower power, Band Aid, organic farming, vegetarianism, acupuncture and alternative medicine, we may detect a common thread — often more emotional than rational — questioning the basic beliefs of the dominant knowledge structure, just as the early scientists and religious protestants questioned the basic beliefs and authority of medieval Chistendom.

It is also characteristic of those with authority in the knowledge structure that they use whatever kinds of power they have, including coercive or legal power, to reinforce their privileged position. They will make entry into their exclusive ranks as difficult as possible, seeking support where necessary and possible from legal systems backed by coercive force. One such strategy in the medieval Christian structure was to insist on the rather bizarre notion of the apostolic succession. The authority given to bishops was restricted to men appointed by other bishops. The scientific state on the other hand was more directly able to use its licensing power to restrict entry into the major professions of law, medicine, the army and the universities. Only when the state itself was in danger were such barriers to entry lowered. The Crimean War and World War I were such occasions on which the British state lowered the barriers of class and wealth to entry in the British Army, allowing in professional career soldiers.

States have also asserted their prior claim on the services of scientists; a claim that scientists sometimes resisted. By the early decades of this century, the barriers of language and of professional legitimacy raised by states had cut down the transnational mobility of scientists. What looked like a reversal of the broader trend towards the consolidation of state power in the knowledge structure came with the Manhattan Project in World War II. By then, the combination of Nazi anti-semitism in Germany and the expanding university system in the comparatively affluent United States had already led to a wholesale exodus of brains from Europe and especially from Central Europe to America. In the Manhattan Project, the US government brought together an international team of top physicists from various countries. But it reserved to itself exclusive control over their discovery of how to apply the principles of nuclear fission to warfare. At the time, and later, some scientists, such as J. Robert Oppenheimer, questioned this political monopoly. Others, like Klaus Fuchs, opposed it. Fuchs secretly conveyed crucial information to the Soviet Union, only to pay dearly for his choice by imprisonment for spying.

There are two alternative interpretations of this episode in the evolution of the knowledge structure. One is that the recruitment by the United States of a multinational team of scientists for its own security was one of a series of benchmarks, registering a gradual change from a knowledge structure in which each state dominated its own part of the knowledge structure, to one that was much more transnational, in which the power of states exercised through their authority in the knowledge structure became much more asymmetric. The alternative explanation is simply that 'science' as the co-existing source of authority with the state was just resisting, even to the point of counter-attacking, as it were, the excessive claims of the state. The scientists did this first by working for the United States, in some cases against their former national authorities, and then in some cases by working against the United Sates in the interests of its major rival, the Soviet Union.

According to this interpretation, the Manhattan Project was only a new twist to an old tale. States had always tried to monopolize scientific ideas and to pen scientists up within their own territorial boundaries. Against the scientists' inclinations, they had seldom succeeded. But when a strong alliance of states was forged, and was sustained by shared belief in the importance of winning the war, then the temporary consent of scientists to its purposes was willingly given. But, with the horrified reaction of many scientists to Hiroshima, that consent was in some cases withdrawn. Even the United States, thereafter, had to take increased powers to punish scientists who pass on 'classified' information and to show increased discrimination in choosing which scientists it could safely employ. On the other hand, the attempt of scientists on both sides of the Iron Curtain in the post-war decades to develop through the Pugwash conferences a countervailing influence to the power of the superpower states had relatively little impact on their relations.

Indications of change

The evidence on this and on other aspects of the changing knowledge structure is conflicting. On the one hand, some potentially important groups are questioning the supremacy of the state in their value systems. The scientists seem to be developing a kind of secular-ecumenical movement that rates scientific truth and progress above the narrow interests of any one nation. Young people in many countries show growing awareness of the dangers of nuclear power and nuclear weapons to life on the planet. Opinions in all kinds of groups around the world are shifting away from trust in the state as the expression of national civil society and towards a wider sense of common humanity. Instead of 'Dulce et decorum est pro patria mori' many people consciously conclude 'Better Red than dead'.

Just putting the two slogans side by side reminds us that nationalism is by no means everywhere in retreat. In most of the countries of the Middle East, and perhaps most notably in Israel, nationalism is still triumphant. And in the United States the reaction of any injury to Americans, even to American armed forces, is such that we can only conclude that, there too, the idea of universal principles, of the collective interest of global community, is rated a very poor second to the pursuit of national interest and the defence of national *amour propre*.

Opposition to the state is itself divided. The environmentalists are often as much anti-science as anti-state. The scientists still believe in material progress and technical advance, in the existence of scientific solutions to economic and even political problems. They want to go forward, whereas the organic food enthusiasts, the advocates of natural childbirth, clear air and clean water, alternative medicine and alternative life-styles want to go back, to reverse and not just to halt scientific progress.

While this uncertainty about fundamental belief systems persists, it would be rash to draw any final conclusions about a permanent change in the locus of power derived from the knowledge structure. It is by no means clear that all states have lost structural power to other sources of authority — to the transnational corporations or to some amorphous international network of scientists.

Interactions of structures

This is not to say, however, that nothing has changed. Some of the consequences of change in the knowledge structure, combined with change in the other structures — the production structure, the financial structure and the security structure — suggest some politically important conclusions.

Firstly, we have to note that the two key technical innovations of the past quarter century have been the development of powerful and sophisticated computers and the development of electronic communication by means of earth-orbiting satellites. Certain ancillary innovations, such as printed circuits and semiconductors, fibre-optic cables, the new fuels and materials used in the launching and operation of satellites and the mechanisms of storing information in what has come to be known as the software for computers have all made vital contributions. (Software, and associated services, for example, now account for 80 per cent of the cost of putting a computer on the market, where twenty years ago 80 per cent of the cost was accounted for by the hardware, the computer itself.)

An immediate and almost universal result of these innovations has been to unify national markets for all other goods and services. National markets for all kinds of goods and services have been replaced by a single global market. The extent of a market in past centuries had always been determined first by the limits of the transport system connecting supplies to buyers (see below, Chapter 8). But it was also always partly determined by the knowledge structure, in the sense that buyers and sellers had to be connected by information and communication systems as well as by transport systems. If a producer did not know about potential customers for his goods or services, the market for them was restricted. Financial markets were the first to be linked by means of the telegraph, even though at first there were all kinds of obstacles to the transnational transfer of funds. The entertainment business was also an early example of technology abolishing barriers dividing the labour market. Instead of being limited to working in theatres for national audiences, actors and actresses could go to Hollywood and act in films. And now, instead of national markets supplemented by a few international ones at the major commercial and financial centres (like the London insurance market, the Baltic Exchange for shipping), almost every commodity, manufacture or service is sold, effectively, on a world market. The new means of communication allow information on market trends to be immediately accessible to buyers and sellers worldwide. They also permit the instant transmission and execution of decisions to sell or to buy.

Several important economic consequences follow, each with highly important political implications. Firstly, the input of information into the production structure is vastly increased. Another way of saying the same thing is that white-collar service jobs replace blue-collar industrial ones. Fewer people work on the factory floor, on farms, in mines, steelmills or shipyards, and more work in offices in front of computers and word processors. This is as big a revolution in the production structure as the shift from agriculture to industry. And, just as the industrial revolution devalued the wealth and power of primary producers, so the information revolution is rapidly devaluing the wealth and power of industrial workers — unless of course they also happen to be producers or processors of information.

The shift has been most marked in the United States where, by 1984,

72 per cent of people employed outside agriculture were in service jobs, compared with 62 per cent in 1960. In the two years 1982–4, 69 per cent of new jobs created in the United States were in service industries. It has been in the United States, too, that the two consequences of the information revolution for firms have been most marked. One is the greatly increased input from the new data processing and information technologies into product design, as a result of the ever-increasing automation of manufacturing processes. Out of $5 billion spent by General Motors to set up a new manufacturing and assembly complex to produce the Saturn car, no less than $2 billion went on the cost of the necessary computer hardware and software. For this purpose General Motors acquired a 'captive' computer company, Electronic Data Systems Corporation.

The other consequence is that large manufacturing firms have been led to diversify into the information sectors. It is significant that the three big American aircraft manufacturers — Boeing, Lockheed and McDonell Douglas — have all set up profitable subsidiaries to sell databank and other information services of all kinds, many of the data banks have nothing whatever to do with the aircraft business. Similarly, big banks have begun to sell information systems developed for their own use on a world market. And many major TNCs have set up captive insurance companies (many based in low-tax Bermuda) to carry out both their own and other people's insurance business.

The net result of these and other comparable developments is that the value to the firm of its employees in service jobs is enhanced at the expense of its old industrial workers. The former are also much more mobile between companies and between sectors of production, so that there is real competition for their services, while the power of the unions to protect the old industrial workers is necessarily reduced.

Another politically important consequence of the change is that the capabilities and power of management in big enterprises are vastly enhanced. One of the important prerequisites for the truly transnational enterprise, developed in World War II by Ford and Kaiser and others, was the ability to exercise close control over distant subsidiaries and affiliates. Yet the information available to management and its power to have decisions carried out were still limited, as Edith Penrose argued in a seminal work, *The Theory of the Growth of the Firm* (1959). They were limited, that is, until satellite communication linking computers allowed the collection of data from the outlying centre. Some examples familiar to most of us are the control through computers of hotel and airline reservations, the central control over chains of retail shops, over wholesale supplies and freight handling, the management of tanker fleets, and the instant transfer of funds between banks and their customers.

Another advantage which the large corporation has in a knowledge structure characterized by rapid technological change is its increased ability to 'internationalize' information. Within the company, it can devote resources to research and development, and any new products or processes so discovered can be kept under close wraps inside the company until it is ready to launch the product on the market, or to incorporate the process in its production. This is why for large corporations industrial espionage is such a threat. In the past, by contrast, the producer used the protection of the state, under patent laws, to prevent competitors 'stealing' his invention. Now the corporation can no longer depend on the state and therefore has to develop its own means for denying others access to the knowledge it has gained.

Sometimes, apparently, its own resources are still not large enough. Alliances, very similar in some respects to the alliances made by states, have to be made with other corporations. These may be complementary — as when a computer company joins forces with a company producing telecommunications equipment. Or the alliance may be between competitors — as when car companies or aircraft companies decide to combine forces to beat their other competitors. Here again rapid change in the knowledge structure is forcing radical change in the production structure.

Some political implications

There are implications for the international political system of the impact which these technological changes in the knowledge structure have had on the production structure. They have centralized power in the big transnational corporations. Not only are these corporations predominantly headquartered in the United States, but the importance of selling on a global market means that even those corporations based in other places — Europe, Japan, Korea — cannot afford *not* to sell on the US market. It is still the largest, richest market under one national set of laws and one national bureaucracy. In short, the technological changes have led to a greater concentration of power in one state.

The same trend to a concentration of authority over the market economy can be seen in the impact of technological change on the financial structure. The Eurocurrency market and the international bond markets, the transnational inter-bank and securities markets, could not have grown so fast and penetrated national financial systems so deeply without the telex, the telephone and the computer systems linked by satellites. All the big banks have been quick to use available technology to improve their competitive position in international foreign exchange and capital markets. For example, Chase Manhattan's communications network links the head office's computer terminal directly with the bank's major branches in Europe and the Caribbean, and via a Cable and Wireless computer in Hong Kong to its other branches in Japan, Singapore, Taipei and other Far East and Middle East financial centres (Hamelink, 1983: 63, Fig. 8). Citibank runs a comparable operation, called Globecom, and spends an estimated $40 million a year on its telecommunications. The politically important point about these communication systems is, of course, that the bank's head office becomes the gatekeeper, controlling access to the system. Control may be less centralized, but it is none the less still exclusive when a number of banks have combined to operate a collective communications system, such as EUREX. This was a joint subsidiary registered in Luxemburg in 1977, liquidated in 1981, which served over sixty banks in fourteen countries. More successful has been SWIFT (Society for Worldwide Interbank Telecommunications), a global inter-bank system established in 1973 and linking banks in New York and Montreal to the major European financial market operators.[4]

The value to the big banks of such systems for instant market dealing in every conceivable type of financial asset is enormous. The systems allow the big operators to gain access to more and faster information about market trends and thus to profit from the opportunities for arbitrage trading in volatile and uncertain conditions. Walter Wriston, former head of Citibank (now Citicorp), has even suggested that 'banking today *is* information' (Wriston, 1986). Similarly, it is the control over, and access to, these global systems that also allows the great grain and commodity trading companies to enjoy such an oligopolistic position as compared with either the producers (the farmers) or the end-users.[5] It does not seem unreasonable to conclude that technical changes in the knowledge structure have served to increase the concentration of power in the financial structure. And there is little doubt among financial circles that the centre of this concentrated financial power lies in the United States (see above, Chapter 5).

Technical change has also had important consequences in the security structure. Knowledge has become more important in the competition between states than either crude manpower or crude gunpower. The superpowers, significantly, were the first to launch earth-orbiting satellites. They were also the first to develop high-powered computers for use in space and for military intelligence and battlefield communication. The results of technical change have been to make both men and machines less important in military strategy than information and information systems. These military and strategic systems are still exclusive to the state, while others, like the satellites owned by Intelsat and Inmarsat, are collectively owned by governments as shareholders. But what is important is that now even the systems reserved to the Pentagon depend on, and could not operate without, the technical know-how and co-operation of the major transnational corporations. The possibility of total control and monopoly by the state (outside the Soviet Union and

China) has seemingly gone for good. The price of such dependence must be some increased susceptibility to corporate influence in policy-making, especially in Washington.

Here, I would suggest, lies at least part of the explanation why the United States has been so obsessively keen on the liberalization of trade in services. This objective has been the motive power behind the United States' insistence, despite European and Japanese agnosticism and Third World suspicion, on launching the Uruguay round of multilateral trade talks in the GATT. It was also entirely due to US pressure that the OECD countries were persuaded at their 1985 annual meeting to agree on the Declaration on Transborder Data Flows, committing them (in principle at least) to minimizing barriers and co-operating to find collective solutions for technical problems impeding growth in this important (and American-dominated) sector.[6]

Part of the answer, of course, is that the United States being the strong trader in all the key service sectors — (banking, insurance, hotels and air transport, advertising, consultancy and information services) — is also predictably the free trader. The fewer barriers raised by other governments, the greater the possibility for the United States of finding in service trade the compensation for the rising US dependence on imported industrial manufactures.

But there is more to it than that. The dominant firms in each of these sectors have wanted and demanded the maximum freedom to compete in the domestic as well as the global market. In each sector, far more than in manufacturing, the advantages — not necessarily economies — of scale mean that the big enterprise has a comparative advantage over small ones. The bigger the enterprise — such as a bank or an insurance company — the lower the risk to the shareholder, to the customer or to its trading partners of a raiding takeover or of financial collapse without state support. Only government regulation of banks, of insurance, and of telecommunications stood in the way. But once Washington gave way on deregulation it became increasingly difficult, as the Europeans and others discovered, not to follow suit. Revision of regulation in the City of London was just the most publicized example; Britain was under pressure to abolish old restrictions and demarcating controls separating the functions of financial operators and to find a new combination of statutory rules and bureaucratic supervision. Unless it did so, it risked watching financial business leak away to New York or to other financial centres that had been quicker to follow the American lead.

Conclusions

I began this chapter by noting that scholars in philosophy and linguistics had a better grasp of some of the concepts necessary to an understanding of power derived from the knowledge structure. They have been grappling for much longer than students of international relations or international economics with the nature of communication, the social uses of language and the relations of dependence made possible by a combination of ideas and belief systems, technology and social and political practice.

Well aware of my own limitations, I have made no reference in the course of this brief survey of the knowledge structures of the international political economy to the active debates conducted by philosophers, especially in Europe, on the nature of knowledge, or the relation between power and communication systems or on the role of ideology in defining the goals of knowledge and thus determining in some degree the findings of social 'science'. Such debates are not on the whole conducted in a language easily understood by me or, I imagine, by most of my readers. They are debates with roots going back at least to Nietzsche, Hegel and Weber, and some would say to Plato and Aristotle. The most influential modern contributions have been Jürgen Habermas, Michel Foucault, Karl Popper and Georg Lukacs. [7] They are also debates that remain largely unresolved.

What the student of international political economy is more immediately concerned with is the nature of power exercised through a knowledge structure, whether past, present or future; with whether the centres of such power are presently undergoing significant change; and with what the 'cui bono' consequences are for states, classes, corporations and other groups. My conclusions (for what they are worth) are that, of the four basic structures of the world economy, the knowledge structure is undergoing the most rapid change. Secondly, that although the final outcomes are still far from clear, there are three broad developments, all of them important to the international political economy, for which there already seems sufficient supporting evidence.

The first of these developments is that the competition between states is becoming a competition for leadership in the knowledge structure. The competition used to be for territory, when land and natural resources were the major factor in the production of wealth and therefore the acquisition of power for the state. Then the competition was for the industrial 'sinews of war' provided by the manufacture of steel, the machines and modes of transport and production based on steel, and later for chemicals, and petroleum and electric power. Today, the competition is for a place at the 'leading edge' (as the jargon has it) of advanced technology. This is the means both to military superiority and to economic prosperity, invulnerability and dominance.

This is something that most ordinary people are already aware of and that is already well reflected in much popular fiction, in films and books. But it is something that has still be be fully absorbed by many theorists, both in international relations and international economics.

This radical change will require an equally radical revision of realist assumptions about the nature of international relations. So far, the only changes in the knowledge structure generally acknowledged by realists to be of importance in the international system as they conceive it are those that have added new weapons to the offensive or defensive military capability of states or that have added new weapons of foreign policy to the traditional means by which diplomacy was conducted. Broadcasting, it is now recognized, began to have importance in World War II; subversion, intelligence using new technologies for surveillance and espionage, and cultural penetration have all been substantially developed in subsequent decades. But other changes that go beyond state–state relations — yet that will ultimately affect both state–state and state–society relations — have been widely overlooked.

The second development resulting from change in the knowledge structure is that of the increasing asymmetry between states as political authorities in the acquisition of knowledge and in access to it. As pointed out above, the US government is itself conscious of its own dominance in all the sectors associated with the knowledge structure, or it would not be so keen on getting others to agree to free trade rules in services. Although American universities and American corporate research centres may be challenged in certain rather narrow fields of advanced technology, their dominance over the broad range is still uncontested. Nor is this asymmetric leadership simply a matter of advanced technologies. It goes much deeper than that. The American language has become the *lingua franca* of the global economy and of the transnational social and professional groups. Whatever the Japanese economy may achieve, the Japanese language will never rival English in importance as a means of interpersonal communication — even if machines may be able, with the digitalization of language, to communicate with each despite the different tongues of their operators. Every language is increasingly being invaded by English words. Literature in English spreads at the expense of literature in other languages. Thus, American universities come to dominate learning and the major professions involved in the knowledge structure not only because they have numbers and resources of libraries and finance but also because their work is conducted in English. By comparison with this predominance in the knowledge structure, any loss of American capability in industrial manufacturing is trivial and unimportant.

Thirdly, change in the knowledge structure is bringing about new distributions of power, social status and influence within societies and across state boundaries. The biggest significant differential between, say, African states, European states and new states like Taiwan is the percentage of the population receiving higher education. Power is passing to the 'information-rich' instead of the 'capital-rich'. Indeed, it is information that unlocks the door giving access to credit, not the mere possession and accumulation of capital in whatever form. Just as industrial workers once came to look down on agricultural workers, so that the very word 'peasant' became one of contempt and abuse, so the 'knowledge workers' are coming to feel superior to the blue-collar workers who carry out merely physical, manual work. Meanwhile, national capitalist classes are being superseded everywhere by a trans-national managerial class in which the social and functional distinctions between state and corporate bureaucracies are becoming rather blurred, and in which the life-styles of each resemble each other more than they do those of state officials or corporate managers who function only in a national milieu.

Part III

The Secondary Power Structures

The next four chapters deal with four aspects of political economy that are both important in their own right and also in some sense structures, defining the options open to business enterprises, minor states, social groups and individuals. They are the world's major transnational transport systems; the trading system; the energy supply system; and the transnational welfare and development system. The choice is a bit arbitrary in that it would be equally logical to include some other secondary structures. For instance, there could be a chapter on international law, except that there is no lack of good descriptive and analytical works by specialists in the subject. There could also be a chapter on the world food system — food for people being as vital to production as energy to machines. But this too has an extensive literature.

The common feature of secondary structures is firstly that, although they are frameworks within which choices are made on the basis of value preferences, they are also secondary to the four primary structures of security, production, finance and knowledge, which play a large part in shaping the secondary structures. In each of these secondary structures the authority of the state — or of some states — plays an extra-territorial role. Within each state, the government usually takes responsibility for seeing that transport by rail, road, river or canal works smoothly and without disruption. Within each state, the limits are set by the government of its power, in peace and war, to command the economy and to oversee the conduct of the market economy and those who are licensed to operate within it. Within each national society, too, provision is made for the welfare of the weaker members of the society. Fourthly, the state takes responsibility, and has done so increasingly in recent decades, for ensuring the future supply from whatever the source of energy for agriculture, industry, transport and domestic consumers. Taking away the departments of government concerned with foreign policy, with defence and the administration of justice, we find that in most countries the authority of the state over the economy and society is vested in ministries of transport, of agriculture and industry, of social security and of energy. In other words, in each of these issue areas in which there is the interaction of the state and the market, there is also a transnational or global dimension to be considered in which national authority has to take account of global markets and in many cases of the transnational influence of other states. Some brief examination of these and some of the questions arising in consequence is therefore necessary for the study of international political economy.

Chapter 7

Transport Systems: Sea and Air

Whether we think of a cluster of remote mountain villages, of our own country or of the whole world, the question of how people and goods get from one place to another is always a highly political matter. Markets obviously play a part. There has to be a demand for goods from other places or from people who want to travel, whether as tourists or on business. But states also play a part. Is the transport system to be provided by the state itself, or by a licensed monopolist, or by private operators responding primarily to market demand? The choice is a political issue. It matters a great deal to different social groups — to traders and shopkeepers, to farmers, to old people, housewives and schoolchildren — so that political choices are in practice made weighing different social values and the competing claims and interests of these different groups. What choice is made for the running of transport systems substantially affects who gets what in the way of benefits and opportunities, and who carries the costs, both the running costs and the capital costs of the necessary infrastructure (ports, roads, canals or railways); and who bears the risks of mishaps and accidents.

It is temptingly easy to take the political economy of transport systems for granted. Once set up, they tend not to change very much. Only a political revolution or a radical advance in technology will reopen the basic political questions of how authority should react to market forces. Between times, it is easy to overlook the usual questions about who governs and with what results both for social groups and for the system as a whole. This is especially true when it comes to the world's transport systems, to international sea transport and to international air transport. Both have for too long been considered to be of only marginal significance, suitable for highly specialized studies or else as a minor branch of economics. Yet, as international trade grows every year faster than world production, and as more and more people move around the world further, faster and oftener than their grandparents would have dreamed possible, the nature of the transport services they use, the layout of sea-routes and air-routes, the prices charged and the terms customarily laid down for the carriage of goods or people becomes a more and more salient issue of international political economy.

In this chapter I shall show that the political economy of international transport has to be looked at as a product of the four primary structures described in Part II. It has not grown up haphazardly or by accident. It has evolved within an international political system in which states have been the major political authorities in charge of markets and at the same time have had to provide for their own survival; people have looked to them for their security, for law and order within the country and for defence against invasion, occupation and subjection. Since the days of the ancient empires of Rome, Persia and China, the first 'transport' interest of the state has been to have roads for armies to march on and for posthorses to carry orders and messages from the central government to the most distant frontiers. The prime purpose of the transport system was to increase the security of the empire and to secure the integration of people within its borders into an orderly, governable society. Just the same priorities have motivated states in the modern world when it came to planning road systems, building railroads or introducing airline routes. Even the remotest regions had to be linked to the centre, and just as 'all roads led to Rome', so rail and air routes have almost always radiated from a nation's capital.

When it came to transport systems beyond these national frontiers, security was still the major consideration for national governments, whether in the management of transport by sea in ships, or later by air in aircraft. And, like those of the ancient empires, the concerns of the larger and more powerful states for their own security have set the ground rules for the international transport systems with which lesser states or newcomer states have had to conform. In other words, the structure of power and security explains in large part the choices made by political authorities over the market for transport by sea and air.

The market has changed very fast in the last three of four decades as production — from farms, mines and factories — has become globalized; that is, as it has become geared to selling on a world market instead of on a local or national one. The internationalization of production together with the use of oil as a prime source of energy (see Chapter 9) has greatly increased the demand for ships and for airline services. The expansion shown in the tables would have been impossible but for a financial structure which not only provided plentiful credit for the building and purchase of ships and aircraft, but also — and no less important — took some of the risk away from the owners and operators of ships and aircraft by means of insurance of cargoes and passengers and of the ships and aircraft themselves. Only in this way could the cost of transport be kept low enough to allow both sea fleets and air fleets to grow as large as they have done.

Nor must we leave out the knowledge structure as a prime determinant of the world's transport system. It has always been important, and a clear example may be seen in the fifteenth century when Henry the Navigator and the early Portuguese pioneers of maritime navigation used not only the stars but also the sun to cross the trackless oceans. It

Table 7.1 World merchant fleet by flags, 1970–1985 (million gross registered tons)

	1970	1978	1982	1985
Liberia	19	49	41	58
Japan	27	39	41	40
Britain	26	31	22	14
Norway	19	26	21	15
United States	18	16	19	16
Soviet Union	15	22	23	25
Greece	11	34	40	31
Panama	5	21	32	40
World Total	247	406	424	410

Source: United Nations

Table 7.2 World merchant fleet by type, 1985 (million gross registered tons)

Tankers	134
Bulk carriers	131
General cargo	74
Containers, lighters	18
Other	53
Total	410

Source: United Nations

Table 7.3 Air transport markets — passengers and freight, 1970–1982

	1970	1975	1982
Passengers (million kilometres)	392	575	964
Freight (m.kms)	10	17	29
— of which international traffic:			
Passengers (m.kms)	159	263	485
Freight (m.km.t)	6	11	22

Source: United Nations

Table 7.4 Air transport markets by region, 1970–1982 (million passenger kilometres)

	1970	1975	1982
North America	231	299	462
Europe	84	134	207
Asia	40	78	189
Latin America	12	22	40
World Total	382	574	965

Source: United Nations

is important now because radio communication by satellite not only increases ship safety but makes the management of shipping much more flexible. And technology, not states, or markets, has often been the source of the most revolutionary changes in transport systems — beginning with the change from sail to steam in shipping, through the development of supertankers and containerships; and in the air, from the change from propeller engines to jets and the introduction of air traffic control systems to manage the fast-growing business of air travel.

What we must now consider in more detail is how each of these primary structures build up a framework for the world's transport. With each, we can ask the same state/market questions that can be asked of any sector of the world economy — from toys to machine guns, from food to art treasures, from diamonds to drugs. Like fruit tarts with different fillings, or soufflés of different flavours, the basic recipe is always the same; it has only to be adapted to the chosen product. We have to start, as cooks do, by assembling the basic ingredients — in this case, the facts about the protagonists, the operators, and the services they are selling to different buyers in the market. We can then ask about the technology they use, and the rules — and who has made them, and why — under which they operate. The interaction thus revealed of rules (mostly, but not exclusively, made by states) and market demands and opportunities will bring out not only who makes profits and losses but also the sustaining bargains, bargains that may be political or economic, or a bit of both. The bargains will in turn reveal the range of issues, of conflicts of interest and policies, and of problems, resolved and unresolved, perceived from different points of view. By this more or less standard route, we can arrive at our own assessment, necessarily and admittedly subjective, of the values given priority by the transport system (or in any other sector), and the distribution of costs and benefits, risks and opportunities that it produces.

Such an analysis will go a bit wider, and raise some different issues, than the kind of comparison of the impact on less developed countries of sea and air transport 'regimes' that has been sketched by Krasner in *Structural Conflict* (1985). This book was an examination of the successes and failures of Third World campaigning for a New International Economic Order. For the transport part of this study, the question was whether the sea transport rules of the game or those for air transport gave more opening to LDCs and better opportunities to participate in the market. The answer was that the air transport system, based on the legal right of states, acknowledged by international law and convention since the 1920s, to bar unwanted intruders from the airspace over their territory, had led to a set of rules already in place before most LDCs became independent states. These rules reserved to them an assured place in an international airline cartel. By contrast, in sea transport, the market was divided among a few monopolies with their own transport facilities that were part of a vertically integrated operation (the steel, bauxite, some oil companies and the socialist state fleets); a private cartel system of liner conferences that seemed to keep primary-producing developing countries in a state of perpetual dependence; and a residual part of the market which was more truly open and competitive. Krasner concludes:

The difference in outcomes is largely a result of the nature of the existing regimes encountered by developing countries . . . In shipping, the existing regime inhibited the development of national carriers in the Third World; in civil aviation, it encouraged it. [Krasner, 1985; 225–6.]

What his study does make clear, however, is that the two transport systems have such different backgrounds that they must be considered separately. Let us start with the oldest system.

Sea transport: the nature of the market

Overwhelmingly, these days, the sea market is one for the transport of goods, not people. The passenger liners of the 1920s and 1930s belong, with stagecoaches, to a bygone age; and the cruise ships that ply the Mediterranean and the Baltic in the summer and the Caribbean in the winter are more like floating hotels than means of transport. Only in a few narrow seas, like the Adriatic, the Aegean and the English Channel, is there a specialized market for ferryboats — hovercraft, hydrofoils and the larger, slower, roll-on roll-off ('ro-ro') ships. Today, the users of sea transport are the exporters and importers of heavy bulk cargoes, like crude oil, grain, iron ore and other minerals, and of the larger manu-factures — cars, machinery, furniture and any other goods suitable for containerization — packaging in large wooden crates that can be mechanically handled and stacked below and above deck.

The producers, the shipping operators, are state enterprises (the Soviet merchant fleet is the third largest in the world), large corpora-tions operating their own fleets, and specialized firms who own (or quite often charter) ships and sell space in them to the shippers. While some of these, the liner fleets, are organized in cartels called liner conferences, others compete on a more open market, such as the Baltic Exchange in the City of London.

The market for sea transport is and always has been highly unstable. Demand has been typically high in boom times and especially during both World Wars when transport of troops and supplies was vital for state security. After each war, and in every major world depression, the market has been hit by severe over-capacity. Freight rates have plum-meted. Ship prices have fallen to a fraction of production costs so that sometimes it was cheaper to lay up ships than to run them at an operating loss. The current slump in shipping has been longer and worse than most. It began in 1975 after the oil price rise hit first the tanker market and then the dry cargo market. It is not yet over. Freight rates fell sharply in the mid 1970s and by 1983 were 25 per cent lower than in 1977. Shipping firms like the Reksten empire in Norway went bust, or sometimes when they were able, quickly diversified into other markets. For example, Britain's old imperial flag line, the Peninsular and Oriental Steamship Co. (P & O), used its accumulated profits to buy up a big housing and construction company and has been able, so far, to survive on its profits even when shipping services have made a loss.

The other striking feature of the market has been the secular fall in operating costs per ton-mile and the increase in the productivity of labour. Where sailors were once a major input, it is now the capital put up by the bankers for ship construction. Where once a large labour-force of dockers or longshoremen was essential for loading and unloading cargoes, machines now do the handling. And, whereas before World War I ships were almost all driven by coal, which also had to be laboriously loaded and stoked, soon after the war shipping companies turned over to oil, which was cheap and cheaply handled — again lowering operating costs.

Technology has sometimes led to a closing of the market and to less competition among the shipping interests, and sometimes to more competition. For instance, the technological revolution in the mid-nineteenth century, when steamships began to take over from sail, quickly led to the organization of liner conferences, which were nothing but cartels of operators designed to maintain prices and limit competition. The greater reliability of steam-driven ships meant that they could keep regular schedules — but also that, unless organized by agreement, they would all compete for the busiest routes, while neglecting the less busy ones. The governments of major trading countries, like Britain, preferred the more extensive and reliable service that the cartels provided, even if it meant letting the shipping lines charge a monopoly rent for it. For what the liner conferences soon learnt to do was to keep outsiders from undercutting their prices by giving customers deferred rebates — in effect, rewards for staying 'loyal' to conference lines. All the major routes across the oceans of the world had their own liner conference. Their total number has for many years been well over three hundred. Now, however, they are in turn threatened by a new technology: the container revolution. This offers shippers combined land–sea transport, often at lower cost and with less risk of loss or damage.

Technology has also revolutionized the building of ships, letting in new shipyards to compete with the old-established ones. In the old days, shipbuilding required an army of men rivetting steel plates together by hand. During World War II, backed by cost-plus orders from the US government and cost-plus defence contracts, an American entrepreneur, Henry Kaiser, developed new methods of prefabricating the parts of cargo ships so that they could be produced more quickly and with more unskilled labour, as well as more cheaply. Further developed after the war, these new methods enabled first Japan, then Korea and Taiwan, Brazil, Yugoslavia and the Soviet Union to invest in large modern shipyards, close to steel mills. They could outsell the British, the Americans or the Germans with larger, cheaper ships (Korean prices are now as low as 40 per cent of European prices). The fact that it is very hard for governments to stop shipping operators from placing orders for new ships wherever they are produced most cheaply meant that this new capacity expanded very rapidly. It also meant that, once in production, all shipbuilders were all the more vulnerable (as we have seen) to a downturn in the market.

Authorities

There is obviously very great inequality among states in the amount of authority wielded over the market for sea transport. Small landlocked states have had little direct interest in sea transport and therefore have exerted little authority over it. States with global or even just regional security interests or with overseas empires or investments have always had good reasons for trying to ensure the security of sea trade: first from pirates and marauders, then from war and the acts of belligerent states, and also from the hazards of wind and weather. It is they who have willingly borne the costs of producing public goods. The worldwide mapmaking done by the British Navy is an example: British Admiralty charts drawn up over a hundred years ago are sometimes still in use. Other public goods are lighthouses and lightships, meteorological services and weather ships. At the same time, the strong maritime states have almost always sought to provide themselves with ships and sailors that can be pressed into service in wartime. Policy towards sea trade — including training, pay and conditions for seamen and safety standards — thus became a branch of defence policy.

The authority of states over ships sailing in the seas beyond their shores and territorial waters derives from one fact and from one fiction. The fact is that all ships sooner or later have to come into port. The fiction is that a ship's deck is part of the territory of the state, and that on the high seas the ship's master or captain stands in as surrogate for its government. 'Port state' authority therefore gives states (other than landlocked states) the power to make rules about the conduct and condition of ships berthing in its harbours. 'Flag state' authority confers the power to make rules governing the conduct of any ship flying the state's flag, including the right to tax the profits from sea transport services.

This dual source of power has led to arguments about whose rules prevail: 'port states' vs. 'flag states'. And it has also led to the anomalous practice known as Flags of Convenience (FoCs). This was a clever American device thought up by smart lawyers in the 1920s to give the US government the maximum call on a merchant fleet in time of war at the minimal cost either to itself or to the shipowners. After the Washington Naval Treaty of 1922 which put agreed limits on British, American, French and Japanese navies, the US Navy was drastically reduced at the same time as wartime Victory ships were scrapped or sold off for what little — in a post-war slump — they would fetch. To cut costs for US shipping companies as low as possible, Averill Harriman — later to become President Roosevelt's chief foreign policy adviser in World War II — discovered a legal loophole that allowed US-owned ships to be registered in Panama, where taxes were low, minimum wage rules non-existent and safety inspections unknown. A year later, in 1924, Ed Stettinius, a future US Secretary of the Navy, did the same thing in Liberia. Thus were invented the Flags of Convenience (FoCs) under which are now registered about a quarter of the entire world merchant fleet. One-third of these FoC ships are American-owned, but a subsequent Act of Congress has ensured that, in wartime, and regardless of the neutral or belligerent status of the flag state, these ships would be subject to recall for war service by the US government. Today, some 40 per cent of FoC-registered ships are oil tankers owned by US and other oil companies; others are the property of large transnational corporations or of international banks.

This FoC practice is criticized by many leading Third World governments with an interest in sea trade. They say it allows rich TNCs an unfair advantage and pre-empts a substantial share of the market which might otherwise fall to their national fleets. And, although the newest FoC ships — including some of the supertankers — are as well-equipped and as scrupulously maintained as any, it is also true (as successive OECD reports have often pointed out) that many others are old and unsafe and would only be licensed to sail by FoC states. The practice is also opposed by labour unions in countries like Britain and Norway on the grounds that their seamen's wages are undercut by cheaper labour from the Middle or Far East and from some Pacific island states for whom repatriated sailors' earnings are a major source of foreign exchange. Yet, however many the complaints, there is little prospect that the practice will be outlawed. So long as the US Navy thinks that it needs this low-cost reserve fleet, the US Congress is unlikely to condemn it, whatever other governments may say. It can satisfy the unions by subsidizing a small high-cost fleet flying the US flag while satisfying the Defence Department that it has a large reserve fleet of FoC ships.

The abdication of authority, which effectively is what it is, by the United States is made more acceptable by the increase in US authority over sea transport that has come with the increased involvement of the US economy with world trade and with the outraged protests of the American environmental lobby over oil spills and other shipborne hazards for American coasts and harbours. As a port state, the US government, operating through an efficient Federal US Coast Guard service, is able to exercise very effective authority over any ships, under whatever flag they fly, that enter US ports. It can deny access to port facilities to any ship which it decides falls below its standards for safety and environmental protection. By this means it has been said that there are two sets of rules for the world's merchant fleet: one for the half that needs to go to US ports, and another, less stringent set for the other half which avoids or does not need to go into a US port.

In 1984, the US Congress took another step extending US authority. The Merchant Shipping Act of that year gave power to the Federal Maritime Commission to impose sanctions on the ships of any other country or organization which excluded or discriminated against US shipowners. The US has always been ambivalent about the liner conferences, tending to criticize and oppose them when US interests were competitive, but tolerating them when they were less competitive and therefore grateful for the protection of the cartel. The new law allows US policy the maximum freedom to have a protectionist cake on some routes while eating the profits of competition on others. The same new law also waived antitrust statutes for large corporations like Ford or General Motors who may want to escape the restrictions of liner conferences by making special tie-in deals with shipping companies to carry cars and auto parts from one subsidiary to another at more or less stable prices.

As Krasner has argued, the opposition mounted by the Group of 77 to the authority exercised over sea transport by the United States and other dominant maritime states has not really been very effective (Krasner, 1985, Chap. 8). Mobilized by the Shipping Department of UNCTAD's Secretariat in Geneva in the late 1960s and early 1970s, the Group of 77 challenged the liner conference system on the grounds that the cartels were using their power to overcharge developing countries for carrying both their exports (mainly primary products) and their imports (mainly manufactures). A long campaign through various UN bodies eventually produced the text of a UN Code of Conduct for Liner Conferences supported by the majority of UNCTAD member states. Its major provision, known as the 40–40–20 rule, asserted that the two trading partners, the exporting state and the importing one, each had the right (if they cared to use it) to reserve to their own flag ships 40 per cent of the trade, leaving only 20 per cent open to competition by ships of other countries — known as crosstraders. Britain, as the leading crosstrader together with the United States, Norway and Greece, totally opposed the Code and refused to ratify it. They declared themselves free under international law to disregard it. Other members of the European Community, who had less to lose and were more concerned to avoid confrontation with developing countries, eventually persuaded Britain to agree to a compromise, the so-called Brussels Package. Under this, the EC states declared themselves, for sea-trade purposes, a single state, thus allowing open competition among all their ships for the trade with developing countries. And they also declared that they would not apply the Code to sea-trade among OECD countries, which was much more important to them anyway than trade with the Third World.

Meanwhile, however, as the depression in shipping persisted and freight rates came down, the resentment of developing countries against shipping lines lessened. Their governments found better means of bargaining with the shipping companies and their enthusiasm waned for building up risky or loss-making national fleets. Like all cartels, the conferences have proved more vulnerable to competition from newcomers outside their circle of members than to political pressure and government controls. In the case of sea transport, their oligopoly position has been undermined by Soviet bloc fleets, by the big container-ship operators, and by the vertical integration of transport in TNC operations.

The only other important source of non-state authority in sea transport is the insurance industry and its old-established practices and institutions like Lloyds of London. This is because the risk of loss at sea of ships and their cargoes was always so great that from the very earliest days there was a strong incentive to spread the risks as widely as possible. It was out of the hazards of sea trade that the whole essential capitalist concept of limited financial liability of partners developed. This rule limited the liability of partners in financing a voyage to the extent of their investment in it. The same idea, encouraging investment and innovation, was later extended in all capitalist countries to any business enterprise. However big the loss, investors would not have to draw on their personal fortunes. It was also in sea trade that the practice of insurance was born. This allowed the partners to spread the risk even wider, paying outsiders a relatively small price for an insurance policy. The insurers, by taking in a large number of small premiums, could accumulate capital reserves large enough to pay out on the occasional claim for loss or damage. Insurers quickly realized that they themselves ran another kind of risk — that of moral hazard; i.e. that the customer would deliberately insure bad risks or even engineer a claim, by setting fire to a losing business, for example. They therefore began to exercise authority by asking for medical examinations in life insurance, by insisting on inspection for fire precautions in insuring buildings, and, in the case of ships, by making marine insurance conditional on an inspection for seaworthyness. It has often been remarked that, because of the cyclical nature of insurance, and especially marine insurance, the underwriters' inspectors were apt to be strict and conscientious when underwriting profits were good, but to be rather less eagle-eyed and pernickety in bad times, when there were too many of them competing for too little business. So, while the authority of politicians may be subject to political cycles before and after elections, the authority of insurance is subject to an underwriting cycle. The whole question, indeed, of who bears the risks of sea transport and on whose authority they are minimized or compensated is so important a part of the political economy of the system that it calls for a short explanatory digression.

Risk

All transport entails risk — risk to the carriers, to the goods or passengers carried, to third parties, and to the environment. (Even the environmental risks are not as new as one might think; it was said that if the increase in horsedrawn traffic in London had continued at the rate it was going before World War I, the problem of sweeping up and disposing of all the horse droppings would have become unmanageable — and the smell quite intolerable!)

All states have responded to the risks inherent in transport systems with different kinds of rules regarding *security* (by setting safety standards) and *efficiency* (by licensing carriers) and *justice* (by monitoring prices). They have also limited the goods and people that can lawfully be carried and have sometimes allocated liability for losses and damage incurred. Insurance has often been made obligatory; for it is no good making a car driver, for instance, legally liable to pay damages to the person he runs over if he may be too poor to pay up. Compulsory insurance is thus the only way to protect third parties from undischarged liability.

States' rules regarding risk management vary a good deal. But the differences do not matter for transport *within* states. They only become a problem when transport (or other service) is sold internationally. Then the states concerned have to agree on a common set of rules. For sea transport, the variation of safety and environmental rules between advanced states and the Flag of Convenience states has already been noted. Two other major issues remain: the allocation of liability for accident, damage or loss, and the extent of the obligation to insure against liability for large claims. Both may seem rather legal and technical, but are actually highly political issues.

The first question — who is to be held legally liable for loss or damage at sea — has been subject since the 1920s to an international agreement known as the Hague Rules. This agreement favours the shipowners by excusing them from liability for loss of the cargo so long as their insurers had declared the ship to be seaworthy when it left port. In the 1920s, the main hazards for ships still came from the forces of nature rather than from human error. Thus, if the captain did make bad decisions at sea or the crew were negligent, this was a minor risk compared with those resulting from the violence of wind and sea. It was up to the shippers, therefore, to insure their cargo — hence the sometimes quite substantial gap between the freight rate charged f.o.b. (free on board) and c.i.f. (cost, insurance and freight).[1]

This old system has recently come under attack from the shippers. They have castigated it as 'the most unconscionable, inequitable liability scheme ever devised by man'.[2] In their experience, losses are nowadays more often caused by human error than by the wildness of the elements; cargoes are lost, damaged by careless handling, stolen or delayed through faults of ship management or negligence, or through the inadequate use of modern communications systems, weather reports, traffic rules, etc. Shippers have urged the US Senate to ratify a new and different set of rules, the Hamburg Rules. The Hamburg Rules are embodied in a UN Convention negotiated in 1978 by sixty–seven states but by 1987 still only ratified by eleven small ones. These rules would oblige shipowners to show that they had taken all necessary precautions to avoid loss or damage to cargoes. They would also substantially increase the maximum allowable claim per package. But they will remain another UN dead letter unless the United States ratifies the convention. Only if it does so is there much chance that enough countries will agree to the change to bring it into force. And in this ongoing debate it is not only the shippers and the shipping operators who are interested parties. The insurance business is also deeply involved. Both the marine insurance companies, who stand to collect less in premiums from the shippers if the liability shifts to the shipowners, and the other major group, the mutual Protection and Indemnity, or P and I, clubs of shipowners oppose the change. For (as pointed out above), although the P and I clubs pay out on behalf of their members, they do little to raise their operating standards, so that the change would either involve them in the expense of doing so or would make them collectively liable for larger claims from their customers.

Nor is this by any means the only policy issue regarding the risks of sea transport. For instance, there is also the hotly debated issue of the rules regarding salvage — when and how the risks run by the salvors are to be rewarded. And there is the management of environmental risk — as with the horses in London. This special kind of risk merits a brief account on the grounds that, like other environmental issues, it is necessarily a very peculiarly transnational issue of the political economy.

Pollution problems

The issue first came to general notice as a result of the rapid expansion in international sea transport of crude oil (and the size of oil tankers) during the 1950s and 1960s: and then of a series of bad oil spills by the new larger tankers off the coasts of Britain, France and the United States.[3]

A legal suit brought by France in a US court held the oil companies who owned both the oil and the tanker liable for the heavy clean-up costs and the loss of French income from fishing and tourism. Like a new, specialized, transnational P and I club, the tanker owners came together to set up a specialized reserve fund against the risk of further claims. It was called TOVALOP (or Tanker Owners' Voluntary Agreement Concerning Liability for Oil Pollution). This was supplemented in 1971 by CRISTAL (Contract Regarding an International Supplement to Tanker Liability for Oil Pollution) and in 1978 by a more comprehensive International Oil Pollution Compensation Fund (IOPC). Aware of their increased liability, the oil companies took better care to avoid spills, while governments, especially the French government and the US government, used naval patrols and coastguards to enforce better navigational discipline.

Yet, all this time, the experts unanimously insisted that nearly five times as much environmental damage was being done by deliberate cleaning out of empty tankers at sea as by accidental spills.[4] Here too the oil companies (as major tanker owners) sided with governments to reduce the pollution as a means of limiting their own liability to prosecution or to suits for damage on the 'polluter pays' principle. They hurriedly developed two new technical solutions — known as COW (Crude Oil Washing) and LOT (Load on Top) — to the problem of how to clean old oil residues out of tankers before reloading without dirtying the sea. The technical details of COW and LOT do not matter; the point was that this was a solution more acceptable to governments than the one originally proposed to them by international officials, which would have involved port states in the expense of providing large waste-oil sumps or disposal areas to take the dirty water. Easier by far to make the oil companies liable, and to track down and prosecute polluting offenders by 'fingerprinting' the chemistry of oil wastes. Governments, therefore, acting together through the International Maritime Organization in London, supplemented the technical solutions with agreement on a set of new rules contained in a 1973 International Convention on the Prevention of Pollution from ships — the MARPOL convention, reinforced in 1978 with a new Protocol which came into force in 1983. These dates show that action through IMO — a UN special agency at which all the maritime states, including the Soviet Union and China, are represented — is apt to be slow and rather laborious. But since IMO works always by consensus, any agreement eventually reached is likely to be accepted by all the important member states and enforced to the best of their ability. (The contrast with UNCTAD, where decisions, taken by the numerical majority of states, can still be rejected and ignored by the most important maritime powers, is striking.) Perhaps the most important step taken by states through the IMO in recent years has been to tighten the rules on liability, making insurance against oil pollution damage compulsory for all shipowners, and opening the courts of all major states to claims for damages. The IMO has also negotiated successive increases of the upper limits of legal liability.

What all this adds up to is that the system of managing risks in the market for sea transport services is one of very mixed, and only partially effective authority. The divergence of environmental as well as safety standards required by flag states means that there is more likelihood of oil spills from a Liberian-registered tanker, say, than from a Norwegian- or a Japanese-registered one.[5] Among the non-state authorities at work, the weakest link in the chain of authority are probably the P and I clubs. These offer their members an insurance facility but they do not bother to check their members' ships or the professional qualifications and competence of their crews. What has affected the market operators, especially the oil companies, is the action of states over the last decade or so in increasing the compensation legally available to victims of pollution, even though this would probably still not be enough to cover damage caused by a very large spill. In the same way, the limited size of the funds available to the global insurance (and reinsurance) industry means that it can exert little restraining authority over behaviour likely to result in such nuclear power catastrophies as the 1986 Chernobyl disaster, or in major damage from gas or LNG explosions, or from major chemical accidents even more serious than the 1985 Bhopal disaster.

The compulsory liability insurance agreed by states through IMO has, however, substantially reduced the amount of oil spilled non-accidentally. It has also led some oil companies to sell off their tankers, thus shifting risk elsewhere — just as the sale of oilwells to nationalized oil companies also offloaded on others the risks of falling crude oil prices. For the foreseeable future, the over-supply of tankers means that the oil companies do not need to own tankers in order to be sure of getting oil from oilfield to refinery to distribution point. Like other large TNCs, the oil companies have been good at spreading to others the environmental as well as the financial and business risks incurred in their industry (see below, Chapter 10).

Even this brief account of the situation in sea transport surely shows that the politics of risk management are far too complex to be captured within a conventional international relations paradigm, whether realist, liberal or neo-Marxist. Conflicts are not always between states, and there are conflicts between capitalists; and between developing countries with different interests; conflicts between seamen of different nationalities; and between different kinds of financial institutions. There is also a complex picture of transnational co-operation, in which the oil companies, private and public, American, Japanese, European or OPEC-owned, share certain interests in common, as do other transnational groups, like the P and I clubs and the insurance companies. These will fight political battles to defend their interests wherever it seems to be necessary — at the level of local government, of national governments and of international organizations. They will also use any opportunity opened up by the market or by technology not just to maximize profits but to minimize risks and to deflect risk or to spread it to others.

Neither a pure political (or political-legal) mode of analysis nor a purely market one is sufficient for the purposes of political economy. To grasp the full reality of the situation, the political economist has to ask some very broad questions. For a start, what are the inherent risks of the operation — for the operators, for their customers, for states and for the shared environment? Are these risks at all reduced by rules? Are the rules made by state or by non-state authority? Whose rules (and on what) apply to the allocation of liability for loss or damage? Are they national rules or rules made by international agreement? Is insurance compulsory or optional? How effectively do insurers influence behaviour and guard against moral hazard? Does the state of the market, the relation of supply to demand and the trend of prices affect the implementation of rules and the impact of authority on the operators?

These are just some of the questions that might be asked. They are questions not only about the who-gets-what in costs and benefits out of the global transport system but also about the four basic values of political economy. Conflicts, for example, have arisen between authorities over whether the system is fair in the way that it opens opportunities for profit, allocates risks and imposes costs. Other conflicts have arisen over the value of freedom and autonomy, over whether there is inequality in the free choices open to the users of sea transport — both enterprises and states. As elsewhere, it seems that greater wealth and/or greater military power confer better bargaining strength in the use of sea transport. On efficiency, at least, the system scores high: it has proved highly adaptable to rapid economic change and prompt in the application of new technologies. It is hard to overrate the importance of its contribution to the creation of wealth in the international political economy by expanding the possibilities of trade and of larger markets. The score on the issue of stability, of maintaining economic order, is less clear, however. Although an open market has allowed prices to accommodate falling demand to rising supply ever since the early 1970s, the waste involved both in unwanted shipbuilding capacity and in unwanted shipping has added to the other unstable factors in the world economy.

Air transport

The first major scheduled international air transport services were introduced in the 1920s by Pan American in the western hemisphere and by (British) Imperial Airways in Europe. Both were aided by government contracts for carrying mail but until quite recently the market has been predominantly one for carrying people, not goods. Goods, however, are now quickly becoming more important and by the mid-1980s the volume of air cargo across the Pacific actually exceeded passenger traffic.

Like sea transport, the way in which the global air transport system is structured rests on a political fiction: the notion that a state 'controls' the airspace above its territory, in the same way that, from the eighteenth century until the second half of the twentieth century, it notionally controlled its 'territorial waters'. These used to extend just three miles out from the shore to the supposed limit of a cannon shot, although now, following a US precedent, states claim authority for certain purposes over territorial waters up to 200 miles from the shore. The notion that any government can control what goes on in the air above it is obviously even more of a fiction than the notion that it can control what goes on far out at sea. It is impossible to stop earth-orbiting satellites from passing over a state's territory. And even before satellites became common, the United States was overflying the Soviet Union with highflying U2 aircraft, one of which was actually brought down and the pilot captured in 1958. The fiction about airspace gained acceptance by governments in the immediate aftermath of World War I. In that war, aircraft had at first been used by both sides as a means of reconnaisance for artillery. They soon got involved in fighting each other above the trenches and then in bombing troop concentrations and strategic targets such as railway stations.[6] The result was that by the end of the war invasion of a country's airspace seemed an 'unfriendly act', especially to an island country like Britain for whom raiding Zeppelins over London had been the first foreign intruders since William the Conqueror in the eleventh century. By post-war agreement, therefore, state authority was mutually agreed to prevail over all air traffic coming into the country from outside. Under the Warsaw Convention of 1929, states could declare certain parts of their airspace reserved for military use and could lay down rules for aircraft coming and going. They could claim the exclusive right to license pilots and commercial operators in the market for air transport.

Once again, as in sea transport, the most advanced industrialized countries always put their security interests first in their policy-making on air traffic. In the 1930s, for instance, the Nazi government in Germany evaded the disarmament provisions of the Versailles Treaty, which had abolished the German Air Force, by training glider pilots at the state's expense. The British government, meanwhile, trained a military reserve of pilots with a subsidized Civil Air Guard training programme. And during World War II strategic interests played a large part in developing both the technology of aircraft manufacture (including the advance from propeller-driven piston engines to jet engines) and the layout of a global network of routes and airports. The US Strategic Air Command, by developing a string of military air bases across the Pacific and also across the Middle East, created the infrastructure on which post-war civilian traffic developed. And as both the Berlin blockade, the Korean War and the Vietnam War showed, any powerful state had to have a reserve of transport aircraft to carry men and supplies to distant war zones.

Authority and the market

Unlike sea transport, the market for air transport is much more directly subject to state authority; non-state authorities such as the International Air Transport Association (IATA), the airlines' cartel, only exist by permission of governments. And, as in international law and international organizations generally, the principle holds in IATA that 'dog does not bite dog'; in other words, that states respect each other's equal rights. Inter-state relations have therefore been much more important to the development of the market than they have in sea transport. This fact was established at the Chicago conference of 1944, when the technical advance of aircraft design during the war for the first time opened up inter-continental travel as a practical possibility in the post-war world. Governments met to discuss how this might be managed. In this, they failed; they could agree only to set up a new specialized UN agency, the International Civil Aviation Organization (ICAO), charged with negotiating safety standards, common navigation practices, traffic control systems, etc. Its wider purposes were later described as 'to ensure that the rights of contracting states are fully respected in every way and that *every contracting state has a fair opportunity to operate an international airline*'.

Indeed, for the United States the Chicago meeting was really a political defeat. In ideological terms, it was also a defeat for economic liberalism, for the United States had ended the war with a virtual monopoly in the production of transport aircraft. It was also the only country with a large, fast-growing domestic market for air travel. The manufacture of aircraft in Europe and Japan had come to a full stop and even Britain had voluntarily agreed earlier in the war to concentrate its manufacturing capacity on building fighters and some bombers and training planes, leaving it to the Americans to make all the transports. No wonder that, as the strongest trader, the US delegation at Chicago was so keen to get the maximum freedom to pick up and carry passengers around the world. But Britain and the other Europeans were just as opposed to the American 'five freedoms' proposal as they were to the opposite Australian–New Zealand proposal for a single world airline service. The Europeans wanted national airlines for national policy purposes. They turned down a supranational world airline; and they would agree only to the first four of the Americans' five freedoms:

— the reciprocally conceded right to overfly another state's territory;
— the right to land in another state to refuel or for other non-commercial reasons;
— the right to pick up people from the home country going to another state;
— and the right to pick up people from another state and bring them to the home country.

They refused utterly to agree to the fifth freedom:

— the right to carry people in either direction between two foreign countries on the way out from or on the way home.

If that had been conceded by the Europeans it would have been the end of all their hopes of building up viable national airlines or of holding against American competition a share of major traffic routes like that across the Atlantic. Their resistance was fundamentally strategic, not economic. For although Imperial Airways had been replaced in 1946 by the less grandiose British Overseas Airways Corporation (BOAC), considerations of empire still strongly influenced British — and also French, Dutch and Belgian — policy. Both in Britain and France, aircraft were designed, developed and built with the long inter-continental routes to Africa and Asia in mind. A greater economic opportunity to develop cheap medium-range aircraft better suited to the nascent intra-European market was missed for what turned out to be totally obsolete political reasons (Wheatcroft, 1956).

The immediate result of European obduracy at Chicago, insisting that US aircraft could only enter European airspace by permission of the local government and in return for a reciprocal right for Europeans in the United States, was deadlock — an agreement to disagree while setting up ICAO as a mere technical and functional forum. A second attempt in 1947 to get a multilateral agreement was also unsuccessful. But by then the bilateral Bermuda Agreement of 1946 had set a precedent which others could follow and which effectively embodied the four freedoms but left individual states free, in a series of other bilateral negotiations, to decide on the degree of openness to foreign airlines and air traffic that they wanted to allow. By an accident of history Britain still had an island colony, Bermuda, quite close to the eastern shores of the United States. Theoretically, therefore, BOAC could fly the Atlantic between British airports.[7] The United States had no such offshore colony on the European side. Britain was thus able to negotiate with the Americans from a position of relative strength. The result was an arrangement by which the two governments agreed on the routes to be flown, but by which each would decide unilaterally which airline or airlines it would license to fly them. There would be no competition on fares, but the carriers could negotiate amongst themselves on the frequency and timing of flights and on the seating capacity to be marketed. Thus, the US preference for competition between privately owned airlines and the European preference for state monopoly airlines could be reconciled.

The overall result of a global network of bilateral Bermuda-type agreements was to set up IATA as an operators' cartel in which, in order to limit competition, even the quality of in-flight meals and the provision of movies on long flights had to be standard. But, at the same time, the United States did get some limited fifth freedom business in as much as the bilateral Bermuda Agreement allowed British airlines to fly to and from New York–London–Frankfurt even though such routes were always subject to *ex post* review by the governments concerned and provided that most of the traffic on the route was genuinely international.

This system, as Krasner has noted, was ready-made for the new states of Africa and Asia who would never have been able to compete at all in a more open market (Krasner, 1985). In the 1950s, as they emerged from colonial status to independence, recognition as fully-fledged members of international society was a major common concern. Membership of the United Nations and other bodies was one such badge of membership; their own national airline, painted with a distinctive national logo, was another and a more visible one. To run their airlines they could draw on a free labour market well supplied with war veterans, experienced and qualified pilots speaking various versions of English, the common *lingua franca* for the air traffic controllers. There were also enough competitive manufacturers eager to sell them aircraft, and banks and export credit agencies willing to lend money to finance their purchase. New and old states, rich and poor, large and small, all could have a share of the market in and out of their territory. In effect, the system established a rough 50:50 rule instead of the 40:40:20 rule sought by the UNCTAD Liner Code. Justice for the state, however, was achieved at the cost of efficiency; customers paid a needlessly high price for many international journeys.

From the late 1960s on, however, the cartel has been slowly undermined by the combined forces of technology and the market, assisted by the connivance of national governments, particularly that of the United States. The changing technology affected the supply of aircraft, introducing by stages or generations more powerful — and more costly — aircraft with seating capacity for more passengers, thus changing the organic composition of capital in the air transport business, substituting capital for labour in the production of each seat-mile. Just as the market for sea transport had been changed and old bargains between operators, between sellers and buyers, had been upset by the change from sail to steam, from coal to oil, from loaded cargo to container handling, so the market for air transport has been radically changed by the move from piston engines to jets and turbo-props. The famous DC6 introduced in 1946 had 80 seats and weighed under 50,000 kilos. The DC7 introduced in 1953 had 105 seats and weighed 64,000 kilos. The Boeing 747 and the Tristar brought in at the end of the 1960s both weighed over 500,000 kilos and had 351 and 330 seats respectively.

Thus, new generations of transport aircraft suddenly increased the supply of seats on any route flown, while imposing on the airlines as operators the cost of depreciating an expensive new investment. The IATA cartel did not allow competition on price, or service, so airlines could only compete on speed (e.g. Concorde on the busy Atlantic route), on comfort and on their reputation for being up-to-date with the newest and best. Where the biggest international airlines (often able to negotiate special terms with the manufacturers) led, the rest found they usually had to follow. Their problem then was how to match demand to supply or, as Anthony Sampson, quoting a memorable remark by Eddie Rickenbacker, puts it, 'Putting bums on seats' (Sampson, 1984: 15).

Before going on to suggest how this technology changed the market 'regime', a few words of explanation are needed about the interaction between the market for transport *aircraft* and the market for transport *services*. For the frantic race between manufacturers to develop new models, often before the old ones were anywhere near worn-out, was no more an accident in the aircraft industry than the IATA cartel was an accident in the transport sector. It was clearly the result of very open competition in the 1950s and 1960s between the three major American aircraft manufacturing corporations — Boeing, McDonnell Douglas and Lockheed. All three had the advantages of a large domestic market, of fat government defence contracts, as well as a head-start on foreign aircraft firms in supplying the international airlines, foreign as well as American. But US government policy ensured real competition between them in research and development, for domestic economic reasons as well as strategic military ones. Unlike most of the European states, the United States had no national railroad system to protect from competition. It had been well served in the nineteenth century by the competition between railroad companies. So it was that the policy chosen for air transport in the 1930s, when the US Civil Aeronautics Board (CAB) was first set up as the federal regulatory authority, also favoured as much competition as was practically feasible. It is a historical fact that transport enterprises threatened by competition from a new form of transport will resist, both by mergers and by seeking help from the state. The state's reaction is therefore crucial. In England, in the nineteenth century, the canal and inland waterway interests sought help from Parliament against the new railways, but they sought in vain; the railway interests were far too politically powerful. So the canals, hampered by regulated prices and other statutory restrictions, lost business, went broke and fell into disuse. In the United States in the twentieth century, the same conflict arose in the competition between rail and air transport. The importance of military superiority in the air had been amply demonstrated in the war against Japan, against Germany, in Korea and again in Vietnam. There was no way in which the US Congress was going to defend the railroads against competition from the airlines. So it was that US railroads lost passenger business, merged and went broke; and the government responded only halfheartedly with some support for Amtrak. By contrast, the open competitive regime for airlines supervised by the CAB created a dynamic and on the whole profitable domestic market in which the competition on all the major routes sustained an expanding demand for each new generation of aircraft. The result for the airlines was that in 1982 the US domestic airlines sold 400 billion passenger seat-kilometres (p.s.k.), only a little less than the 485 billion p.s.ks sold on *all* international routes outside the Soviet Union. The result for the American manufacturers was that they had ample funds to spend on research and development and could dominate the market even when European governments tried to combine forces to finance a rival European aircraft industry. By the 1980s, although Lockheed had folded by then, Boeing still held 60 per cent of the world market (excluding the Soviet market served by the Aeroflot monopoly), McDonnell Douglas 19 per cent and the European syndicate, Airbus Industries, despite tremendous efforts, only 15 per cent. (The remaining 6 per cent held by Brasilia indicates the future possibility of yet more change — a shift of aircraft manufacturing to NICs comparable to the shift already experienced in textiles, steel and shipbuilding.)

What this suggests is the interconnection of a sector such as air transport services with the four basic structures of security, production, finance and knowledge. It also shows the interconnection of air transport with other sectors (aircraft manufacturing, computers, fuel), which provide it either with the necessary inputs or else with the necessary markets. In this case, it is the tour operators and the big hotel chains that provide the necessary demand for the airlines — just as cereal growers provide the demand for fertilizers.

The advantage of trying to sum up the network of bargains affecting a sector in this way is that it makes it less easy for the political economist to overlook some important exogenous factor, whether coming from a market, from technology or from an authority, either of which may have a substantial impact on the who-gets-what of the particular sector. It also serves as a reminder of other policy issues, whether for governments or other authorities, which might otherwise be forgotten or disregarded.

Although I have concentrated so far on the issue of efficiency and competitiveness in air transport, there is also — as in sea transport — an important policy issue of safety. In this, the shared common interest of governments in minimizing the risk of air crashes makes ICAO an important authority even though it presents no significant threat to state sovereignty. But national authority also plays an important part. Just as we saw that, in oil pollution caused by tankers at sea, the French government found it more effective to sue the oil companies in a Chicago court rather than a Bordeaux one, so in the case of a Turkish Airlines crash in Paris in the early 1970s, a suit was brought to a Californian court by lawyers employed by *The Economist* — their Paris correspondent had been killed in the crash — against McDonnell Douglas for design defects in the aircraft. US courts were used, and were an effective means of getting the manufacturers to pay more attention to safety, not only because the manufacturer was American but also because US laws on product liability (and for that matter professional liability) were much stricter than most European laws. A further result of both is that liability is shared by the airline and the manufacturer and therefore both have more need of insurance. Once again, the insurance industry acts as a non-state authority by determining the cost and the availability of cover against legal as well as against real risk.

Meanwhile, the authority of the IATA cartel has been affected by technological change — the introduction of jumbo jets — by the consequent expansion of the market, bringing tourists into the picture. The jump in seating capacity of new jets gave a big incentive to the airlines to cheat on the cartel rules in order to fill their empty seats, even if this could only be done by lowering prices. The first really big loophole in the rules was opened by a national authority, that of the United States.[8] The US government in any case had never been wholly convinced that an international airline cartel was either necessary or desirable. Then, during the Vietnam War, the need to take troops to Vietnam and, once there, to relieve them from time to time with periodic respites from the horrors of fighting on such alien ground against such determined resistance led the US military to contract with a new kind of transport operator, one that did not seem to be in direct competition with the regular scheduled service airlines. But the R & R ('rest and recuperation') market so created in the Far East adventitiously gave a great boost to the idea of using the new larger aircraft to satisfy a totally new market and to carry a new traveller, the holiday-maker. For holiday-makers would be flying, not so much to the great cities and business centres of the world, as to the holiday resorts of Europe and the Caribbean — or for Japan, to Korea, Indonesia and Thailand. So it was that the CAB began to license tour operators at first for an experimental period of five years and then more permanently. At first, there were all kinds of limits put on the new market. The airfare had to be combined with hotel charges, the group travelling had to be a genuine club or affinity group of some kind. But these limits soon proved hard to police. The profits to be made by getting 'bums on seats' proved highly attractive. The scheduled airlines, while publicly deploring the 'illegal' bucket shops selling phoney tour tickets, were tempted to join in the game themselves, selling cheap air tickets not only to Majorca or the Bahamas but to New York and Chicago.

The result was that tourism in the 1970s and 1980s became a principal source of growth in the market for air transport.[9] But because of social and economic factors on the demand side, that growth has been far from even or uniform. For example, it is a fact that, in the early days of tour operations, Britain generated as much as 40 per cent of the entire tour or charter traffic. This may have been partly due to London being an entrepôt airport, partly that the British government allowed very free competition among travel agents and tour operators to keep prices as low as, and indeed often far below, what the rules allowed. But it may also have been that British families could more easily be tempted to holiday abroad than, for example, French or Italian families. A poor summer climate, a seafaring tradition, an island location, the very fact that successive post-war British governments had tried hard to check foreign travel for balance of payments reasons, may all have helped to make the difference. But, whatever the reasons, where the British tour operators led, the Germans, Dutch and Scandinavians followed. And their destinations were also apt to be affected by government policies at the receiving end. For example, for many years, fares to Greece were cheaper than to Turkey, and tourists flocked to Athens in their millions. The difference was that the Greek government allowed the charter companies to compete freely with Olympic, the state airline, while the Turks, until recently, did not. And Spain was more popular a destination than Yugoslavia, partly because the government allowed the exchange rate to fall, making it cheap, and also because it allowed foreign investors to finance a vast expansion in the construction of seaside hotels and apartments.

Transport and trade

In this chapter I have touched on some of the issues of political economy to emerge from recent developments in the world's sea and air transport systems. They are sufficient, I hope, to show the impact of the four primary structures of the global political economy on the availability of these services and on the terms on which they are sold in the market. Much more than the road and rail transport systems, which, being land-based, fall more directly under the authority of each territorial state, sea and air transport systems reveal a greater degree of asymmetry in the authority exercised by some states as compared with others over that market. Powerful states can agree on rules, or can delegate their authority to the operators. What they do will influence the distribution of profit, the incidence of risk, and of cost, to the users.

It is important in political economy not to take this unequal distribution of authority over transport systems for granted. Some textbooks on the politics of international economic relations deal with trade and the issues over which trading states disagree, without so much as a mention of the transport system. Yet, trade between states cannot take place unless goods can be carried from one state to another. Mediterranean trade, from the Roman Empire to the nineteenth century, was checkered by periods when marauding pirates made trade so hazardous that it virtually ceased. Although aircraft hijackers are comparatively rare, the reaction of governments to this threat shows the importance they attach to the safety and reliability of air transport services. As in the past, states with strong trading interests exert an influence on the patterns of air and sea routes in accordance with their need for markets and for secure supplies. This pattern then becomes a secondary structure within which other trading states have to operate. Thus it seems logical to consider transport systems before trading systems.

Chapter 8

Trade

Trade and war are the two oldest forms of international relations. Both are topics on which people's attitudes and opinions differ widely. In international political economy, indeed, there is no other subject besides trade on which theories diverge more widely, or in which most theories diverge further from the facts. The theories diverge from each other for the simple reason that they are so closely connected with normative doctrines that their explanations of what *is* reflects different doctrinal opinions about what *ought* to be, and therefore each theory is much affected by the priority given by its supporters to different values such as efficiency, equity, autonomy and security. This also explains why there is so much divergence between what actually happens in trade relations in the world economy and what is supposed to happen according to the various theories.

This is why, in order to get some overall grasp of the structure of trade, it is best to begin with the facts, so far as they are known, and then to proceed to the conflicting theories, rather than the other way round as so many textbooks of international economics are apt to do. The facts will also help to put into perspective the way in which the flows, the content and the terms of international trade are so heavily dependent on the four primary structures of security, production, finance and knowledge.

The result of this dependence on the primary power structures is that exchanges in international trade are not simply the outcome of market forces, of relative supply and demand. Rather, they are the result of a complex and interlocking network of bargains that are partly economic and partly political. These bargains involve the trade-off for states of their security interests and their commercial interests. They involve the unequal access of trading partners to both finance and technology. They involve domestic political bargaining over the access to be granted to national markets, and corporate decision-making regarding secure as well as profitable sources of supply. In this interlocking set of bargaining relationships, there is no way in which the economic can be separated from the political, or that superior bargaining power can be described as either political or economic. Yet, the balance of bargaining power over trade will be found to be more decisive than the debates conducted in international organizations.

Conventional texts on international politics, when they deal with trade, often tend to start with the relevant international organizations.

But this gives the false impression that it is the trade 'regime' — the rules and arrangements agreed between governments — that is a prime determinant of what actually happens. Instead, so-called 'rulebooks' are in reality a rather peripheral influence, reflecting the interests and bargaining power of the most powerful states on the conduct of the most effective traders.

Facts

There are six major facts about world trade of the last hundred years that can be deduced from the statistics available to us. They are as follows:

(1) Trade between national economies has grown very fast — faster than production.
(2) It has grown very unevenly.
(3) The goods and services traded have changed substantially.
(4) The main participants have changed; and some national economies have become much more involved in foreign trade than others.
(5) The way in which trade is carried on (the authority–market relationship) varies widely between national and international markets and consequently between sectors.
(6) The terms on which goods and services are traded also vary very much.

Let us review the evidence for each of these major facts.

Fast growth

During the whole of the present century trade between countries has grown faster than their total production. That is to say, the proportion of production sold across state frontiers has steadily risen. Before World War I, international trade grew at an average rate of 2.5 per cent per year, while output grew at an average annual rate of 2.2 per cent. In the last half-century, the rate of growth has accelerated, even allowing for inflation, as the following figures of the total value of world trade suggest: 1938, $25 billion; 1945, $58 billion; 1958, $114 billion; 1975, $903 billion; 1984, $1,915 billion. An even more astonishing fact is that in one decade, from 1960 to 1970, the volume of world trade almost doubled. Another is that, in the mid-1980s, in a period characterized by the same slack commodity prices, the same difficulties with foreign debt, the same trend towards protectionism that also characterized the depression years of the 1930s, world trade, instead of falling, as in the 1930s, actually grew in 1984 by 9 per cent over 1983. In 1985 and 1986 it grew a bit more slowly, at 2.5 per cent. In recent decades, trade has usually grown faster than world production.

What the available figures do not tell us with any degree of accuracy is whether trade is growing faster, about the same, or more slowly, *between* countries than it is growing *within* countries. The trade within countries can be deduced rather roughly, from the volume of retail and wholesale sales and the estimates of gross domestic product (GDP). But the first two sets of figures will include a certain amount of double counting and the GDP can miss out on many exchanges that are not recorded and not declared for tax purposes. (At one time in the mid-1980s the Italian government, for instance, decided it had been grossly under-estimating the value and volume of these exchanges in the so-called 'black economy' and arbitrarily increased its estimate of the Italian GDP by something like 15 per cent.) In developing countries, the total of internal exchanges will be even more of a 'guesstimate'.

The question of fact on this point is not unimportant, for internal trade is free of restrictions, at least in market or semi-market economies. No one bothers to count the balance of trade between Texas and Massachusetts, for example, or between Minas Gerais and Rio Grande do Sul. If it grows it is because production is growing, because purchasing power is growing, because the use of money and the volume of credit to finance the exchanges is also growing, and (not least) because there is a transport system that can move the goods and people reasonably cheaply and easily from one place to another. All these factors also contribute to the growth of international trade — and may actually be contributing more than the reduction of trade barriers to

Table 8.1 Manufacturing: production and export shares by country group, 1965, 1973, and 1985 (*per cent*)

Country group	Share in production			Share in exports		
	1965	1973	1985	1965	1973	1985
Industrial market economies	85.4	83.9	81.6	92.5	90.0	82.3
Developing countries	14.5	16.0	18.1	7.3	9.9	17.4
Low-income	7.5	7.0	6.9	2.3	1.8	2.1
Middle-income	7.0	9.0	11.2	5.0	8.1	15.3
High-income oil exporters	0.1	0.1	0.3	0.2	0.1	0.3
Total	100.0	100.0	100.0	100.0	100.0	100.0

Source: World Bank

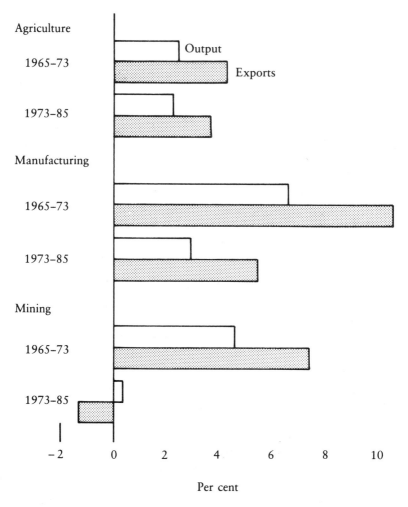

Source: World Development Report 1987, p. 43
Figure 8.1 Post-war growth in world output and exports (percentage)

the recorded fast growth of the last fifty years. Because we know from analysis of the production structure that in most countries more and more producers are producing not just for the local or even the national market but for a world market, it seems likely that external exchanges in many countries may be growing faster than internal exchanges, though comparative economic growth-rates suggest that this may be more true of developed than developing countries. In the latter, the extension of the money economy, the provision of credit and the urbanization of populations may be having more dramatic effects on internal exchanges.

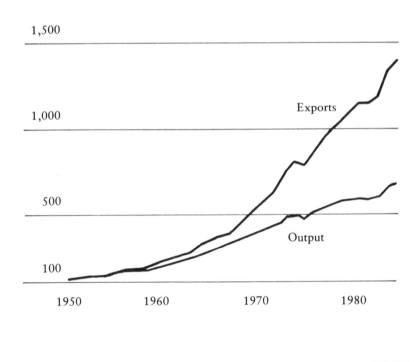

Source: World Development Report, 1987, p. 43
Figure 8.2 World manufacturing output and exports

The question is also worth raising because there is no intrinsically good reason why analysis of the exchange structure in the world political economy should be limited to exchanges across frontiers. An exchange structure is the network of *all* the bargains struck between buyers and sellers of goods and services. It is a political accident that governments monitor imports and exports that cross their frontiers more closely than they monitor exchanges that go on within them. They did this first because tariffs on foreign trade were a source of revenue for the state; and then because the state needed to know about the balance of its trade with the outside world since if this were in deficit it could affect the external value of its currency and the state of its monetary reserves, or both. The economic literature about trade has therefore concentrated on international trade. Yet, many of the political economy questions concerning the consequences of trade — the distribution of costs and benefits, of risks and opportunities — and

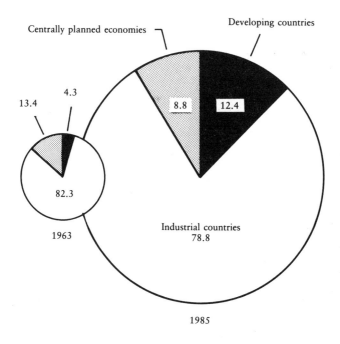

Centrally planned economies

Developing countries

4.3

13.4

8.8   12.4

82.3

1963

Industrial countries
78.8

1985

Source: World Development Report 1987, p. 147, using GATT figures in current US dollars
Figure 8.3 World exports of manufactures, 1963 and 1985 (*percentage shares*)

concerning the political results when people produce goods and services for exchange rather than for themselves or their families, or because they are directed by the state agencies to do so, will be equally relevant and important within states as they are within the world economy.

Uneven growth

The second major fact about international trade, which probably also applies to internal or intra-national trade, is that over the last fifty years it has grown in jerks, unevenly, much faster in some years than in others. There have even been times when the volume of international trade has fallen from the year before. Such times have been when there was a world war going on or when the growth of the world economy was slowed down by economic depression, as in the 1870s and the 1930s. In both wars, merchant ships were attacked and sunk, or prevented from trading by naval blockade, or they were commandeered for war service, transporting troops and armaments to war theatres, by the US and British navies. Inevitably, peaceful trade suffered and continents like Latin America and Australia were obliged to substitute local production for imports. Nothing, in short, has such a dampening effect on international trade as war. The state of the security structure, whether conflict in it is local or general, whether it is modified, as in the superpowers' cold wars, or total, as in both world wars, will have direct results on the patterns of trade.

Between times, between the 1870s Great Depression and World War I, in the 1920s and again after World War II, international trade grew rapidly. And the paradoxical fact is that in these periods of faster growth there were always some major trading countries that were following policies of severe protectionism and restraint on trade. Before World War I, for instance, trade was growing rapidly, even though all the fastest-growing industrial countries — the United States, Japan, Germany and France — were all highly protectionist in their trade policy. The forces of the market appeared to triumph over the policies of states: in all these countries imports grew as well as exports. In each of the three decades before World War I, the volume of world trade grew by an average of 40 per cent (34 per cent per head of world population). In the inter-war period, trade was slow to recover and was too soon cut back by the 1929 Depression, so that over the two inter-war decades, world trade grew by an average of only 14 per cent per decade (or 3 per cent per head of population).

Changing content

The third fact is that the composition of international trade has undergone very great changes over the last hundred years. From being an exchange structure in which most of the exchanges were of goods, and most of the goods were food, minerals or other raw materials, it has become an exchange structure dominated by the exchange of manufactures. Instead of primary products accounting for two-thirds of world trade as they did in the nineteenth century, by 1966 they accounted for only one-third; and that fell by 1983 to only 17 per cent of total world trade. David Ricardo's classic example quoted in so many economics textbooks of trade between two countries, which was the exchange of English wool for Portuguese wine, is therefore totally obsolete and atypical of modern international trade. The commonest international exchange is not even raw materials for manufactured goods. Even the developing countries are becoming less and less committed to exporting primary products. By 1984, these made up even less than a quarter of exports from African countries and only 15 per cent from Asian ones. The eighteen commodities which the Group of 77 (the organized lobby of developing countries) selected as deserving of commodity stabilization support from other members of the United Nations were in reality, even in the 1970s, rather unimportant in world trade as a whole. Individual commodities, like copper for Zambia, cocoa for Ghana and jute for Bangladesh, may be a major export for particular countries, but taken together primary products accounted for only 10 per cent of world trade in 1970 and, by 1983, for only 5 per cent.

The only important primary product still traded internationally is, of course, oil (see below, Chapter 9). But that commodity hardly figured at all in trade statistics before World War I, while some commodities that were then quite important (natural rubber, guano, copra, furs and ostrich feathers) have practically disappeared from the scene. All kinds of electronic products, computers, aircraft and other manufactures undreamed of fifty years ago are now traded actively on the world market. So are all kinds of services, like advertising, consultancy, and education. International trade, in short, is a moving picture, never static in its composition from one year to the next, but always reflecting — just as it did in the ancient world, in the Middle Ages, in the eighteenth and nineteenth centuries — the purchasing power of the relatively rich and the relatively powerful.

Unequal participation

The involvement of people in different countries in the global trading system is very unequal. The reasons for this are both economic and political.

The economic reasons are that, because income is unevenly distributed in the world, so, therefore, is purchasing power. It is people in the richer, industrialized countries who can afford to buy more manufactured goods and services than people in poor, developing countries. So, the manufactures that now make up the bulk of internationally traded goods are mainly imported and exported by the industrialized countries. Despite faster growth-rates in developing countries, this domination of world trade by the developed market economies has been a consistent trend. The share of industrialized market economies in world trade at the end of World War II was nearly 60 per cent. By the 1960s their share had risen to 70 per cent and by 1985 it was 72 per cent. In that year, despite their far greater numbers, the non-oil developing countries of the Third World were still only exporting just over a quarter of the exports of developed countries.

The political reasons are of two kinds. The first and most obvious is that some states in the international political system are small and others are large. Continental states, like China, the Soviet Union and the United States, can more easily satisfy their needs by trade from within their own wide frontiers. By contrast, small states — ranging from the (Dutch) United Provinces in the seventeenth century to Singapore and Hong Kong in the twentieth — have found that trade is a good way to grow rich. They have therefore actively sought to become very much involved in it.

The second political reason for unequal participation is that states' policies towards trade with others have always been governed by their security concerns. They have encouraged trade with allies and dependents, and discouraged it with potential rivals and enemies. Never has this simple fact been more evident than in the last forty years when the cold war between the superpowers has affected their respective trade policies towards each other and towards their respective allies. At the end of the 1940s, the US Congress passed a law which severely restricted the goods that could be sold by US enterprises to the Soviet Union and its East European allies. Next, the US government set up in Paris a committee on trade with Communist states (COCOM). This was an organization of its NATO allies directed to draw up and apply a co-ordinated list of forbidden export items. At the same time, in all the East European countries, the governing Communist party governments were indicting people for the crime of advocating or conducting trade with the West. The result was that world trade really consisted of two systems — a market-oriented and a state-planned system — almost entirely insulated from one another. By the 1960s, when East–West trade had grown, two-thirds of the exports of countries in the Soviet bloc, euphemistically referred to in GATT statistical tables as the 'Eastern Trading Area', still went to other countries in the bloc. Even in the early 1980s, when East–West trade had been nourished by generous Western credits to Poland and other East European countries, the proportion of Soviet bloc exports going inside the bloc was still as high as 50 per cent. At that time, only 17 per cent of the bloc's exports was going to all the developing countries put together and 30 per cent to developed market economies.[1]

At the same time that the United States in COCOM was using its political influence over its allies (derived from their dependence on US defence) to discourage trade with the Soviet bloc, it was actively working to develop trade links with the alliance. American opposition to the closed imperial trading systems set up by the Europeans with their overseas colonies went back a long way. President Wilson in his Fourteen Points statement of war aims after World War I had included in them an 'open door' policy for world trade. The Roosevelt Administration in the 1940s shared the same ambition. Secretary of State Cordell Hull was ideologically convinced that freer, non-discriminatory trade was a necessary condition for world peace and good order; while American business interests could see that extra profits could be made by expanding US exports not only of wheat, cotton and other primary products but, even more, of manufactures. The United States' avowed purpose in trade policy was 'to make real the principle of equal access to markets and raw materials of the world, and thus the preservation of peace'. A major target was the reduction and if possible elimination of the British imperial preference system consolidated during the 1930s depression by the Commonwealth's Ottawa agreements of 1932. Negotiating with Britain was therefore a vital first stage in setting up an open post-war trade system. It was made easier by the fact that, although Anglo–American agreement on common resources for a common purpose — that of winning the war — had set up Combined Boards to allocate ships, armaments, and all kinds of supplies of goods and raw materials to where they would best serve the common aim of victory over Germany and Japan, this principle had never been applied to finance. Britain, having run its monetary reserves of gold and dollars right down to pay for American arms in the early part of the war before Pearl Harbour, and having raised dollar funds by every conceivable means, including leasing its Caribbean bases to the United States, melting down silver sixpenny coins and commandeering private investments in US company shares, was finally totally dependent on American goodwill and self-interest. As recounted by Gardner (1969), the concessions necessary to US post-war trade policy were successively wrung from Britain, first in the negotiations over the Lend-lease Agreement in 1942, then in the negotiations prior to the Bretton Woods Agreement in 1943, and finally and irrevocably in the deal over the British Loan (formally, the Anglo–American Financial Agreement) in 1945. Stage by stage, Britain paid for its military and financial dependence on the United States with a political commitment to support American plans to build a non-discriminatory trading system and, if not to dismantle the closed imperial ones, at least to see that they would be slowly phased out.

But trade ties once established between countries for political reasons do not easily wither away. One reason for this is the close economic connection between investment and trade. The financial structure that ties a colonial currency to an imperial one and that unites its banking system to that of the dominant country exerts a powerful influence on trade flows. And these links do not vanish when colonialism ends and the flag of independence is run up. The result is that trade figures for African countries thirty years after independence still show a marked partiality for trade with France, or Britain, as does Indonesian trade with the Netherlands. Similarly, the predominance of US investment in Latin America, and of Japanese investment in South-east Asia is reflected in trade flows in both directions which favour the investing country.

One result of these political and economic influences from the past is that South–South trade flows (that is, trade between developing countries) still amount to only just over 3 per cent of total world exports, and are only about a third as large as their exports to the industrial countries.

No standard rules

Once we think not just of international trade but of the exchange structure that operates throughout the world economy, within as well as across national frontiers, a striking fact that emerges at once is the stark contrast between the rules that apply to trade within states and those that apply to trade between them.

Within the broad categories of products exchanged, there have been other big changes. Some raw materials like cotton and wool have become much less important; others like oil and bauxite much more important. Some kinds of manufactures have given way to others, as first textiles were supplanted by steel and engineering products and then as chemicals, cars and electronic manufactures took over larger shares of the total export market. The latest growth area for international exchange is the 'invisible' or service sector, which includes all the transnational exchanges involved in entertainment, tourism, education, advertising, consultancy and other professional services.

Within states, governments have always laid down rules for the conduct of trade, rules that put certain social and political objectives and certain social and political values above the total freedom of the market. Socialist states go further still, taking over as far as possible from the market and subjecting most important exchange transactions to direction by the central agencies of the state. But even the most liberal, free-enterprise oriented governments have all tried to govern trade in such a way as to produce more security and stability for the whole national production and consumption system than the unlicensed market would produce by itself; more safety for employees and more stable prices for consumers than there would be if no restraint at all were put on the pursuit of profit; and more equity, certainly, than there would be if no laws governed the performance of contracts, the settlement of debts, the description of goods and the general conduct of corporate enterprises. Within states, too, there will be more severe prohibitions, and severe restrictions on what may be exchanged. Rules will vary, but may ban trade in alcohol, or drugs; in prostitution or child labour; in guns and explosives and in poisons. Certain trades may be reserved either to the state or to a chosen monopoly; others perhaps will be open only to nationals of the state or to specially licensed operators (tobacco, railroads, posts and telephones; medical, legal and banking services). And participants in different national exchange transactions will be further constrained by local peculiarities of the tax system, by anti-trust or competition policies; by national labour laws, or by patent and company law. All these rules will temper the efficiency of the market system by an imposed concern for greater security and stability and also for greater equity. It need hardly be added, though, that national governments have been far more concerned with the pursuit of these values within their own jurisdiction, and for their own people, than they have been for others beyond their jurisdiction. Indeed, in trade policies, greater security within the state may quite often be obtained only at someone else's expense. But, in a political system based on state sovereignty, the fundamental right of states to act in this way is not questioned.

Even if the government of a developed and a developing country both imposed identical rules on internal exchange and if both followed identical external trade policies with an identical mix of free trade and protectionism, the very size of the developed country and the importance of its extensive market would mean that its self-interested regulation would carry more weight with the developing country's exporters than vice versa. This basic asymmetry between the power of governments in developed and developing countries to ensure their own economic security through trade arrangements and regulations, and between associations of manufacturers and primary producers to do the same, is yet another fact of the world's trade structure as it exists in the real world, as distinct from the world of economic theory.

Terms of trade

The final point to be derived from the facts is that the terms on which exchanges are made vary very much from sector to sector in international trade as well as between internal trade and international trade. Developing countries often allege — and believe — that the terms of international trade have become more unequal (see below, pp. 175–78) and that they operate increasingly to their disadvantage. As a generalization, this allegation is hard to sustain and economists have spent hours arguing the point. Much always depends on the period chosen for comparison. For instance, if one were to compare the terms of trade for LDC exports in 1951, at the height of the Korean War, and the associated boom in commodity markets, with their terms of trade in the late 1950s when the same markets were hit by recession, or if one were to compare 1972, say with 1982 or 1983, either set of figures would support the LDCs' contention. But equally, if one were to choose as base years the years of recession and low commodity prices, an exactly opposite argument could be made.

All that can be said with any confidence from the factual evidence available is that markets in commodities — oil, coffee, sugar, tin, copper, cocoa and so on — have been much more volatile, moving both up *and* down more violently than markets in manufactures. One reason is that manufacturers, as Galbraith put it, 'administer' prices. That is to say, they have a list price which they announce to customers. Though they may be obliged to respond to poor demand or competition by lowering their list prices, that is not quite the same as being at the daily mercy of a market system of trade over which the producer has no control and in which, in many cases, speculative trading can move prices up or down even when neither supply nor demand have changed in any way.

Another fact, of course, is that producers, like states, seek security in the market, and producers of manufactures find it easier to organize cartels and to maintain restrictive practices than do primary producers. There are usually fewer of them and they can more easily co-ordinate their 'administered' selling prices. An American estimate made as long ago as the 1930s put the total number of known international cartel arrangements at 179, of which 133 involved manufactures. These ranged from petroleum products to chemicals, steel and aluminium, to matches and light bulbs (Berle and Means, 1967). Interrupted by the war and restrained by US antitrust proceedings, such cartels were less evident in the 1950s and 1960s. But by the 1970s they began again to multiply. And this time they have often been encouraged and endorsed by governments anxious to maintain domestic employment by negotiating Voluntary Export Restrictions (VERs) and Orderly Marketing Arrangements (OMAs) with their foreign competitors. It is also a fact that such agreements between governments have been easier when the producers — as in steel — were few in number and already well organized nationally.

The internationalization of production has been another important development affecting the terms on which goods are traded across frontiers. Whether a TNC's global strategy involves the setting-up of 'relay' affiliates abroad reproducing the production processes developed by the parent company at home, or whether it sets up a 'workshop' affiliate responsible for one stage in the production of a product destined for the world market, the firm is internalizing trade across political frontiers (Michalet, 1976). Some estimates even in the 1970s attributed 70 per cent of US exports and 75 per cent of British exports to intra-firm sales, planned and conducted by a central management according to its corporate global strategy.[2] As competition has intensified in world markets, large firms have merged or mounted takeovers, or else have negotiated joint ventures, even with rivals, in order to spread the risks and to cut development costs by sharing them. The result is that the 'nationality' of a car, a computer, an overcoat or a man's suit, an aircraft or a television set is nowadays rather unclear. Not only in international trade is there a lot of inter-industry trade — that is, Swedish cars being shipped across the North Sea to Britain or France while French and British cars pass by in other ships headed for Sweden — but there is also so much intra-firm trade that the 'Swedish car' (in the case of Volvos) may actually contain more parts and components made outside Sweden than it contains parts and components made in Sweden. Clearly, the terms on which such parts and components are supplied to the assembly plant — which again, as with Ford or General Motors, can be in a country other than the company's headquarters — are a matter of complex negotiation in which tax advantages, labour union pressures, transport systems and market destinations are some of the many factors affecting the transaction.

Against this complex and necessarily very abbreviated summary of the factual background, let us now turn to consider the rival theories and doctrines concerning trade in the world economy.

Theories of trade

There are three main schools of thought about international trade, but none of the theoretical explanations of why trade occurs across state frontiers entirely fits the foregoing set of facts about world trade. Each reaches a different conclusion about the proper role of the state as regards the markets for goods and services that are traded internationally. Since what is 'proper' is essentially a political question, it is no mere coincidence that these three schools of thought broadly coincide with the three schools of thought about inter-state relations.

In the study of international relations the three are known as the realist, the pluralist and the structuralist (Little and McKinlay, 1986; Gilpin, 1957; Barry Jones, 1983). In international economics, they go under somewhat different labels — mercantilist (or neo-mercantilist), neo-classical or liberal, and Marxist (or neo-Marxist, or in Latin America and other Third World countries, *dependencia* theories). Reduced to the simplest essentials, the difference between the three schools lies in the value that ought to be given priority and, conversely, the defect of the system that most needs correcting by the intervention of political authority and the use of power — power to coerce, to bargain or to persuade. The realists, or mercantilists, hold that in an insecure world the most important value is security. Survival is the chief aim of the state, and if a world market economy threatens that survival, policy should be directed to achieve whatever is necessary for the survival of the state. Social cohesion is the foundation of the state and so it may be worth paying quite a high price in the sacrifice of other values to achieve or to maintain that social cohesion, just as it is worth a high price to defend the state against a foreign invader.

The liberals or pluralists hold the creation of wealth by the efficient combination of the factors of production to be the ultimate objective of a materialist society. States as well as firms need wealth in order to be powerful and to survive. So efficiency is the prime value. Policies aimed at avoiding economic inefficiency should have priority and as few restrictions placed upon the functioning of the market in order to ensure the greatest creation of wealth at the lowest possible cost.

By contrast, the main concern of the structuralists, radicals and *dependencia* school is with justice — or rather the injustice — of the system. Correcting an unjust bias in the system has priority over other values. There is a moral imperative, too, on political authorities in all states to act positively now to correct the injustices resulting from the way in which both the international political system and the international economic system have functioned in the past. One produced colonialism and the other produced under-development.

Inevitably, the difference over ends leads to great differences over political means. And for this reason alone we can be mercifully brief in outlining the main elements of the three theoretical schools. If they are really more political and ideological than scientific — in the sense that they do not proceed to their conclusions simply through the observation of objective facts — and if none satisfactorily fits with the facts, then it is unlikely that any of them will prove an entirely reliable guide to any student or scholar addressing specific problems or specific issues of trade in the world economy, whether these concern a particular pair or group of countries engaged in trade or whether they concern the states and enterprises engaged in a particular sector of the world market economy. All the student of international political economy really needs is to be familiar enough with the underlying concepts and arguments of each school so as to be able to recognize them when encountered in the literature or in debate.

Liberal theory is by far the most dominant among American and, indeed, most European and Japanese economists. Its central tenet is the Law of Comparative Costs. This states that wealth for both trade partners will be maximized if each specializes in the production of goods or services in which it has the greatest comparative advantage. In a two-country, two-product model, the law goes further and states that if one of the countries is better than the other at producing *both* products, then both countries will maximize wealth if the more efficient country specializes in the production of that good in which it has the greatest comparative advantage. Although there were forerunners the credit for formulating this concept is traditionally given to David

Ricardo, the early nineteenth-century London financier. It was derived from the same labour theory of value that was also the foundation for Marx's ideas about the extraction by capitalists of the surplus value contributed under capitalism by workers, incorporated in their product and resulting in profit to the capitalist.

Out of a truly vast literature developed by neo-classical economists, two important derivative arguments may be mentioned. One is Jacob Viner's theoretical defence of trade liberalization within an inner group of countries. Known as the Customs Union theory, this explains that the net addition to welfare/wealth from such an exclusive arrangement has to be calculated by comparing the trade-creating effects of the liberalization effected between them with the trade-diverting effects of trade transferred from more efficient producers outside the group to less efficient ones within it. If the sum is positive, the customs union can be defended on liberal principles as a second-best solution to multilateral liberalization.

The other is the Heckscher–Ohlin model elaborated by two Swedish economists before World War II. This suggests that the comparative efficiency of countries in producing different goods is derived from their differential endowment with the factors of production — capital and labour. Trade between developed and developing countries is explained by the fact that the former are well endowed with capital, the latter with labour. The different combination of factors will cause capital-intensive products to be produced both for home consumption and for export in one country and labour-intensive products to be produced both for home consumption and for export in the other.

Much empirical work has since shown that this model does not necessarily hold good. Wassily Leontief, in the 1950s, for example, demonstrated the paradox that the United States — where labour was comparatively scarce and dear and capital comparatively accessible and cheap — actually exported products that required less capital per worker-year than goods imported into the United States. More fundamentally than that, however, the liberal theory of international trade makes the major false assumption that firms, especially large firms, in planning production, and states in deciding commercial policies, can both afford to disregard questions of security, and of survival, in order to give priority to the most efficient allocation of resources.

Realist theory, being based on the contrary assumption, does not make that mistake. While liberal theory has dominated the academic scene, realist theory has dominated the political one: more states in the history of the last hundred years have acted in accordance with realist theory than in accordance with liberal theory. Its basic assertion is that the survival and autonomy of the state is the prime objective of policy but that the interests of firstcomers and latecomers in industrialization do not coincide. While free trade may suit the former, the latecomers will never be able to catch up in open competition. For successful industrialization they will therefore need state intervention and commercial protection. The realist case was forcefully argued by Alexander Hamilton in the newly-independent United States of America, and by Friedrich List in Germany in the decades before Bismarck united the country in 1870. The close links between government and industry developed over the years by both France and Japan were equally based on the common assumption that competitiveness in world markets can be substantially assisted by government intervention and the judicious use of protection, subsidy and other non-tariff barriers, by the selective allocation of credit and sometimes even by the suppression of competition. Pragmatism in the choice of policies at different times and in different sectors is implicit in realist analysis. As Dudley Seers, a development economist recently converted from liberal economic principles, wrote, 'Policies . . . can only be derived from national need, not from internationalist premises about an international community which does not exist.'[3]

Structuralist or dependencia theory also starts from the assumption that the market is not neutral and that history, and the uneven economic development of different parts of the world have introduced a bias against the developing countries of Asia, Africa and Latin America. This bias is intrinsic to the system and therefore justifies a redressive or compensatory set of policies assisting the Third World to catch up and to become more equal trading partners with the industrialized countries of North America, Europe and Japan.

Greater equality is the value given priority, and the policies advocated for the achievement of a New International Economic Order in the 1970s all had this element in common; that they sought change which would go some way to alleviating the inequality, whether by commodity stabilization, by increased aid and easier credit, by commercial preference or by the management of sea transport, as explained in the last chapter.

On these objectives and on the basic assertion of the intrinsic bias in the trading system there has been wide agreement in developing countries. The credit for articulating such a broad approach must go to Raul Prebisch, the Chilean economist who headed the UN Economic Commission for Latin America and used the findings of the Haberler Report of 1958 on the post-war trends in world trade to such effect. It was Prebisch more than anyone else who used the facts regarding the relative decline in international trade in primary products, and the asymmetric terms of the market for Third World exports and imports to fashion a series of policy aims leading to the calling of the first UNCTAD in 1964. But, theoretically, it has to be said that there is rather a wide divergence of views among neo-Marxists, structuralists and *dependencia* writers about the ultimate causes of the inequality and the dependence. One respected structuralist, Arghiri Emmanuel (1972), for instance, argues that it is the relative immobility of labour, reflecting the immigration policies of states, compared to the mobility of capital, reflecting the interests of investors and banks, that is the root cause of the disparity. The West Indian economist Arthur Lewis (1978) put his finger more firmly on the original difference between the productivity of labour in agriculture in Europe and in the plantations in the tropics that produced low prices and low wages in Third World countries. Yet others like Amin (1976) or Gunder Frank (1978) see the economic inequality as the reflection of an inequality inseparable from a capitalist system sustained by the use of political power, both nationally and internationally.

It is hardly surprising, as indicated earlier, that different explanations lead to, and legitimate, different policy prescriptions as to how states should respond to the world market economy. The shortcomings of all three main bodies of theory when set against the facts can now be summarized. None of them, firstly, satisfactorily accounts for the very marked structural convergence of national economies — and especially those of the industrialized countries. All these countries tend to produce the same mix of products and then to exchange them with each other. Nor does trade theory account for the second stage of structural convergence, which may be described as multinational *composite production.*

Secondly, none accounts satisfactorily for the wide divergence of policy responses among states and even among groups of states at similar stages of economic development. It is not enough for economists to dismiss such substantial differences as due to irrational decisions of various kinds by politicians, for there is more to it than that, including economic factors as well as historical and geographical ones.

The diverse performance of developing countries in international trade is even more striking. Empirical work explicitly inspired by liberal trade theory has shown that import substitution policies for industry, especially in Latin America, have been associated with slower economic growth-rates and less competitive production and performance than those achieved by the export-oriented economies. But liberal theory by itself does not explain why some LDCs felt confidence enough in the first place to take on the risks of export-oriented policies and why others did not. The performance of the four East Asian Newly Industrialized Countries (NICs), for example, has never been satisfactorily explained on the basis of any of the main bodies of trade theory. Even economists have ended up referring vaguely to the common factor of Confucian philosophy as the basis for the active entrepreneurship shown by Chinese and Koreans.

Nor, finally, are the theories at all helpful in explaining the wide variation in the state–markets relationship concerning trade in different goods and services. There are sectors that in other respects are quite similar but in which states intervene more purposefully in one than the other. Think, for example, of coal and oil, of sea transport and air transport, of steel and aluminium, of textiles and clothes compared with radios and television sets.

In short, the common weakness of trade theories, whatever their ideological bias may be, is that they seek to explain and to treat trade in too great isolation. They do not sufficiently take into account the impact on exchange relations between states (as on exchange relations between people) of the four major structures of political economy. If such exchange relations are the result of variable influences coming from the four structures, it is not surprising that the search for a general theory to explain all trade links in the world economy proves unrewarding and unsatisfactory.

Attention to the facts of any one country's performance and trade policies, or to the trade patterns in any one sector of the world market economy, reveals this very clearly. Firstly, there is the influence of the security structure. Alliances and conflicts evidently link or distance trade partners. Concern with state security reinforces other factors — such as income distribution and consumer demands — leading to a convergence in patterns of industrial production. It is a striking fact that the same basic industries, all considered vital for defence reasons, have been nurtured whenever necessary by the governments of leading industrialized economies (Sen, 1984).

Secondly, there is the influence of the production structure in which, as explained in Chapter 4, all industries have experienced the increasing capital cost and decreasing life-expectancy of plant, machinery and often the products themselves. The shortening span of time before obsolescence sets in impels all producers of goods and services to seek wider market outlets and quicker profits than they can hope to find within national economies. This imperative of industrial production brings more and more firms, and more and more states into the world markets. It is also the reason for the trend to co-operation agreements between rival enterprises, particularly in the development of the next generation of a product or service, when this is likely to make demands both on financial and human resources beyond the capability of any single firm to satisfy.

Thirdly, there is the financial structure in both its aspects, that is to say, as a structure in which national currencies co-exist but are exchangeable and as a structure within which credit is created both by banks and governments and is highly mobile internationally. The impact of the financial structure on trade has for too long been obscured or overlooked as a result of specialization by economists in either trade or money. The realization has been slow to dawn that the two must be taken together. A poor performance in trade can easily be the result of an exchange rate pushed higher by the inflow of foreign, internationally mobile capital — the experience of the United States in the years 1982 to 1986 is a classic example. Conversely, a weakening market in one sector of the world economy could cause a country's trade balance to deteriorate, and the supply of new foreign capital to dry up, with the result that, in order to finance essential investment and perhaps government spending, a deflationary monetary policy becomes necessary just when other indicators call for the opposite strategy. In the years 1985–7 Nigeria and Indonesia had such an experience as oil exporters.

The instability and the uneven growth recorded in trade statistics over the century have been primarily a reflection of the uneven creation and availability of credit in the world market economy. All the boom times in world trade have been times when credit was being freely created by banks or by governments, or both, and made available internationally either directly or through international capital markets. All the slumps have followed a drying-up of credit, sometimes due to the diversion of credit flows from international to domestic capital markets — as in the United States in 1928, when the flow of short-term credit to Europe was diverted to Wall Street, or when US banks, from about 1984, began prudently diverting their capital from the international loan markets to rebuilding their own capital–asset ratios, thus exacerbating the credit-famine already hitting the Latin American debtor countries. Trade theories have been slow to see that the protectionist responses made by governments in such situations were the symptoms of financial disorder, not the cause of depressed trade.[4]

Lastly, the impact of the knowledge structure on world trade has already been implicit in the point about the accelerating rate of technological advance and therefore of the obsolescence of products and of production processes. But there are other effects too. There is a close correlation between the availability of knowledge through education and performance in export trade. Taiwan by 1987 had built up its monetary reserves through successive years of trade surpluses to $62 billion, and had one of the highest proportions in the world of its population in full-time education. African countries have much lower percentages of literacy and this is an important limiting factor in their ability to export successfully.

There are also the trade effects of the ways in which knowledge has been made accessible for industrialization. The patent system developed in Europe and the United States in the nineteenth century imposed on Japan a cost for the acquisition of their industrial know-how which the country was still repaying in the 1970s. But, by that time, this particular aspect of the knowledge structure was being changed by the large transnational corporations who, to preserve their own market positions against their competitors, were increasingly internalizing technical knowledge acquired in their research and development divisions, and spending more on security systems to prevent industrial espionage from robbing them of its possession. The efficacy with which, in this new structure, knowledge could be kept from would-be competitors among the LDCs was subject to much more variation by sector and by country than the old system of technology transfer; and so, in consequence, were their prospects as exporters of manufactures.

Much of the above is only common sense. But the net result is that because the impact of any one primary structure on the trade prospects of any one country at any one time will vary so much, the combined effects on that country of all four structures, some being favourable to it and others unfavourable, will vary even more. No two countries' prospects — its opportunities and its constraints, the costs and benefits — will be the same, and even the same country's prospects will change with changes in global structures. Consequently, its competitiveness in the market and its bargaining power outside the market with, for example, a powerful transnational corporation interested in investing in new plant in the country, or again, outside the market, its bargaining power with the governments of other states will together determine its place in the trading system. To take one example, a large counter-trade deal worth some $4 billion exchanging Nigerian oil for Brazilian sugar and manufactures was negotiated in the mid-1980s. The incentive obviously came from the credit in the financial famine hitting both debtor countries and from the surplus capacity in relation to demand in the world production of both crude oil and sugar. Although it was deplored as discriminatory — which of course it was — the deal proved attractive partly because of the size of the domestic market which each was able to offer to the other. Third parties who deplored it were unable to prevent it since countertrade, long-practiced and tolerated in East–West trade, was by then proving an important escape route for many countries afflicted by scarce resources of foreign exchange.

International organizations

This point about bargaining power in determining the terms of individual international exchanges, and about bargaining power itself being a complex outcome of multiple factors emanating from the primary structures, can be usefully applied to the recurrent questions, 'Who governs?' Is it markets, or states, or international organizations? Have the latter so 'embedded' liberalism in the trade structure, as Ruggie has argued, that states are really constrained by the rulebooks in their exercise of bargaining power — political and economic (Ruggie, 1983)? How far is the trade structure of the world economy dependent on governments' continuing support or on the multilateral agreements reached through international organizations like the GATT? The answers call for some clear thinking about the exact role of international organizations and their relation to state policies.

Firstly, it must be remembered that, in making agreements and setting up international organizations, states have had multiple objectives, often mutually inconsistent. They have agreed and co-operated to make some trade — as for slaves, or narcotics — illegal; or to severely punish interference with trade, as by pirates. They have agreed to co-operate in denying trade to enemies or potential enemies, as in COCOM. They have persistently chosen to discriminate in favour of associates, and in consequence against others, both in groups, as in the European Community, or Asean or Carifta, and bilaterally as in the US–Israel or the US–Mexican trade agreements. They have agreed to co-operate in liberalizing trade on a non-discriminatory basis, as in the GATT. And they have agreed to discuss policies on trade and development that might benefit less developed countries, as in UNCTAD. And the astonishing fact is that some states subscribe to almost all these organizations except the regional ones from which they are excluded. *The notion that international organizations relating to trade are based on a liberal consensus is therefore a gross over-simplification.* The states that are members of some organizations profess a commitment to liberal principles for trade, but that is another matter.

Secondly, *the objectives of international trade organizations are set by the most powerful state in the group or on the basis of a bargain between two or more powerful states.* That state or group of states will therefore set the limits to the co-operation to which they commit themselves through the organization. The objectives of the GATT as explained above were set by the United States, reinforced by the wartime bargain struck with Britain. It is also important to remember that they were also constrained by limits set for the Administration by the Congress. It was the US Senate that, by refusing to ratify the Havana Charter for an International Trade Organization, was responsible for the executive agreement initiated by the Truman Administration and later known as the General Agreement on Tariffs and Trade. And the processes adopted by the High Contracting Parties (as GATT members are formally known) were set within limits laid down by the Congress in the Reciprocal Trade Agreement Act of 1934. This for the first time gave the President power to negotiate commercial agreements independently of the Congress — but only on condition that these were 'paid for' by reciprocating concessions and that tariffs would be cut by no more than half.

Champions of trade liberalization through the GATT have described the system as resting on 'four pillars'. As described by the Curzons, these were: (1) the principle of non-discrimination (and thus the no-new-preference rule for European imperial trade relations); (2) the most-favoured-nation principle applied multilaterally, so that concessions made for one applied to all; (3) the principle of recriprocity applied multilaterally so that through multilateral bargaining country A's concession to country B could be 'paid for' by a concession from country C — who would in turn hope to be repaid with another concession from country B, D, E, or F, etc. The fourth and final pillar on which the whole agreement rested, was a general acceptance of the trade exceptions and escape clauses by which, monitored in the forum of GATT meetings, states under certain circumstances could depart from the three first general principles. In practice, of course, the loopholes could be (and were) used by the United States for itself or on behalf of its allies as national interest dictated, so that the structure supported by the pillars was not nearly as stable and unchanging as the metaphor implied. The third point to remember, therefore, is that *international trade organizations' role and impact have consequently tended to change over time* and to reflect the changing priorities and concerns of its most powerful member state or group of states.

The record of GATT has been full of contradictions and anomalies. The first pillar of non-discrimination, for example, was perhaps the most oddly interpreted. In order to foster the economic recovery of Western Europe (which, in the cold war, the United States badly needed for strategic reasons), the Americans immediately allowed the Western European countries to discriminate against US exports by applying quota and licensing restrictions against them. And, because Britain found itself in financial difficulties after the war, the United States allowed the sterling area to apply discriminatory exchange controls which proved much more effective as trade barriers against dollar imports than the imperial preference tariff structures to which the United States had so bitterly objected in the wartime negotiations. American assistance to the European countries was also made conditional on their collaboration with the United States in a major strategy of trade discrimination — the strategic embargoes on trade with China, the Soviet Union and East European countries enjoined on the US government by the Battle Act of 1951 and enforced through the multilateral COCOM organization.

Even between GATT members, there were big loopholes in the network of rules. One major one was the freedom to use increased tariffs for balance of payments reasons. Another was the waiver procedure allowed for in Article 25 of the GATT, which was used both to allow trade discrimination by the European Coal and Steel Community (ECSC) and later by the European Economic Community (EEC). It was also used by the United States in 1954 onwards to allow restriction of trade in agricultural products. Yet another was Article 19 on 'the difficulties in particular sectors', which allowed suspension of tariff concessions in special circumstances provided it was on a non-discriminatory basis. And there was Article 6, which allowed defensive levies to be put on imports considered to be dumped (i.e. sold below the home price), to the detriment of the importing countries' domestic producers. Mostly, these loopholes were used by the United States, or, with its agreement, by other allied industrialized countries to suit their own economic interests. About the only time the rules were altered to offer special tariff preference to the developing countries was under the so-called Generalized Special Preference System (GSP). This was rather reluctantly accepted by the United States, Europe and Japan in 1971 as a result of continued pressure for developing countries. But it was so hedged about by qualifications and restrictions that its practical importance has been negligible (MacBean and Snowden, 1981).

The fourth and last point is not so much a general observation as a 'DIY' or 'how-to-do-it' point. It is that, in order to assess realistically the prospects of any international trade organization (or any set of negotiations conducted through it, such as the Uruguay Round, for instance), the important point to start with is *the extent and the limit of the bargaining power of the most important state or states*. The United States has dominated and directed the negotiations in the GATT, for example initiating the Multifibre Agreement negotiations and first blocking and then accepting under limits the GSP. It has been able to do so partly because of its implicit bargain with its NATO/OECD allies that gave it a free hand in monetary management and trade negotiations in return for a nuclear defence umbrella; and partly because of the bargaining power conferred on it by its control over so large and rich a domestic market. Access to this prize was so valuable to the other industrialized countries and to the developing countries that, like unrequited lovers, they have again and again turned a blind eye to reinterpretations of the original bargain rather than be barred from it altogether. In the 1980s, however, European and Japanese firms have taken a leaf out of the American book and have literally sought access to the US market by establishing, either by investment or by takeovers, bridgehead-affiliates within the United States. These moves reduce somewhat the bargaining power of the United States by giving foreign firms more possibilities of flexible response to US protectionism. At the same time, the unilateralist trend in US trade policy towards repeated reinterpretations of what constitutes dumping or unfair competition or serious injury to domestic industry closes new gates to the internal market, and thus reduces its value in inter-governmental bargaining (Winham, 1987; Destler, 1986).

It may also be that, despite the launching of another trade round of negotiations, the real significance of such negotiations for many of the important participants in trade is actually diminishing. As trade moves into intra-industry and intra-firm trade, the level of tariffs or quotas merely means that the firm rather than the government reaps the benefit of the higher prices made possible by restricted supplies. When the location of production of components and therefore the flows of intra-firm trade are dictated by companies, government restrictions will be only one variable in their decision-making. The negotiations may still be important for exporters in developing countries; but, as the record of UNCTAD proposals and North–South discussions on trade have repeatedly shown, the bargaining power of the Group of 77 has been insufficient to wring more than token concessions from either the United States or, despite protestations about the Lomé Agreement, from the European Community or Japan. Analysed on the basis of bargaining power, it looks as though the LDCs with large markets, stable governments and educated work-forces can improve their trading prospects by negotiation with foreign corporations rather than by fruitless lobbying in inter-governmental organizations. For those without such bargaining strengths, however, the slow erosion of the multilateral trade 'regime', such as it was, may spell rather narrower prospects and more limited opportunities.

Chapter 9

Energy

The fifth factor

For all developed economies, whether planned, mixed or market-oriented, energy is a vital factor of production. The basic industries in every modern economy — steel, chemicals, engineering — all need large inputs of energy, whether this comes from oil, coal, gas or nuclear power. Nor can any modern economy function without transport. Road, rail, sea and air transport are all heavy users of energy. And when there is a breakdown in the supply of power to homes and factories, a modern society comes almost to a standstill.

The classical economists identified only three factors of production — land, labour and capital. This was natural enough in economies where most wealth came from the land, and where most people were still employed either in farming or its allied trades, as blacksmiths, wheelwrights, carpenters, thatchers, coopers, etc. Yet even at the time when Adam Smith and David Ricardo were laying the foundations of modern economics, they really should have counted two more important factors: technology and energy. Even then, in agriculture, the wealth produced by a given combination of land, labour and capital could be substantially improved with the further addition of technology. Even before the Agricultural Revolution of the seventeenth and eighteenth centuries, the productivity of land and labour had been substantially raised in North-west Europe, by all kinds of technological improvements — such as the iron ploughshare, windmills and watermills, better drainage of wet lands. All required not just capital, but know-how. Later, laying the economic and financial foundations for the Industrial Revolution, had come the four-course rotation system popularized in England by 'Turnip' Townsend, and the improved livestock breeding methods made possible by the enclosure of common land.

Hand in hand with the technology that contributed to greater wealth went an additional input of energy. According to Cipolla, before the Industrial Revolution, 85 per cent of the energy used in the whole world came from muscles — the muscles of men and, increasingly in the richer societies, of animals (Cipolla, 1962). Even the Doomsday Book, compiled by William the Conqueror in eleventh century England as an aid to better tax-collection, recognized the importance of energy as a factor of production. Recorded in it are the number of oxen — they were then the main draught animals — kept in every English village. Later, when the technology of harnessing horses — easier than oxen to feed and keep through the long hard winter — was improved, the productivity of land was raised enabling farmers to raise and keep more horses, while waterpower and windpower could be used instead of animals for grinding corn into flour. Thus, energy in its primitive forms was an essential factor in the Agricultural Revolution.

That energy was also an essential factor in the Industrial Revolution is something every schoolchild knows. The steam-engine replaced windmills and watermills in industry and allowed workers to be concentrated in cotton and woollen mills where the new machines, financed by capital, could turn out bales of cloth instead of yards. Steam engines had first been used in mining, and were later adapted to produce the railway engine. And steam required coal. So it was that the geographical pattern of industrialization in nineteenth century Europe closely coincided with the geological distribution of coal beneath the ground. Industry grew up in the Midlands and the North of England where there was plenty of coal, not in the South. It developed in the north-east of France, not in the south-west, for the same reason; and in the Ruhr and Silesia in Germany, not in the northern plain. Italy, which had led Europe in technology and wealth in the fifteenth century, now found itself handicapped by two tremendous disadvantages: political disunity and a lack of coal. In Italy, as in Greece, people stayed longer on the land and industrialization really hardly got going until after World War I.

By then, states had come to recognize the importance of energy supplies for their security. France's insistent demands for reparations from Germany in 1918 were made on the grounds that the bloody four-year struggle in the mud of Flanders had destroyed or made temporarily unusable the large coalfields of north-eastern France. Such a loss called for compensation. Germany must pay — and in coal as well as money. They should cede the Saar coalfield to France. But this demand was one that cut clear across the principle of self-determination proclaimed by President Wilson and generally accepted by the Allies as the legitimate reason for breaking up the old Austro–Hungarian empire and setting up the new states of Czechoslovakia and Yugoslavia — and for that matter the Baltic states of Estonia, Latvia and Lithuania wrested from Russia in the wake of the 1917 Revolution. But the entire population of the Saarland was German-speaking. The objective test of nationality used by frontier commissions throughout post-war Europe was language. President Wilson was so outraged by this French demand that it was the one issue that nearly broke up the whole Paris Peace Conference. The captain of the presidential ship at Le Havre was ordered to get up steam and the President threatened to leave Paris and return home in disgust. But diplomacy prevailed and the result was a Franco–American compromise that made the Saar a League trust and allowed a (French)

League of Nations commissioner to administer the Saar as part of France for fifteen years, after which a plebiscite was to be held to decide its future.[1]

Just to stress the point that possession of coal as a vital source of national energy for industry was by then recognized as a major objective of foreign policy, there was one more issue at the Paris Peace Conference in which concern with coalfields became a hot political issue. The coalfield was Silesia. It lay awkwardly, partly in Poland, partly in Germany and partly in Czechoslovakia. Perhaps fortunately for the legitimacy of the Commission entrusted with mapping a new frontier between the three states, the national identity question was extremely confused, with haphazard pockets of German and Polish-speaking people making it impossible to draw a neat frontier on the basis of nationality. The defeated Germans, however, remained convinced that once again the veil of Versailles legitimacy had been used hypocritically to deprive them of an important industrial resource. France's reoccupation of the Ruhr coalfield in 1923, when Germany, in the throes of hyperinflation was unable to keep up reparation payments, only served to confirm these suspicions.

Nor did this perhaps simplistic notion that coal was necessary to national industry, and industry — especially steel — was necessary for military power quickly disappear. During World War II, Roosevelt's Secretary of the Treasury, Henry Morgenthau, came up with what he thought was a radical solution to the 'German problem'. 'Pastoralizing' the industrial areas of Germany and closing down the Ruhr coal-mines would rob Germany of any possibility of starting yet another European war and, for the third time, dragging in the United States. Without German coal there would be no German heavy industry; without heavy industry, no powerful German Army and therefore no temptation to bully or threaten neighbouring states to the east, south or west: QED. But Britain, the exiled governments of Europe and wiser American heads knew better; they saw that such a post-war strategy would also impoverish Germany's neighbours. It would undermine and delay economic recovery throughout Western Europe, and incidentally would also leave Germany defenceless against a newly powerful Soviet Union. The Morgenthau Plan was dropped.

Even after the war, when both navies and armies were using oil, not coal, and oil was already a key issue in international politics, the obsession with coal persisted. Once again, France tried hard to wangle a takeover of the Saar coalfield, swiftly acting to lure the Saarlanders to forget their language and cultural ties and vote for French rations rather than scantier German ones. Meanwhile, Britain came up with a proposal for an International Ruhr Authority to oversee post-war use of this vital energy resource. Both moves led to diplomatic trouble, and both were only resolved by the inspired suggestion from Robert

Table 9.1: World consumption of energy by source

	Oil	Natural gas	Coal	Hydro	Nuclear	Total
1979	45	18.4	28.5	5.9	2.2	100
1981	42.4	19.3	29.2	6.2	2.9	100
1983	40.3	19.2	30.3	6.8	3.4	100
1984*	39.3	19.7	30.3	6.8	3.9	100

* Estimated
Source: Union des Chambres Syndicales de l'Industrie du Pétrole, *L'industrie Française du pétrole 1984*, Paris, p.28.

Schuman in 1950 for a European Coal and Steel Community and a High Authority with supranational powers. This would not only settle the question of who owned and controlled the coalfields but, by removing so old a bone of Franco–German contention, would make war between them impossible (Diebold, 1959).

As things turned out, the ECSC never proved such a pathbreaking initiative as Schuman had hoped. The High Authority never fully succeeded in replacing national governments in the management of either industry. Its neo-functionalist assumption that the ECSC would generate European loyalties strong enough to bring political union in by the back door, so to speak, were over-optimistic. Political union was resisted — and not only by France under General de Gaulle. The European Economic Community of the 1960s remained by common consent a loose confederation or association of states, most effective when united against a common external threat.

But the reason why the European Coal and Steel Community no longer held centre stage by the 1970s was much more economic than political. By that time, oil had taken the place of coal as the object of national strategy and international diplomacy. Energy was still 'high politics' — but energy came from a different source. And until the North Sea oilfields were developed, all the European states no longer controlled within their own frontiers their chief source of industrial energy, but were all in the same boat as net importers of oil and gas. Where most coal had been produced and consumed on national markets oil, as the new major source of energy, was being produced and sold on a world market. (Poland, still a major exporter of coal today, was one exception to this general rule.) The politics of how this was done, the terms on which it was acquired, the means by which it was discovered and marketed were matters of international political economy rather than international diplomacy and foreign politics. In other words, the domestic policies of the states concerned came newly into the picture, as did the conditions of the market and the nature of the major market operators.

What distinguished oil from coal as a source of energy and therefore one of the five primary factors of production in an industrializing world economy was that it was so much more mobile. This is an important point, for one of the features of the global economy is the unequal mobility of different factors of production. In the days of coal, energy was largely immobile. Land was also immobile, though it could be acquired by conquest or, occasionally, by purchase. Labour was only partly mobile: it was more mobile before World War I than afterwards, when the United States and others began to close their doors to new immigrants, and when economic as well as political factors brought the practice of buying slaves and bringing in cheap and indentured labour to a virtual end. It became more mobile again from the 1960s onwards when legal or illegal *gastarbeiter* were recruited to work at more menial jobs in Europe and America. In the days of coal, capital was mobile, but, like technology, it became very much more so in the oil age with the improvements of transport and communications systems and with the global integration of international capital markets and banking systems. On balance, therefore, one might say that the relative ease with which oil could be moved across continents by pipelines and across oceans by supertankers reinforced a net increase in the mobility of the major factors of production. But, as consideration of the main sources of energy in the world economy today will show, being more mobile does not mean that it is any less political; only that the politics become transnational.

Facts and theories

Fortunately, unlike trade, the analysis of the political economy of the world's energy supply is not obscured by a lot of obsolete economic theory. On the other hand, it is a still largely undeveloped field. Until well after World War II the acknowledged experts on coal or oil were people working in or advising either corporations or national governments. They were essentially practical people working on particular problems, not academics in search of a general theory. Even today, experts in oil and energy matters, whether they are working in business or in government, are not particularly worried about theory. Their main attention is on the short-run prospects for the market — a volatile and unpredictable market — and with the question of how governments and corporations can best respond. The economic theorists, on the other hand, are not much drawn to applying theory to energy markets. They can see that these markets are highly susceptible to strong forces that are essentially political. For instance, the 'oil shock' of October

1973, when prices in the market were quadrupled almost overnight, coincided with, and could hardly have happened without, the Seven Days War between Israel and her Arab neighbours. War or the threat of war in the Middle East is a market factor difficult to incorporate in any economic theory. Even in 1987, the possibility of conflict spreading from the Iran–Iraq war into the Persian Gulf and affecting oil supplies from Kuwait as well as from Iran and Iraq was the main factor raising the oil price in a few months by 25 per cent from below $15 a barrel to over $20.

Nor, on the whole, have general theorists in political science or international relations had much to contribute. Those who have written about the oil business in political terms have often come to it as experts on Middle East politics. This is obviously one indispensable part of the picture. But it is not the only one. Political line-ups in the US Congress, for example, or in the Politburo, can be just as important. And, although it is clear that state policies with regard to energy are much concerned with the question of energy security, the political theorists who work on security matters still tend to think of strategy as something pertaining mainly to military security, to defence policy and not to energy policy. The concepts and methods of strategic studies (and for that matter of the mirror-image, peace studies) are not easily applied to the political economy — the who-gets-what-and-why — of the world energy system. In short, it seems to be a classic case of the no man's land lying between the social sciences, an area unexplored and unoccupied by any of the major theoretical disciplines.

What is needed — since the politics and economics of energy in an industrialized world economy are obviously so important nowadays — is some analytical framework for relating the impact of states' actions on the markets for various sources of energy, with the impact of these markets on the policies and actions, and indeed the economic development and national security of the states. Because of the subject's importance, there is no lack of facts to draw on. The bibliographies of published material, books, journals and current news articles on oil, gas, coal and nuclear power — not to mention the 'alternative' energy sources of wind, waves, solar energy, etc. — are already vast. The problem is one of selection: what to look for in the haystack of facts and opinions. As E.H. Carr observed about the writing of history, the question is like the fish displayed on the fishmonger's marble slab. Which fish out of all the thousands swimming in the oceans are selected, caught and sold? There has to be some reason, or set of reasons for selecting certain kinds of fish, or certain specific facts, and rejecting others. How that selection should be made so as to answer the kind of political economy questions raised in this book can perhaps best be suggested by a short historical review of the state–market interaction over the past fifty years in the supply and demand for oil. We can then return to look for the comparable facts in the other energy sources, to see how they suggest similar or different answers to the basic questions.

To do all at once would be very complicated and probably confusing; and oil is by far the most important energy source in the world economy. It is therefore the one that most affects the demand for and use of the others. When oil gets dearer, or its supply uncertain, state policies smile on coal or nuclear power; but when oil looks plentiful and cheap, those policies tend to cool. Both the dominance of oil and the greater volatility of oil markets are easily seen from the facts.

For, while some of the facts about energy — the extent of reserves of non-renewable energy resources, for instance — are subject to expert disagreement and constant revision in the light of changing costs and prices, there are some facts of geology and economic history concerning oil that are unchallenged. One is that the accidents of climate and rock formation have distributed oil reserves — and reserves of coal and gas — very unevenly underneath the surface of the earth. Over 52 per cent of the known reserves of crude oil in the world in the mid-1980s were in the Middle East. Over 40 per cent of the known reserves of natural gas were beneath the Soviet Union and Eastern Europe and by far the largest reserves of coal in the world were in the United States (28.7 per cent) and the Soviet Union (27.7 per cent). Although new discoveries can still be made, the broad orders of magnitude of these uneven resources of coal, oil and gas are unlikely to change substantially.

The other fact about oil is that taking it out of the ground is cheap. Of all the sources of energy, the cheapest is Middle-East oil — a fifth of the cost, on average, of North Sea oil and perhaps as much as forty times cheaper than getting oil from the tar-sand beds of North America, or of imported liquefied natural gas. This economic fact explains the dominant position of Middle East oil in the world energy system. In 1984, nearly 40 per cent of energy consumed in the world was derived from oil, and 33 per cent of that came from the Middle East. The proportion coming from oil was less then than it had been in 1979 when it had accounted for 45 per cent of the total, but the Middle East was still by far the most important source of supply.

The historical facts are also important. First, that the total world demand for energy in the sixty years 1925 to 1985 increased by a factor of about five — far more than the demand for food, or steel or any other raw material. Over that same period, demand continued highly uneven, the demand from the industrialized countries far exceeding that from Africa or even Latin America, and the demand from North America being far greater than that of all Western Europe, the Soviet bloc, or Japan.

It is also a fact that, in all the industrialized countries, there has not been a constant relation between the input of energy and the output of

Table 9.2 World oil production*, 1973–1985 (barrels daily)

	World	OPEC	OPEC/world %
1973	58.5	31.3	53.5
1974	58.6	31.1	53.0
1975	55.7	27.5	49.4
1976	60.1	31.1	51.7
1977	62.6	31.7	50.7
1978	63.0	30.3	48.0
1979	65.8	31.5	47.8
1980	62.7	27.4	43.7
1981	59.4	23.4	39.4
1982	57.0	19.9	35.0
1983	56.7	18.5	32.6
1984	57.8	18.3	31.8
1985	56.9	16.5	29.0

* Including natural gas liquids.
Source: Mikdashi Transnational Oil, p.65

Table 9.3 World oil refining capacity by region, 1975–1982 (m.m.t.)

	1970	1975	1980	1982
North America	858	1,063	1,248	1,081
Europe	795	1,085	1,123	1,009
Soviet Union	304	420	525	575
Asia	446	683	1,123	1,009
South America	140	187	214	211
Africa	38	64	119	118
World	2,617	3,545	4,114	3,884

Source: United Nations

industry. In other words, the efficiency of energy use in transport and in industry has substantially increased even while total demand was still growing. This has been most marked in the years since the big oil price rise of 1973, and perhaps most marked in Japanese industry. But, even in the United States, the most profligate oil consumer in the world picture, the ratio of energy used to gross domestic product fell by about a quarter in the decade after 1975. The credit can be shared between the market that put the pressure of higher prices on the users and governments that used conservation policies to make it still more attractive to use energy more economically.

One final historical fact is worth emphasizing. It is that over the last fifteen years there has been substantial divergence between the 'real' price of oil and its nominal price. While the nominal price, denominated (as oil mostly still is) in US dollars, went from under $4 in the early 1970s to $34 and over in 1979, the inflation and the consequent depreciation in the value of the US dollar meant that the real price rose only to about $15. And, thereafter, as US monetary policy tightened and the dollar strengthened, the fall in the real price of oil was not nearly as precipitous as the fall in the nominal price. Bearing these facts in mind, let us now look at the relationship of states, markets and the oil corporations as they have changed historically over recent times.

Companies, governments and markets

Governments, companies, markets: these are the three key players in the oil business game. For the most part, in political economy, it is legitimate — and certainly convenient — to simplify the concept of an authority–market nexus by talking in shorthand of the state–market relationship. But, in oil, the most important authority has often been not the state, as represented by the national government, but the oil company or a group of oil companies effectively managing the market. And both companies and governments have been, at different times and to different degrees, at the mercy of the market.

In the early days of the oil business, that market was for all practical purposes an American one and the only government that counted was that of the United States. The technology of oil was such that a well drilled into the earth could draw crude petroleum from an underground area much larger than the surface area of the concession. United States laws, based on mining for coal and metals, assumed that a concession granted to an entrepreneur would, while it lasted, be exclusive. But it was not: adjacent concessionaires drew on the same pool: quick exploitation and quick sales maximized profits. The first result was cut-throat competition in the market between neighbouring concessionaires, leading to volatile prices and the vulnerability of weak entrepreneurs to stronger ones. John D. Rockefeller's secret in the oil game — a secret later shared by all the big oil companies — was to see the strength to be gained from vertical integration. The cut-throat market soon gave way to the Standard Oil trust. The political backlash to that, in turn, brought in the US government with decisions of the Supreme Court in the 1890s to make inter-state oil business illegal, freeing the market to match oil supply to growing demands.

The national phase of the game ended with World War I. That had demonstrated the need of all armies and navies for supplies of oil and had accelerated the oil-using technologies in transport and industry, especially chemicals. It had also brought about, or hastened, the demise of the Ottoman Empire and its replacement in the Middle East with weak states like Syria, Iraq and Palestine that the victorious Allies decided should be 'mandates' under the supposed supervision of the League of Nations. Their governments were in no position to contest the extension of the concept of oil concessions to much larger areas than the pioneer oil concessionaires in the United States had had. (The first of these, the D'Arcy concession, had been given by Iran in 1901 to one of the founders of what later became Anglo–Iranian.) A large concession meant that there was less danger of competitive exploitation of new finds of oil and cut throat marketing to sell the oil at anything above cost before the reserve was exhausted.

Thus, the second phase of the game was dominated by the companies. The concession states were poor, so poor that they were grateful for the small rewards in the shape of royalties on output that companies offered. And they were powerless, for lack of finance and know-how and marketing outlets, to take over the business for themselves. The consumer governments were indifferent to what went on so long as their own interests were not jeopardized. Britain and France were only concerned to keep any other major state out of the Middle East and to keep their respective spheres of influence. (In 1916 they had even drawn an invisible frontier, the Sykes–Picot line, dividing the post-war spoils between themselves.) Their only other concern was to secure their strategic oil supplies in case of war. This same concern brought the Republican Coolidge Administration in the late 1920s to support US oil companies' claims to share in the concession game in the Middle East — a share which their market size and wealth caused to progressively grow. Otherwise the US government was not too concerned about the authority exercised by its powerful oil companies over the international trade in oil so long as this did not compromise the antitrust rules and the concessionary regulations imposed on the US domestic market.

For almost fifty years, therefore, the international market was virtually at the mercy of the Seven Sisters, as the major oil companies came to be called. Only that part of the market supplied from oil production in the Soviet Union and Mexico — the first example of selective oil nationalization in 1938 — lay beyond the reach of the big oil companies. Vertical integration, putting all the operations from exploration and drilling for crude oil, through transportation, refining and marketing direct to consumers, made these big companies rich. And wealth made them interested in staying rich by restricting competition on everything but price. The group effectively coordinated pricing of various grades and types of oil in relation to an agreed 'posted price' for Saudi Arabian crude. The rulers of these oil states had little or no say over the rate of oil extraction, over the production processes or over the market for oil. It was the companies who could decide to burn off gas from an oilwell, to carry it by pipeline to their own terminals, to load it into tankers under their control and sell it at prices determined by them and the other majors.

World War II may have brought big changes in the balance of power between states in the Middle East, but it brought little change in the balance of power between companies and oil-producing states. Britain and France effectively retreated from the Middle East, leaving Israel and the Arab neighbouring states in an uneasy and unstable situation of unresolved conflict. The United States, more acutely aware than ever of its strategic interest in the area, at first tried under Truman and Dulles to build it into a global alliance system aimed at the containment of the Soviet Union. But, as Soviet expansionism southward seemed less threatening, United States policy aimed only at a superpower stand-off, combined with intermittent attempts at pacification between the Arab states — whose continued compliance was necessary for the secure supply of oil — and Israel, whose preservation as a Jewish homeland claimed massive political support in the US Congress.

The implicit bargain between the US government and the oil majors was that they would continue to have a free hand in their relations with each other outside the United States and with the Middle East states, provided their profits were applied to exploration sufficient to secure an ever-expanding supply of oil to meet the growing demands of Europe and Japan. From the 1950s onwards, they were even freed from any obligation to pay American taxes on these profits. They were allowed to offset royalty payments to the oil states against tax liability to the United States. In the long run, the only significant change in the post-war decades was brought about by the attempt by Iran under Mossadegh in 1951 to nationalize the Anglo–Iranian and break the power of the oil companies. The global production strategies of the oil companies managed to replace Iranian oil with oil from Kuwait and Iraq, just as they managed to keep the oil flowing to Europe by sending it round the Cape when the Suez Canal was closed in 1957. All that happened was that the eventual settlement with Iran after the fall of Mossadegh undermined the Seven Sisters' cartel by letting in a number of independent newcomers as members of a consortium in an important oil-producing state.

In a Third World perspective the decade of the 1960s might seem to be a new, distinct third phase in the market–company–state game. Another view is that it was not the *formation* of OPEC that was the important historical landmark, but only OPEC's effective intervention in the market over a decade later. In 1960, the oil-producing states, led by Venezuela, had reacted to a decision by the oil companies which reduced their revenues from oil royalties. They then set up the

Organization of Petroleum Exporting Companies (OPEC). Recession in the world market economy in 1958–9 had produced a temporary over-supply of oil, causing the companies to lower prices and incidentally (and perhaps unthinkingly) to cut government revenues by 13.5 cents a barrel. OPEC's purpose at that moment was not particularly ambitious; it aimed merely 'to study and formulate a system to ensure the stabiliza-tion of prices'. It did not start out by trying to move the market. The original members (Saudi Arabia, Iraq, Iran, Venezuela) were soon joined by the other Middle East oil states and by Algeria, Liberia, Gabon, Nigeria and Ecuador. Mexico, the Soviet Union and Britain stayed outside. But, although by 1973, OPEC was producing 53.5 per cent of total world oil output, its power to move the market was still minimal. It was only when its members used their political authority over what went on within their territorial frontiers that the balance of power with the companies and then with the market was substantially changed. The lead was taken by Libya. In 1969 Colonel Mu'ammar Gaddafi overthrew the King and set about raising the state revenues by threatening to expropriate any company in Libya that did not cut production and raise prices. Helped by Armand Hammer's Occidental — not one of the Seven Sisters — Libya had raised output even ahead of Saudi Arabia and was in a position to negotiate a new deal on the state–company share-out.

The Libyan example was soon followed by other oil-producing states, all claiming a larger share of the companies' profits. The companies, able to offset their royalty payments against US tax and doing well in a period of buoyant demand, did not resist strongly. They were glad enough in the Tehran Agreement of 1971 to concede a fifty–fifty split with the governments in return for the latters' promise to raise prices by no more than 2.5 per cent a year. That agreement, however, did not anticipate Nixon's dollar devaluation later that year, nor the partly speculative boom in commodities in 1972 that reflected the general uncertainty and post-Smithsonian lack of confidence in the dollar-based monetary system (see Chapter 5). With the outbreak of the October War in 1973, the stage was set for the disgruntled member states of OPEC to use the consequent uncertainty in the oil market to declare the quadrupling of oil prices, combined with the threat to embargo oil exports to consumer countries thought to be too friendly to Israel.

Thus, by stages, from 1969 to 1973, began the fourth phase of the tripartite bargaining relationship between governments, companies and markets. In this phase, the companies appeared to lose power over the market and the market in turn seemed to be subjected to the direction of state policies. Nor was it only the policies of the OPEC producing states that dominated the situation in this new phase. The consumer governments also stepped in. In Europe and Japan, aware of the effect of the fourfold oil price rise on their import bills, most governments increased prices by imposing new taxes to discourage consumption. The United States alone failed to do this for fear of Congress, and in 1974 introduced a complex price-control system designed to 'protect' the US market from OPEC decision-making. Yet, in practice, this policy worked perversely, encouraging imports and discouraging new exploration for oil at home, thus making the United States doubly vulnerable to the global oil market.

The failure to raise prices at home was also a major reason for the failure of the US government's bid to rally an effective international organization of consumers in opposition to OPEC. The International Energy Agency proposed by Secretary of State Kissinger in 1974 was intended to interfere with the oil market by keeping prices down, just as OPEC was trying to interfere to keep them up. It was an odd move from a government that had hitherto studiously kept out of the international oil market, and had consistently opposed (on the grounds of the highest liberal ideals) any suggestion from developing countries that it might be a good idea to stabilize commodity prices by operating buffer stocks or quota commitments by producers or consumers. Yet, building oil stocks and pursuing conservation policies were the major prescriptions urged by the Americans on member states of the IEA.

In fact, far more effective than the IEA in 'defeating' OPEC were the unintended side-effects of US monetary and financial policies. Inflation and the depreciation of the dollar between 1974 and 1978 took most of the gilt off the gingerbread of higher oil prices. The Iranian revolution of 1978–9, tempted the OPEC members to try the same gambit again — using a political event to jack up prices. But the second oil price rise was quite soon defeated, not by other governments but by the market. By March 1983, OPEC found itself obliged to agree on a climb-down, a $5 reduction in oil prices by which it hoped to show it was still in control. But, this time, the market took charge. Prices fell still more, despite the cutbacks self-imposed by Saudi Arabia and agreed by other OPEC states. The fourth phase of state domination was definitely over.

The reasons were clear enough. The producer states had taken over production of crude oil (and of some downstream production of petroleum products) from the oil companies; but they had not fully taken over the high-cost, high-risk responsibility for exploration. The companies had directed their exploration efforts and their financial and technological resources to non-OPEC oilfields, to Alaska, the North Sea and Mexico. OPEC's market share of world oil exports fell from 70 per cent to 30 per cent. Consumer states and their industries had meanwhile invested in alternative sources of energy, in nuclear, hydroelectric and coal-fired power stations, and had worked unforeseen miracles in energy conservation. Countries like Japan had entered into long-term bilateral contracts to secure supplies. A debtor country like Brazil had negotiated countertrade deals with oil-exporting fellow-debtor Nigeria, bartering sugar and machinery for oil. Maintaining a price-fixing cartel in such conditions was bound to be hard.

The fifth phase, therefore, was one in which the market returned to play a much more significant part. But, although, as Morse argued, this was a 'return to Liberalism'. it did not mean that either the oil companies or governments could be entirely left out of the picture (Morse, 1983). The companies still had control of the technology of exploration, of offshore production, of refining and marketing; and they had the capital necessary for risk-taking in an essentially risky business. Some had actually increased their financial and technological resources by selective mergers and acquisitions of other companies (IEA, 1986). Some poor debtor states thus now found themselves competing to woo reluctant oil companies into new forms of partnership with buy-back and contract-free terms. Many producer states (including Britain), which had taken control through national oil companies, could not easily divest. The choice between oil, coal, hydroelectric (when possible) and nuclear power remained the responsibility of government even in non-socialist states. So long as there remained a volatile world market for imported oil, and so long as the major oil companies stayed in the top ten or twenty of transnational corporations, the complex triangular balance of state–market–company was likely, in some form or other, to persist.

The impact of four structures

That triangular balance, it is very clear from the above brief summary of developments in the last fifty or a hundred years, has been subject to very substantial and, in recent years, often rather sudden change. Explaining this dynamism is not easy. One approach first suggested by Keohane and Nye (1977) and subsequently adopted rather widely in the American literature in international political economy was to look for the reasons for 'regime change'. Regimes, it will be recalled, are generally now held to be defined in Krasner's words as the 'principles, norms, rules and decision-making procedures around which actor expectations converge in a given issue area' (Krasner, 1983). Although it looks like a broad definition, that particular formulation tends in practice to direct most attention to inter-governmental mechanisms and agreements on policy objectives and thus to the decision-making procedures of international organizations. Indeed, since the approach was developed precisely in order to answer the question, 'Why do international organizations like the IMF or the Law of the Sea change their character over time?', it is not to be wondered at that the method focuses so strongly on what goes on within the organizations, or in the negotiations *between governments* concerning the nature of international 'regimes'. Broadly and intelligently used, it can still lead — as the results show — to good analytical work that combines attention to the economic forces emanating from markets with the political forces emanating from governments and other authorities. But there are dangers of narrowness inherent in it. It starts, as it were, at the wrong end, at developments in international organizations. Just because such organizations are slow to change their avowed principles and objectives, or to adapt their established procedures, they can easily be rather distorting mirrors — as indeed is the case with the main international organizations in the energy structure, OPEC, the IEA and the IAEA as the central supervisory agency in the nuclear power business. What the regime change method of analysis too often overlooks, or underrates, are, firstly, the forces of the market as they affect state policies, domestic and foreign, and therefore, indirectly, distributional outcomes; and, secondly, the forces of technological change as they affect both state policies, domestic and foreign and market conditions — and for that matter, market shares for companies, and for states.

The impact of four structures

The analytical framework, or method, suggested in this book tries not to leave these things out of the political economy picture. It therefore suggests *starting* with change in the four primary structures — instead of starting at the other end with the reflections of change in the doings of inter-governmental organizations. (In the final chapter, for further clarification, I shall try to set out the steps in this method as if they were written for a mechanic's manual or a cookbook recipe.) But, for the oil business, as the most important part of the global energy supply system (or sub-structure), we can use what has been written so far in this chapter to demonstrate briefly how the method works. What we do is to look first for the changes in the four primary structures described in Chapters 3, 4, 5 and 6, which have had a substantial impact on policies of powerful states, on company strategies, on market conditions and on the overall triangular balance of power over outcomes between states, companies and markets. Having done that, we can ask, in turn, about the secondary or spin-off effects on the policies of other states, on outcomes in international organizations and on the political economy of related markets — in the case of oil, particularly, on its near substitutes, coal, gas and nuclear power.

The reader at this point can legitimately object that all I am doing is going in at a different point on the circle — and perhaps with a broader range of who-gets-what questions. This is fair comment, for a common theme of the four chapters describing the primary structures was that none was divinely ordained, nor did it come to be what it was by blind accident. States, as the dominant authorities in command, in mixed and, ultimately, in market economies made the policies — or refrained from making them — that shaped the structures. In defence of my approach, I would reply that, although I agree that there is a circularity of cause and effect, I still think it better to start with the part least liable to sudden change, i.e. with the structures, rather than with the policies or market conditions.

In the *security structure* there were two major changes that fundamentally altered the state–company–market relationship. One was the redefinition of the necessary conditions of security for the state, especially by the United States, after the first OPEC oil price rise of 1973. The other was the result of a change in the knowledge structure when it became known that the technology developed for atomic weapons in World War II could be applied to the production of electric power for industry.[2]

Let us take the first change. It is summed up in a statement of Henry Kissinger:[3]

In the last three decades we have become so increasingly dependent on imported energy that today our economy and well-being are hostage to decisions made by nations thousands of miles away . . .

The energy crisis has placed at risk all of this nation's objectives in the world. It has mortgaged our economy and made our foreign policy vulnerable to unprecedented pressures . . . it has also profoundly affected our national security by triggering a political crisis of global dimensions.

The language may be a bit over-dramatic, and the assertions somewhat exaggerated, but the perception of a fundamental change in American security is plain enough, and also fairly typical of popular American reactions to the 1973 price rise. This changed perception was much more acutely evident in the United States than in some other states. Switzerland, for example, had long before reacted to its own perception of energy insecurity by investing heavily in capital-intensive hydroelectric power supplies and in costly strategic stockpiles of oil. But Swiss perceptions and policies had much less significance for other states, and for world markets in oil, than did those of a global power like the United States.

What Kissinger was saying was that the security of the United States did not just require that it had sufficient military capability to prevent invasion of its territory or attack by other states. It was threatened in a new way. Energy insecurity could undermine both its defence policies and its foreign policies. Therefore, against this new threat both defence and foreign policies and domestic energy policies had to be mobilized, for reasons of state security. What he did not say clearly — though it was implicit — was that a deficiency or weakness in carrying out one leg of a tripartite security strategy would have to be compensated by strengthening one or both of the others. In economic terms, policies were substitutable at the margin. It would be the same if, in olden days, a town were threatened with siege. Three kinds of policy could reduce the risks of starvation and subsequent defeat. One would be 'domestic', to ration food or tax it enough to cut demand, and to stockpile supplies. One would be 'foreign', to seek allies, military and economic. And a third would be military, to anticipate and defeat the besiegers. In the oil story, US policies after 1974 similarly looked to three sets of policy. The foreign and domestic were closely linked. For, to increase US security, to decrease its susceptibility (in Keohane and Nye terms) to energy insecurity, it was necessary not just to reduce demand in the US market, but also demand in the world market. Hence the IEA. But when US demand was not cut as much as Kissinger and others had hoped, the effect of others' cuts was modified. The effectiveness of the consumers' alliance organized by Kissinger through the IEA was undermined by US domestic policies, for these did everything except restrain current demand for oil. They were chiefly directed to getting American industry to substitute coal and gas for oil, so as to reduce dependence on oil imports. A further aim was to build and store underground a larger strategic stockpile of up to one billion barrels of oil. But, for domestic budgetary reasons, this goal was never reached. The result was that the United States has had to look more to its defence and foreign policies to achieve the security it wanted. Its concern with the security of Middle East supplies was evidenced by reflagging of Kuwaiti tankers in the Persian Gulf in 1987, which made it necessary to increase its military and naval commitments in that area. In this way, domestic failures were reflected in the global security structures in which (as we saw in Chapter 3) the Middle East is a high risk area.

Nor was the changed perception of the parameters of the security structure for states uniquely American. After the first OPEC price rise, other states' concern with this new *problematique* of security — how to secure supplies of energy for the country's industry and transport systems — led, as we saw, to greater state intervention in markets and to much greater diversity of state policies towards energy sources other than oil.

The IEA publishes an annual review of energy policies and programmes of its member states. It is evident from this that those states that produce oil can continue to use it, but that those who have to import it have had to make great efforts (within the limits of their resources) to diversify into other kinds of energy. It is striking that, in the countries most dependent on imported oil, or on imported oil and gas, like France, the switch to dependence on nuclear power has been largest — and public toleration of the risks involved has been greatest. The governments of such countries have also shown strong political resistance to attempts by the United States and the Soviet Union to maintain (through the IAEA) a system of surveillance to prevent the application of nuclear fuel to the manufacture of nuclear weapons; pro-nuclear in energy, they are inclined to be pro-nuclear in defence.

This system was initiated as long ago as 1953, when President Eisenhower made his Atoms for Peace offer to countries which, in return, would abjure the manufacture of nuclear weapons. The policy eventually resulted in the Non-Proliferation Treaty of 1964 signed by 111 states. This set up a surveillance system over nuclear power plants and entrusted inspection to the UN's International Atomic Energy Agency based in Vienna. But the NPT was not signed by China, France, Israel, South Africa, Taiwan, India or Pakistan. What these countries had in common was not a non-aligned or neutral foreign policy, nor any great pretension to military might. Primarily, it was that all of them, except China, depended on imported energy supplies. By the 1980s, when energy security had become even more imperative, the prognosis for the NPT 'regime' looked less sure, despite attempts to reinforce it through the 1976 London Nuclear Fuel Cycle Evaluation Programme. In a very real sense, the uncertainties of the oil business had broadened states' perceptions of what constituted insecurity; and the responses of states had in turn both increased some of the risks (of nuclear proliferation) in the security structure and multiplied the uncertainties in the oil market.

One of those uncertainties derived directly from the production structure. The opportunity for OPEC to exploit the rapidly increasing market demand for oil was directly due to the exceptionally fast economic growth of the 1960s and the consequent outrunning of oil demand over oil supply at 1972 prices. The oil market has always reacted quickly to the state of the world economy. Poor prices in the mid-1980s were in part due to diversification, as noted above, but also to the slackening of growth-rates in the major industrial countries, which are also the major consumers of energy. Future prospects will also depend on the level of economic growth, of industrial and agricultural production, and on its location and direction. One of the major imponderables in the future is the demand and supply of energy in the Soviet Union. Economic reforms, if successful, would require an accelerated production of energy for industry and much of this would have to come from increased outputs of coal, gas and nuclear power. The same is true of China. No analysis of Western markets, therefore, can ignore the part played by the two great planned economies, for even they are now much more closely integrated into a global energy structure than ever before, with the Soviet Union supplying gas to Europe and Japan getting coal from China. Not the least uncertainty is how the Soviet Union will react in its nuclear programme after the Chernobyl disaster of 1986.

Two points in particular about the impact of the financial structure on the energy system are worth recalling. One is that the volatility of oil prices and of national currencies — especially the US dollar — have acted and reacted upon each other, adding to the uncertainties both of the financial structure and of energy supply and price prospects. Because most trade in oil has been conducted in dollars, even when sold by Saudi Arabia and bought by Japan, it was possible in the early 1980s for oil prices to fall but for the cost of oil to increase for other consumers whose currencies were weakening in terms of dollars. Nothing could do more to stabilize oil prices than long-term stability in the purchasing power of the dollar — or, alternatively, a stronger move to price oil in a basket of currencies or according to some index of prices of manufactures and services bought by oil exporters. The second point is that the financial structure is such that it makes credit more easily available to the 'haves' than to the 'have-nots', to the large global oil companies than to some of their oil-poor customers. It is true that in order to avoid worse damage to the health of the world economy the United States and its fellow members of the affluent alliance of industrial and oil-exporting states (especially Saudi Arabia) have provided special credits through the IMF Witteveen Facility to enable NOPEC countries to buy oil when the price went up in the 1970s. But such emergency aid was still miniscule compared to the financial resources of the major oil companies. Just as, in recent years, the investment strategies of the oil companies steered clear of political risk areas like the Middle East and went for high-cost but lower-risk areas like Alaska or the North Sea, so, in the future, much will depend on their investment and development decisions. These decisions in turn, inevitably, are affected by a comparison of the anticipated profits to be made from long-term investment in production with those from short-term financial transactions by management. For, by taking full advantage of the possibilities of arbitrage in the currency markets or of lending to capital-hungry governments, the oil companies might decide that their money would be more profitably employed in the financial structure than in the production structure.

If finance has been one of the sources of corporate power in the global energy structure, so has corporations' command of knowledge — knowledge of geological formations and the chances of finding oil from new wells, knowledge of every other aspect of a business with which for so long states did not involve themselves. For instance, when the technology of offshore drilling was first adapted to North Sea conditions, only the oil companies had information about the costs of drilling from offshore rigs and the prospects of finding oil. The British government, wishing to impose a tax on the companies so as to share in the benefits, was at first disadvantaged in knowing how much or how little it could ask for. Other governments, especially those of developing countries, have found that, in bargaining with foreign oil companies, they have had to make concessions in recognition of the companies' command of technology, especially in exploration and product development.

Generally speaking, it is the companies' superior knowledge that has enabled them to gracefully surrender the riskier parts of the business to others, while maintaining control over the more profitable processes in between. By nationalizing the oil fields, the OPEC states took upon themselves the risk of a downturn in the market for crude oil, of increased competition from non-OPEC producers, of all the difficult bargaining involved in a collective cutback in surplus capacity if prices were to be stopped from falling.

In a wider sense, too, the energy structure has responded to changes in the knowledge structure. In the 1960s, people believed and acted as though the supply of oil was inexhaustible and would continue to flow uninterruptedly for ever. The effect of the first 'oil shock' in the early 1970s was reinforced by the publicity given at the time to the Club of Rome report called *Limits to Growth* (Meadows *et al.*, 1972). This predicted that the combined effects of population growth and economic growth through spreading industrialization would exhaust the earth's stock of non-renewable resources and would do so at an accelerating pace so that the oil price rise was not a temporary phenomenon that market forces could soon correct but rather the first of many milestones in a secular trend towards scarcer and therefore dearer oil. It was this belief that led both to the over-optimism among OPEC member states about their ability in the long term to control the market and to the readier acceptance among the consuming countries of the need both for conservation and for diversification in dependence on oil and especially OPEC oil. Without such changes in dominant beliefs, OPEC as an international organization capable of effective market management might have lasted longer and so might the IAEA as an international organization capable of effectively policing the use of nuclear fuel as an energy resource.

Table 9.4 Percentage of population with electricity supply: some LDC examples

Taiwan	99
Mexico	81
China	60
Brazil	56
Philippines	52
Senegal	36
Indonesia	16
India	14
Kenya	6
Bangladesh	4

Source: World Bank, *World Development Report*, 1985

Thus we can see that, although energy is the *sine qua non* for the exercise of power in the international political economy, and neither security nor wealth can be achieved without a secure supply of energy, yet change in the world's energy system has taken place within, and under the influence of, the four primary structures described earlier. These were in place in broad outline before the change-over from coal to oil, hydro-electric and nuclear sources of energy, and from steam to diesel and electricity. Although it is true that there is some circularity at work here, and that there is a feedback process from the energy system to each of the four structures, it is nevertheless true that before energy became quite so crucial a factor of production as it is today, there already existed an international political system in which the state was entrusted with the provision of security. There was already in being a capitalist system of production in which factors of production were combined to produce goods for sale on an international market as well as on national ones. And there was also a ready-made financial system of banks and capital markets that made credit available for production and trade. Finally, there was the sustaining knowledge structure in which the pursuit of profit, of wealth, of greater material comfort — to all of which more and cheaper energy could greatly contribute — were all widely accepted as desirable and legitimate.

Chapter 10

Welfare

Welfare consists not just of the hand-outs that governments give to the unemployed, the old and the destitute. There is more to it than that; just as there is more to welfare in the context of the global political economy than the foreign 'aid' (as it is rather euphemistically called) made available by rich countries to poorer ones. Many textbooks on international political economy devote a good deal of attention to the subject of foreign aid, but in doing so they imply that they are dealing with the welfare issue in the world economy. If fact, all they are doing is to spotlight one small aspect of the whole welfare picture. Foreign aid — even when it is not just a fancy name for loans at more or less commercial rates — is not the only form of resource transfer. And resource transfers are not the only form in which welfare is provided, either within states or in the wider world system. Welfare, indeed, is such a broad all-embracing term that it has to include both the benefits and opportunities available through the market and the benefits and opportunities made available through the political intervention of states or other authorities. It is impossible in political economy to separate the 'economic' kind of welfare from the 'political' kind.

What I shall try to do here, therefore, is firstly to clarify what exactly a welfare system is; and, secondly, to answer at least some of the questions that ask what kind of welfare system operates in the world — how is welfare allocated by the combined action of the market and authorities? Which authorities intervene most? And to whose benefit? What kind of welfare is provided, to whom, and by what means.

The answers will have some bearing on a long-running debate among people interested in world affairs and international law and politics. It might be described as the idealist–realist debate (or, in functionalist language, the *gemeinschaft–gesellschaft* debate). The idealists have argued passionately — and continue to do so — that although progress may be slow, we are nevertheless witnessing the gradual development of a sense of world community and the slow emergence of a global welfare system. One international lawyer has even asserted that 'The world community is bound to become a welfare community just as the nation-state became a welfare state'.[1] The idealists claim to see the seeds of such a developing welfare system in the UN's Development Decade in the 1960s and in the acclaim given in the 1970s by the World Bank to the idea of financial support for basic human needs. As early as the 1950s, the UN's second Secretary-General, Burma's U Thant, declared that 'the adoption of a target . . . shows that the concept of shared resources is beginning to enter the philosophy of states in their relations to other states'.[2] Awareness of common problems, aided by the visual impact of television, it is argued, is slowly changing people's perceptions; from belonging first and foremost to the nation, to belonging first and foremost to the human race, regardless of colour, culture or political persuasion.

Realists disagree. The only real society, they resolutely insist, is the society of states, linked by the possibility of conflict and the opportunities for commerce, but essentially locked into a competitive game. In this game, all governments belong to a kind of cartel of authority, they all have in common the jealously guarded privileges of rulership. This 'governors club' has a common interest shared even by the strongest states to preserve the pretence, however flimsy, of state sovereignty. Intrusion on it by international organization must be resisted; and the responsibility of the state for the provision of welfare will not easily be shared with any international agency.

Like trade, transport and energy, the structure providing welfare will largely reflect the nature of the primary structures of security, production, finance and knowledge. Each of these is a source, as we have seen, of structural power in the international political economy. That power, and the uses to which it is put, are likely to determine to a large extent the allocation of welfare among states, among classes and other social groups. To that extent this too is a dependent, or secondary, structure. Once again, we shall be looking at 'who gets what' in a broader way than is possible through the state–state perspective that still dominates so much of the literature of international political economy.

What is a welfare system?

One of the key attributes of any authority is that it has the power to allocate welfare — that is, to give benefits in the form of special rights or privileges, as well as benefits of a more material kind. Fathers and mothers allocate welfare in a family. Teachers allocate welfare in schools. Governments allocate welfare in national societies. In every case, the allocation is an essentially political act.

Authority is exercised to allocate welfare in quite a different way from how it would be allocated if left entirely to the forces of the market. The market will reconcile demand and supply through the price mechanism. It will allocate scarce resources in such a way as to satisfy some wants while denying others. Authority may go along with this allocation, or it may use its political power to countermand, as it were, the dictates of the market. It may decide that, if a certain group cannot afford to buy food, say, or the services of a lawyer, none the less that group shall be allocated free or cheap food and legal advice. A perennial question in political economy at any level, therefore, is how much welfare is derived from the working of the market and how much is allocated by the political intervention of authority? That authority may be the state. Or it could be an international organization. Or it could be a religious hierarchy, a charitable foundation or trust or even (oddly enough) a business enterprise, when it is not acting in direct accord with the market and the maximization of profit. The authority it exercises may be derived partly from its coercive power, from its great wealth, from the consent of others in the society or, of course, from a combination of all three.

In looking at any welfare system, it is important not to start out with the preconceived idea that it must always be what the policy-makers would call 'progressive' — that is, taking from the rich and giving to the poor. The allocation of welfare is not necessarily synonymous with what most people would call 'doing good'. It can be 'regressive' — taking from the poor and giving to the rich. There are authoritarian states today in which the loot filched by the rulers from the people and stashed away in foreign bank accounts and real estate far outweighs any crumbs reluctantly dispensed to the poor. The Shah of Iran was such a ruler; so was Bokassa and so were Ferdinand and Imelda Marcos. It is a debatable question whether religious hierarchies allocate welfare regressively or progressively. The Catholic Church will not disclose the extent of its finances, let alone the value of treasures accumulated through the centuries, yet it continues to lay claim to the pennies of the poor even in the poorest of Catholic communities. Business corporations, too, usually allocate more welfare, in the shape of stock options, to their directors than they spend on sports facilities for their lower-paid workers. Even in the aid agencies, supposedly devoted to using the resources of rich countries to give a helping hand in the economic development of poor countries, there are plenty of instances where more money has been spent on the salaries and comforts of the administrators than ever percolated through their hands into those of the people they were claiming to help.

The second point is that welfare systems, even when uncorrupt and progressive, are seldom entirely motivated by altruism. There is usually some kind of implicit bargain, a political/economic exchange that serves as much to reinforce authority as it does to alleviate wants. Governments, for instance, use the allocation of welfare (to farmers, perhaps, or to pensioners) to win the support of a useful constituency — people who, in return for the welfare benefits received, will support and sustain those in authority. Recall that in the desert-island tale at the beginning of this book, the market system gained the support of the mothers when old Tom was put in charge of the children. By organizing a child-care service, the community gave the mothers more time to gather food and to fish, thus adding both to collective productivity, to their welfare and to Tom's. Similarly, in the old Tammany Hall days in New York City, the political bosses arranged to distribute winter coal and food to needy families, the better to secure their votes at election time. Control of City Hall and the police made it possible to operate a welfare system within a system, an allocation of welfare that was based not just on need but on need plus a political exchange.

Welfare systems are apt to be most altruistic when they are allocating welfare to those whom no one can bargain with — to past or future generations rather than to those presently alive. Welfare economics may not have much to say about either the dead or posterity as recipients of welfare but in fact many societies, even some advanced industrialized ones, devote substantial resources to the dead. Prayers for their souls, tombs and flowers, monuments and memorials can allocate real resources from the living to the dead. And, in a real sense, environmental measures that look to long-term benefits that will pay off for posterity long after those paying for them will be dead, charitable bequests and even rules against abortion are all welfare allocations in favour of the unborn.

When we try to analyse how welfare is allocated in the world economy, and by whom, it will help to distinguish, and consider separately, the three ways in which welfare is allocated by states and other authorities. Firstly, it may be done by making protective rules; secondly, by the transfer of resources; and, thirdly, by the provision of public goods. Clearly, just looking at foreign aid programmes, whether bilateral or multilateral, channelled through international organizations like the World Bank and the World Health Organization, is not enough. We have to ask what other international and transnational resource transfers are being made. And we have to ask what protective rules are made, within states and internationally; and what public goods, providing what particular welfare benefits, and to whom, are being provided.

A few examples will illustrate each of the three ways or channels by which welfare is allocated by authority, and will immediately bring home two important points: that states are the main source of allocated welfare, so that welfare is predominantly, though not exclusively, a national matter; and, as a corollary, that there is very great disparity in the welfare that can be and that is allocated by different national governments.

Protective rules may be negative or positive. Negative rules will be made in some — but not all — countries to prevent the exploitation of child labour. Little boys in England are no longer made to climb dark, sooty and dangerous chimneys in order to clean them, as they were in Dickens's time. Yet, in some countries today child labour is still being exploited and no protective rules are there to prevent it. Other negative rules will prevent the insanitary dumping of rubbish, or the pollution of the air, of rivers or beaches — although, even within Europe, there is still great variation in the strictness with which such rules are enforced. Positive rules can also protect both particular groups and the collective interest. In some cold countries it is obligatory for householders to clear the snow off the pavements in front of their houses, not in others. In most advanced countries there is a rule that children must be sent to school; not in many African countries. In the United States and most European countries — though not in Italy — there is a rule that car seat-belts must be worn to minimize injury in case of accident. In some countries pedestrians are partially protected if they become the innocent victims of car crashes by rules that make third-party insurance compulsory for all car-owners. But in other countries there are no such rules; if you are unlucky enough to be knocked over and injured by an indigent car-owner you may get no compensation.

Resource transfers — which may be of money, of goods or of services — vary between national societies even more: just consider old-age pensions, child allowances for unmarried as well as married mothers, rent subsidies, unemployment payments. Goods transferred may be food, especially if transfer payments to farmers have produced an embarrassing surplus of cereals, butter or cheese; or they may be subsidized housing, free condoms – to cut down the spread of AIDS — free or subsidized medicine, or school-books. But, in poor countries, many fewer of these goods will be transferred by the state. People will depend more on their families for welfare support, on private charity and on religious organizations. All these will provide more than governments can in the way of both goods and services — professional services of lawyers, doctors, teachers, nurses — and emergency services. Such services, when generously provided, tend to qualify as public goods; that is to say that, if supplied they cannot be denied to anyone in the community, nor will use by some leave less for others. State schools and the services of a body of teachers would be one example; police forces to preserve public order and the fire services to prevent the spread of fire are two others. Most of a society's economic infrastructure — roads, for instance — will be public goods. But in poor countries it is obvious that the economic choices between provision of police and hospitals, between schools and roads, between airports and public parks or nature reserves, will be much more acute; for public goods, though equally available to all, may not be equally used by or useful to all. Economic choices between different public goods, therefore, are also necessarily political choices, favouring some needs over others. And the resources available to states as welfare-allocating authorities will be less or more according to the performance of the country in world markets. We can hypothesize that the authorities in control of the wealthiest economies will be in a stronger position, therefore, than those in charge of poor economies to decide in a global context how much welfare is allocated transnationally as well as intranationally, and in all three forms: as protective rules; in transferred resources; and in a particular selection of public goods.

Rules for global welfare

These rules are few and they are not, so far, very effective. As noted above, opinions differ as to whether they ever will be, so long as nation-states dominate the security structure and are more concerned with their own survival than with abstract principles of justice and human welfare.[3]

The most comprehensive and ambitious statement of welfare principles for world society is to be found in the Universal Declaration of Human Rights. This was in origin the brainchild of an international lawyer, Professor Lauterpacht, himself a wartime refugee from Nazi oppression in Cambridge. He formulated a first draft with the intention that after the war governments would find it harder to violate certain fundamental human rights if these had gained general ratification and support. In 1948 the United Nations General Assembly passed the Universal Declaration without a dissenting vote, including in it a long list of unexceptionable liberal principles in defence of individual rights and freedoms. The declared intention of the proposers was that the formulation of these universal protective rules would proceed progressively, to an international agreement accepted by states as legally binding, and, finally, to an agreement backed by powers of enforcement. In the event, it never got beyond the first stage. Articles 4, 5 and 9 of the Universal Declaration, for instance, proclaim in part that, 'no one shall be subjected to torture or to cruel, inhuman or degrading treatment . . . shall be held in slavery . . . shall be subjected to arbitrary arrest or detention'. To take only the last 'rule' concerning arbitrary arrest, it is almost an understatement to say that it is more honoured in the breach than the observance. All states with military governments or one-party systems, such as the Soviet Union and its socialist allies, automatically claim the countermanding right to arrest people arbitrarily on some vague charge such as 'hostility to socialist principles', 'subversion', or even 'parasitism'. Other states, by apparently constitutional means, assume 'special powers' to arrest their opponents — as in Liberia, Nigeria, Egypt and Morocco. Still others, which actually have national statutes supporting these global principles, then 'temporarily' suspend them with 'emergency laws'. Some examples are Singapore's Internal Security Act, Thailand's Anti-Communist Activities Act, India's National Security Act, Zimbabwe's Temporary Emergency Powers Act — and this is only a selection from many. Disappearances in Argentina, torture in Chile, degrading treatment in Soviet psychiatric 'hospitals' — the practice of many states which are UN members makes nonsense of the Universal Declaration; as it does too of the 1949 Convention on Genocide and the Helsinki Agreement on Human Rights negotiated as part of a broader agreement on European security and explicitly guaranteeing freedom of exit and freedom of conscience to the citizens of the Soviet Union. Although the UN has a Commission on Human Rights that solemnly sits in Geneva every year to hear reports, it is bound by Article 2 (7) of the UN Charter, which protects member states from any intervention in their domestic affairs. So, the Commission makes recommendations in the certain knowledge that few, if any, governments will take notice of them. And although the 1949 Genocide Convention made no mention in its text of the right of states to make reservations about its rules, an advisory opinion by the International Court of Justice in 1951 ruled that reservations could be made — thus opening the door to brutal massacres of Tsutsis, Nagas, Hereros and many other minority racial groups.

Several observers have come to the conclusion that the only authorities with even a slight capacity to move repressive governments are the non-governmental organizations like Amnesty International, which use publicity and direct personal intervention with politicians, judges and officials to try to improve the fate of political prisoners and prisoners of conscience (Vincent, 1986: 34; Vasak, 1982). Only in Europe, in the European Commission on Human Rights set up by the Council of Europe in 1950, is there the appearance of an international body with powers to reverse state decisions in matters of human rights. But, although states in the 1950 Convention have undertaken to execute the decisions of an impartial European Court of judges, the progressive achievement is really one that had already taken place within states, prior to the agreement. Conforming to the Convention has only been possible because these were states already confident enough of their own survival not to fear substantial opposition.

The only two groups that might be said to have gained some minimal protection from internationally agreed rules for their greater welfare are prisoners of war and diplomats. But in both cases it has not been the existence of formal agreements between governments that has ensured that protective welfare rules have been — at least at times — observed. It has been the reciprocal vulnerability of the state's own soldiers and diplomats to ill-treatment by other states that has restrained it. Even so, as both soldiers taken prisoner and diplomats taken hostage have found to their cost, there still remain governments and circumstances in which the principle of reciprocal vulnerability does not work.

Resource transfers

Concessional foreign aid — that is, free grants of money or goods (or money or goods transferred at less than market prices) — is a very small and relatively insignificant part of all the resources transferred in the world economy. As described above, most of the welfare transfers, like the welfare rules, made in the world are made within the boundaries of the state; and even within the richest states the progressive transfer of welfare resources often forms only a small part of total transfers. In command economies, like that of the Soviet Union, more welfare per head is allocated by those with status and power to their own class, the *nomenklatura* — people whose names are on lists which give privileged access to foreign-currency shops, to the best dachas and holiday resorts, to special education for their children. In capitalist and market economies, too, more welfare accrues to the already rich by purchase in the market — for second homes, for the most expensive clothes and consumer goods, for education, medical and legal services and for travel and entertainment. In neither system does the proportion of income taken in tax and reallocated for welfare transfers have much significance since both systems allocate income unevenly in the first place — under one system according to status and standing in a hierarchy of power, and under the other according to the rewards offered by a labour market (and a capital market, to some extent), which is itself highly discriminatory.

Given these rather important provisos, how much transnational transfer of welfare resources actually takes place? The short answer is that nobody knows because the statistics are incomplete and unreliable. The OECD's annual report compiled by its Development Centre for the Development Assistance Committee (DAC) purports to give the latest statistics of financial flows from developed to developing countries. It is widely used and quoted, but the figures do not include the return payments of profits and dividends, though they do include outflows of foreign direct investment (FDI). At the same time, those figures of FDI may be an understatement in as much as they only count investment capital actually transferred across the exchanges — as when a company raises funds at home, and transfers them to an LDC, where it builds and equips some kind of industrial plant. If — as frequently happens nowadays — the company's major investment is in research and development and this takes place in the company's home state, while the technology is actually applied in a production plant in a developing country, that 'investment' — which may easily amount to billions of US dollars — may not show up at all in the FDI figures. In fact, of the many new forms of investment (NFI), from turnkey contracts to production buybacks, only a small proportion are reflected in the conventionally accepted figures for foreign investment (Streeten, 1987).

But, as we said in the chapter on the financial structure, what is clear is that most foreign investment, whatever its form, goes to the most developed and therefore *least* needy of the developing countries. There is less risk there and more opportunity for economic growth and therefore profit, so that finance flows to them far more readily than to the least developed countries. Even if we only take the figures for transnational bank loans to developing countries (which are more reliable even though they too include some doubtful elements and some grey areas where guesses have to substitute for certainties), it is at once plain that these transfers for private profit and gain have in most recent years been much more important than the official loans transferred by governments and counted as 'foreign aid'. In 1983, for instance, the total amount of US foreign aid was recorded as $8 billion. This was the largest amount transferred by any one government — and incidentally more than twice the amount transferred by the Soviet Union and all its COMECON allies. But it was also less than a quarter of the total recorded amount of international bank loans.

In that particular year, 1983, however, the drastic reduction in bank lending to developing countries resulted in the anomalous situation that the countries of Latin America, which had been able to borrow heavily from the banks in earlier years, were now making reverse transfers, in the shape of interest and repayments on old loans, that were actually more than the new money coming from the banks. An UNCTAD estimate put this net reverse flow in 1983–5 from Latin America to the international banks at over $100 billion. Transfers via the market, in short, though they may at times be much larger (especially for the better-off) — and are usually freer in the sense of not being tied — than transfers allocated by governments under their aid programmes, are also a good deal more unreliable.

Resource transfers from governments are no more altruistic than transfers from corporations or from foreign banks. On this one point, the writers on foreign aid for economic development are pretty much agreed even though they couch their common conclusion in terms that range from the outright vituperative and condemnatory to the sorrowfully regretful (Hayter, 1971). In giving aid, governments have mostly had in mind either political bargains, serving their strategic and foreign policy interests, or economic bargains, serving their export industries and employment objectives. You might not guess as much from reading the rhetoric about foreign aid, or even some of the OECD/DAC reports. For, although international official loans, i.e. loans from governments to governments, were not unknown in the nineteenth century, and although a few were arranged under the sponsorship of the League of Nations in the inter-war period as rescue operations for central banks in Central Europe, the idea of aid as a permanent feature of international relations in fact only dates from

World War II, and from the post-war objectives proclaimed by the alliance that called itself, from 1942 on, the United Nations.

The Preamble to the UN Charter speaks of the common determination 'to promote social progress and better standards of life in larger freedom'. It refers to the 'economic and social advancement of all peoples'. In Articles 55 and 56, the Charter even asserts that 'conditions of stability and wellbeing . . . are necessary for peaceful and friendly relations among nations'. The signatory states bind themselves to act individually and collectively to promote, together with human rights, 'higher standards of living, full employment and conditions of economic and social progress and development' — not to mention 'solutions of international economic, social health and related problems and international culture and educational co-operation'.

It is now not much short of fifty years since these words were written into the UN Charter. In all that time, the governments of the 'aid-giving' countries have persisted in the rhetoric of a global welfare system, accepting targets for successive UN Development Decades and persistently regretting that unfortunately they were still not able to reach the original 'target' of 1 per cent of GNP devoted to aid — or even the later and lower targets. (The US percentage in 1983 was less than a quarter of 1 per cent and Japan's was just a third of 1 per cent. The CMEA collective figure was 0.17 per cent of GNP.) Not once have any of them denied their commitment to the original concept of a world welfare system that transcended the boundaries of the state.

Practice, however, has told a different story. Every aid 'donor' — 'creditor' would be more accurate a description since aid is predominantly lent, not given — has preferred to make the loans available bilaterally, not multilaterally. That is, they have given loans to developing countries directly, not through multilateral international institutions like the World Bank, the UN Development Programme or the International Development Association. By this means they have been able to decide for themselves which countries they will assist and which they will not. And they can negotiate with them as to the purposes for which the money will be spent and, very often, where it will be spent (i.e. it will be 'tied' to the donor's exports). Just to illustrate this, the 1983 figures gave a total of $26 billion of bilateral aid, and only $7 billion of aid channelled through international organizations. Even the OPEC countries, which for a time in the early 1980s looked like the most generous of donors, allocating almost 3 per cent of GNP to foreign aid, still preferred to give the lion's share to poorer Muslim friends and Arab and African neighbours. Although Saudi Arabia was able to push the Western countries into setting up an International Fund for Agricultural Development, and although they did give the IMF $2 billion for the Witteveen Facility for NOPEC countries — Witteveen asked in vain for $5 billion — they too gave about three times as much in bilateral aid as they did in multilateral aid.

Their motives, just like those of the United States or the Soviet Union, were predominantly strategic. Like Tammany Hall bosses, aid donors too have hoped to buy political support with their money. In the 1950s and 1960s, the distribution pattern of US aid was primarily determined by its strategic defence objectives. The containment of the Soviet Union in Europe produced money for the Marshall Plan. Later, after the Korean War, US aid went to the Asian peripheral states to the south and east of the Soviet Union and China — to Pakistan and India, to South Korea and Taiwan.

As McKinlay and Mughan (1984: 34) observed, it was clear by 1950 that containment was to be the principal US response to what it perceived to be a global ideological and military threat posed by communism in general and the Soviet Union in particular. What is more, official transfers were to be the principal, although not exclusive, means by which the containment strategy was to be implemented.

The Soviet Union, with less to offer, has been even more discriminatory, giving aid to only about half a dozen countries on whose political support and military cooperation it hopes to depend. European donors have been more captive of their past political associations. Each of the former colonial powers has given priority in the distribution of aid to its former colonies — Britain to the new Commonwealth countries, France to francophone Africa, the Netherlands to Indonesia. According to Mahbub ul Haq, about 25 per cent of total resource transfers in the mid-1970s were still governed by special relationships with a few former colonies and dependants rather than by the relative poverty or growth needs of the developing countries (Mahbub ul Haq in Sauvant and Hasenpflug, 1977: 249).

More recently, the strategic objectives of the rich countries have been commercial as well as military and political. That is to say, aid has been used to promote the donor's exports and with less hope of buying either military allies or votes at the UN. As seen from Table 10.1, the importance of export credit in the financial flows of developing countries has grown substantially of late. Most of this export credit — essentially a bridging loan to give the exporter immediate and certain payment for goods dispatched abroad but not yet received or paid for — has an element of subsidy. The risk of non-payment is insured at less than commercial rates, thus encouraging exporters to sell to poor and politically unstable countries. *Cui bono*? The importing country gets a better choice of foreign goods at a cheaper price than if the cargo had been insured commercially. But the exporters also benefit by extending their risk-covered market at the taxpayers' expense. An alternative method of export-promotion is, of course, to give 'tied' aid — that is, aid that may only be used to buy the donor country's goods or services. This method is favoured over subsidized export credit by the United

Table 10.1 Official development aid (ODA): groups of donors, 1975 and 1983

		Volume of ODA ($ billion*)	Shares of total	% GNP
1975–6	OECD	20.5	63.3	0.35
	OPEC	9.0	27.8	2.61
	CMEA	2.2	6.7	0.14
1983–4	OECD	28.4	76.8	0.36
	OPEC	5.0	13.6	0.95
	CMEA	3.1	8.5	0.21

* at 1983 prices and exchange rates
Source: OECD

States, and is particularly effective where military aid is concerned. Indeed, since the early 1970s, US arms sales to Third World countries, often on promotional price or credit terms, have exceeded both US economic aid and direct military assistance (ibid., p.41, Fig. 2.1).

This suggests that aid programmes are not simple welfare transfers of resources, military or civilian, from rich countries to poor ones, but rather transfers which benefit particular constituencies in the donor country as well as in the receiving country.[4] Those constituencies, moreover, mostly do not consist of poor people. Official aid is given by governments to governments. Military aid, in the form of weapons, missiles and aircraft, benefits the arms industries of the donor country and the armed forces of the receiving country. Food aid to developing countries also benefits farmers in the donor countries as much as it does consumers in the developing countries — and in the long run even that is not certain since dependence on cheap imported food tends to depress returns to local farmers, thus discouraging agricultural investment and keeping productivity low and costs high.

Welfare for the needy

A key question with any welfare system is how well it provides for those in real need — the most destitute and those suffering most hardship. Here again, the global system is long on rhetoric and conspicuously short on action, including real resource transfers. Let us look briefly at the treatment of children and of refugees.

In 1959, the United Nations Assembly unanimously adopted a Declaration on the Rights of the Child — health care, free education, housing, protection from cruelty and neglect, etc. Yet, in 1986, forty

years after the UN had set up a special agency — the United Nations
International Children's Emergency Fund (UNICEF) — an estimated 5
million children died from lack of minimal protection against child
diseases like measles. Millions more lacked schooling or proper housing. And UNICEF was one of the least well-funded of all the UN special
agencies, and depended for a large part of its budget on voluntary
contributions or the sale of pretty Christmas cards. (At one time in the
1960s it was also the agency with one of the highest percentages of its
budget spent on administration costs.) Despite the rhetoric of the
Declaration, the relief provided by UNICEF and by governments was
rather less than the relief provided through religious organizations and
voluntary agencies like the Save the Children Fund.

But if the welfare of children has been sadly neglected, the treatment
of victims of war and other refugees — or as they were euphemistically
described at the end of World War II, 'displaced persons' — has been
much worse because efforts to get international cooperation have been
frustrated not only by indifference but by violent political conflicts.

After World War I, there had been a near-chaotic situation in central
Europe, with serious outbreaks of typhus, a lethal influenza epidemic,
and severe food shortages. These had been dealt with by a private
consortium of charitable organizations under the leadership of the
Hoover Committee. Fears of what might happen if the same chaos
reigned after World War II led the allied United Nations to draft an
agreement in 1943 for a multilateral organization to be set up for the
relief of post-war hardship. Having demanded the unconditional
surrender of the Axis powers in 1942, there was no doubt where responsibility for the relief of post-war hardship and misery would lie. The
principle was accepted that relief would be given by the Allies without
political discrimination and only at the request of receiving governments. A kind of tax principle was accepted which arranged that the
contributions to the United Nations Relief and Rehabilitation
Administration (UNRRA) would be based on 1 per cent of each state's
GNP in 1943, and that these resources would be subscribed one-tenth
in convertible currency and nine-tenths in kind.

In the early post-war months UNRRA worked remarkably effectively
and the danger of disease and disorder taking over in Central Europe
gradually receded. But UNRRA was killed by a decision of the US
Congress, which absolutely refused to pick up the bill for a politically
neutral welfare organization, i.e. one that helped people with
communist governments as well as plural democracies. The United
States' share of votes in UNRRA was 6 per cent; but its contribution to
UNRRA's resources was 72 per cent. And although UNRRA's officers
protested that Yugoslavia had a relatively good record of fair and honest
distribution of food while Nationalist China, Greece and Italy all had
rather bad ones, the onset of the cold war committed the United States

Disbursement
as % of GNP

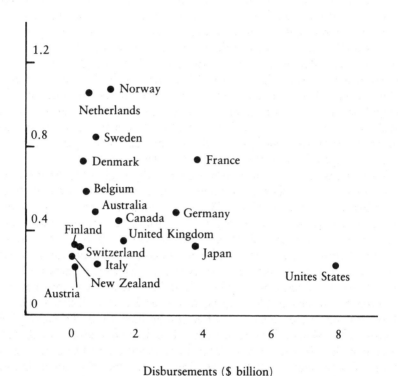

Disbursements ($ billion)

From: *World Development Report 1985*, p. 101 OECD figures

Figure 10.1 ODA disbursements 1983

to keeping up its assistance to the last three but persuaded the Congress that it should cut it off to the Yugoslavs. And although Kindleberger (1987) suggests that Canada, Britain and the Soviet Union also shared some blame for the collapse of UNRRA, there seems little doubt that the main responsibility lay with the United States. As always, the development of a world welfare system could proceed only if the leading power and the biggest contributor saw the development as consistent with its own national interest.

The treatment of refugees by the world community illustrates many of the same points. Under the League of Nations, the Nansen Office (named for the Norwegian explorer who ran it) did much to temper the rigidities of nationality laws, by issuing identity papers to stateless persons — mainly those who had fled from Eastern Europe without

$ Billion

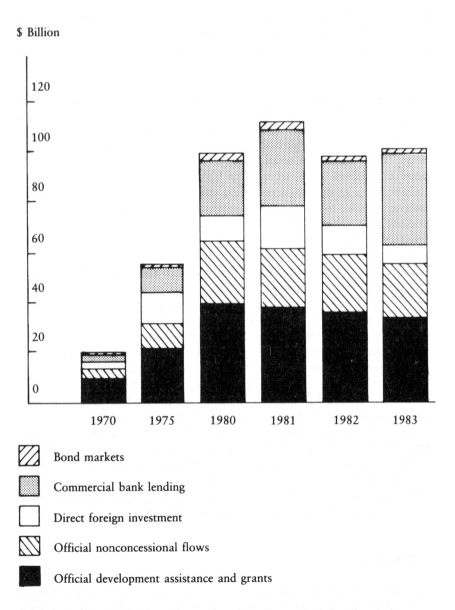

From: *World Development Report 1985*, p. 86

Figure 10.2 ODA and other sources of finance for developing countries

passports. After World War II, when UNRRA collapsed in 1948, the International Refugee Organization (IRO) was inaugurated as a UN special agency with a budget dependent on the contributions of member states. Those states that found themselves with large refugee camps were anxious to pass the refugees on to other countries as quickly as possible. They argued in the IRO that the refugees' plight should be dealt with by a levy on all member states to finance their resettlement and that each member country should be allotted a quota of refugees so as to share the indirect costs. But when it came to the point, the rich states would not be taxed, and the empty, sparsely populated states (even when, like Canada and Australia, they agreed to take large numbers of refugees) still wanted to be free to pick and choose, to take the healthy and productive and to leave behind the old and the sick. The Soviet Union even insisted on its right to repatriate refugees against their own wishes — and got the Americans and British to help them do so.

The result of all this disagreement was that the IRO collapsed into a rump organization consisting of a UN High Commissioner for Refugees with limited funds and even more limited powers. He acted as an unhappy and ineffectual mediator on behalf both of European refugees and, in the aftermath of the first Arab–Israeli war in 1948, of the Palestinians. There again, the conflict of interest between the states, like Jordan, which found themselves with the refugees, and others like Syria, which could have accepted them had they not strong political as well as economic reasons for keeping them where they were, made sure that nothing was done. The same unhappy story followed the war between India and Pakistan, the Korean War, the Vietnam War and many other international and civil conflicts. As with those wounded in battle, the refugees came to look not to political authority but to private voluntary charities for the relief of hardship. And, as mentioned earlier, forgotten political prisoners have similarly had more help from Amnesty International than from any inter-governmental body.

Public goods

The international political economy has no central public authority, so it is not to be expected that it will be provided with many genuinely public goods in the sense in which the term is usually applied to goods or facilities which a government or some other central political authority has decided shall be supplied freely for general use. The nearest thing to real public goods consists only of the incidental benefits enjoyed by others as a result of goods or facilities provided by individual state authorities primarily in their own national interest. Such, for instance, is the benefit of such security as may be enjoyed by others as a result of the defence policies of the superpowers and the fact that these forces appear to be in a state of more or less stable balance. Similarly, one might say that the international political economy has the use and benefit of an internationally acceptable and usable currency — the US dollar. But, as with the military balance, it is accidental, or coincidental, if the benefits publicly enjoyed from the use of this widely available facility are more or less important than the costs and risks to other users of their vulnerability to changes in US monetary management.

The other approximation to public goods in the international political economy — but it is not really a very close approximation — is those goods and services which are in part provided or subsidized by governments and made generally available for sale on the world market. Such for instance are the sea and air transport systems described and analysed in a previous chapter and the communications systems developed on the basis of earth-orbiting satellites. All three exist primarily to serve the world market economy, and the benefits go mainly to those in the production structure who depend and sell on world markets. The sea and air transport systems are indeed supported by certain infrastructural aids that are in fact public goods — for example, the air and sea traffic control systems, weather reports on the basis of satellite pictures processed by computers, beacons and lighthouses. The cost of making these available to allcomers is mostly borne by states while the benefits accrue to the major traders and carriers.

The world communications system is rather different. Some communications satellites are privately owned and operated — by banking syndicates, primarily. Others are owned by national governments — the Soviet Union, India or Indonesia, for example. And besides these, INTELSAT is a curious hybrid between a commercial corporation and an international organization — perhaps the nearest thing to an agency supplying the public good of communication facilities.

Besides these rather marginal and minor provisions of public goods useful to international commerce and communication must be set the loss of the one public good that was freely accessible to all for centuries, the high seas. Today there is very little of the surface of the world's major oceans that is not claimed as an exclusive economic zone by the government of some state. This was one matter on which the UN Conference on the Law of the Sea could effectively agree. Significantly, where it could not agree was that the resources of the sea-bed constituted a common heritage of mankind and therefore should be treated as a public good, exploited by an International Sea-bed Authority and the proceeds used as if they were international revenue.

Conclusions

From a global perspective the welfare system is far less well developed than the transport or trading systems — trade in energy included. These serve the integrated world market economy, while welfare primarily serves the citizens of the individual state. Both trade and transport are sustained by strong transnational interests and encouraged out of self-interest by the governments of the most developed economies. By contrast, the positive provision of welfare by states across these frontiers, to people in *other* states, is either strategic in motivation or symbolic in character.

One exception here might be internationally agreed environmental controls like the MARPOL conventions. Progress where collective co-operation is necessary, however, has proved painfully slow. The principle that 'the polluter pays' can be worked into national legal systems and enforced in national courts. It is not so easy to enforce between states. Take acid rain, for example. Britain is reluctant to act to save German and Scandinavian forests, as the United States is reluctant to do it for Canada. Conventions to arrest the destruction of the ozone layer of the atmosphere may be agreed more quickly in principle than executed in state practice.

Some transnational welfare is provided independently of state authority by religious organizations or non-denominational organizations inspired by charitable emotions and altruistic beliefs. This part of the global welfare system, though small, seems to be growing, suggesting a gradual change in that part of the knowledge structure that concerns people's perceptions and beliefs. But it is a change that so far has had little impact on state behaviour.

Indeed, as the security structure has changed so that the acquisition of foreign military and air bases has become less important and the development of new and advanced inter-continental defensive and offensive systems has become more important, so the use of foreign aid (including military aid) as a tool of economic statecraft has lost some of its appeal on grounds of political self-interest. The strategic motivation for most semi-concessional lending for most 'donor' states is far more to capture or preserve market shares than to acquire or preserve military bases. The only exception, perhaps, to this general trend is to be found in the continued superpower interest in naval bases, especially in the Pacific, but also in the Indian Ocean. For example, when the Soviet Union purchases repair and supply facilities from mini-states in the Pacific like Vanuatu, the United States is soon moved to respond with similar or comparable offers of aid, equally inspired by strategic considerations.

Over the past four decades, it is clear that there has been a broad trend away from aid as an effective policy instrument. This has been particularly marked in the older donor states like the United States — far the largest single aid donor — and in Britain and Canada. The effect of this loss of interest has been obscured in the overall statistics by the rising importance of 'new' donors like Japan, Italy, Germany and even Switzerland. It is also obscured by the inflation of the 1970s, when aid measured in (depreciating) dollars seemed to rise rapidly. But, in the 1980s, the total of official development assistance levelled off and even declined, though non-concessional lending continued to rise. In the same period, what has grown and multiplied without cease has been the volume of symbolic protestations of concern by the rich for the plight of the poor. Such symbolic responses come cheap, but in the long run may prove politically explosive.

Part IV

Pick Your Own, or Suit Yourself

Chapter 11

Questions and Answers

The aim of this book has been more to suggest questions than to provide set answers. The intention all along has been to direct attention to a broader range of considerations than are encompassed by the state–state perspectives of international relations, and to do so by posing a partially new set of questions regarding, especially, the basic structures of the international political economy. The intention was to leave it to the reader to supply his or her own answers, according to individual value preferences and subjective political choices. It has been an invitation to Pick-Your-Own strawberries, not to buy a basket of ready-picked and packaged fruit.

In practice, this has proved difficult; especially as we passed from the four primary structures to the secondary or dependent structures, the mere description of what had emerged in trade or transport, and how it had developed out of past policy decisions and market changes inevitably selected one set of answers instead of another. This was particularly so with the chapters on transport systems and on the supply of energy in the world economy. Both became essays in sectoral analysis, even though both oil and sea transport, for instance, are not just sectors of the economy but are also infrastructural, providing the necessary means and inputs to a whole range of other sectors. Both lie on the borderline between structures and sectors. A larger, more comprehensive book, or a second companion volume, could logically proceed across that border to outline the political economy of a whole series of interesting sectors. Several of these, like the political economy of cereal production, trade and consumption, are very important, politically and economically. Others — whales or timber, for instance — would highlight new aspects of the concept of authority in relation to the market. Tempting as this is, it would tend to dilute still further the idea of a book of questions rather than answers.

For those who may wish to find their own answers in a sectoral analysis, however, a brief recapitulation of the steps to take, expanding and explaining the procedures followed in brief in earlier chapters on oil and transport, may be helpful.

Take six eggs

A cookbook recipe starts by telling you what you will need to have ready to make the dish. A manual or handbook, whether for changing the oil in an engine or for assembling a kit of some kind, will start with a plan or map, showing the relevant components and where to start work. In political economy, for sectoral analysis, we could start with a matrix. On the horizontal axis of the matrix, we have the changes, if any, in the four primary structures. On the vertical axis, we have the four components of the authority–market relationship. See Figure 11.1. Logically, there should be only three categories on the vertical axis — states, markets and the balance between them. But since in some sectors there are important non-state authorities coexisting with state authorities and having an important impact on who gets what at the end of the day, it is easier to deal separately with them from the start. (In oil, it was the major oil companies; in the world market for art treasures, it could be the big international auctioneers, and the experts they employ to validate and value the pictures, furniture, memorabilia, etc., put up for sale.) Optionally, and if you really think that an international bureaucracy has an influence on market forces separate and distinct from the influence of the national governments that belong to it,

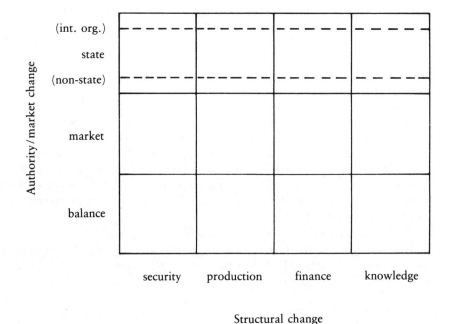

Figure 11.1 Structural change and the authority/market nexus

the international bureaucracy would make a fifth category and another row of boxes to fill. For instance, in the case of the market for discounted developing country debt, one could argue that the attitude of the IMF bureaucracy towards the country's economic policies was a separate factor from the attitude of the United States, and was a factor independent and distinct from change in the financial or credit structure which related more to the vulnerability of creditor banks in general than to uncertainties in the structure. Or, in the case of the mostly state-managed market for radio programmes, you could say that in the registering role of the WARC (World Administering Radio Conference) the actions of the bureaucracy were to some degree independent of the policies of states towards the competition for wavelengths. But only if there is real evidence that the agency has some technical capability, or some special authority legitimated not by the approval of governments but by the consent and respect of those affected should it be considered separately from state policies. It is only too easy, misled by the public relations efforts of international organizations, to confuse, for instance, the authority of NATO with that of the United States, or that of COMECON with that of the Soviet Union. 'Market conditions' may or may not be vulnerable to change in the primary structures. Obviously, it matters whether the market is in a stable or a volatile condition, whether the trend of prices is rising or falling, whether there are a few producers (aluminium, soda ash) and many buyers; or alternatively, many producers and few buyers (cocoa beans, wheat); few producers and few buyers (aircraft engines); or many producers and many buyers (cotton knickers, plastic bowls, cutlery). In each case, the 'geometry of the market' being different, this will make a difference to the impact of change in the primary structures. Higher interest rates will affect small buyers (or sellers) more than large ones, and this will affect what has to be said at Stage 2 of the analysis.

Stage 2 proceeds from the bottom line of the first matrix — the balance of power over outcomes between authority (or authorities if plural) and market and asks what distributional consequences follow from the market being more or less subject to political management (i.e. manipulation or intervention for essentially non-profit-oriented, not strictly economic, reasons). Evidently, there will be a subjective element in deciding what net effect of this balance will follow from contrary changes — changes in the opposite direction — emanating from more than one of the four primary structures. For instance, it is possible that, in the market for a particular kind of weapon or military equipment, change in the security structure — perhaps some increase in perceived insecurity — will lead to a tightening of authority control over the market for those particular weapons. But, at the same time, financial deregulation will make it easier to finance purchases of the same weapons.

Despite the occasional difficulty of this kind, in Stage 2 we try to decide what are the secondary effects of structural change as filtered through states' responses and market responses and the balance between them. In diagrammatic form, we could represent this balance as a see-saw, subject to different pressures emanating on the market end of the see-saw and on the major authorities in that market — which may be one state, an alliance of states or a cartel of market managers — like the Seven Sisters in the oil market of the 1950s. In Figure 11.2, the primary structures are represented as interlocking circles because, as seen earlier, it is impossible to deal with any one of them in isolation from the other.

In Stage 3, we try to work out the distributional consequences of changes in the see-saw. We have to ask what the net effect of a change in the angle of the see-saw is likely to be for social groups within and across state frontiers. Are the workers better or worse-off? Are consumers carrying new risks? Or are producers? Are creditors more secure, or are debtors under tougher pressure? And next — given that we are mostly looking at integrated world markets in which only a few states will have much influence on the market–authority see-saw — what are the consequences for other states? For other non-state institutions? For international organizations? What too are the repercussions of change in this market–authority balance on related markets? For example, a deregulation of air transport, a loss of authority by the IATA cartel over the market of air travel affected the market for tourism, and consequently the local market for construction companies building hotels, which might be local or transnational.

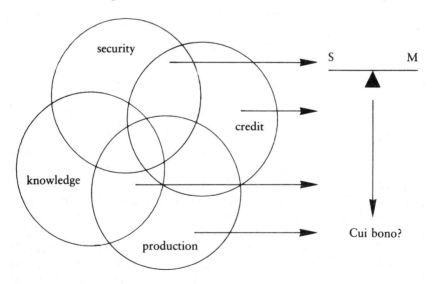

Figure 11.2 Interlocking Structures

Unresolved problems

However painstaking and unbiased the research in international political economy, we have to admit that there are always going to be more questions than answers. There are problems that students are likely to encounter that probably can never be fully resolved, open questions to which there are not necessarily answers. There are three in particular, of which it is as well to be forewarned.

One question is whether, even short of the chimera of a general theory of international political economy, there are any reliable rules of thumb that say which structure is dominant and thus which, in any given sector or situation, are likely to be the decisive structural changes. It seems to me that it is just not possible to be sure that changes in the security structure, for instance, will always have more effect on outcomes than changes in finance or in ideas or access to information in the knowledge structure, or even than change in the way in which production is organized. It is therefore all the more important to keep an open mind. By way of illustration, take the spread of information on the manufacture and uses of small computers. This spread — basically a change in the knowledge structure in which more people had access to knowledge that had previously been limited — results in change in the CoCom (i.e. Coordinating Committee) rules on trade in strategic goods from NATO countries to the Soviet bloc. Options for states in the security structure are consequently constrained, opportunities for enterprises enlarged. Or take the expansion of international bank lending and of official credit for arms sales to developing countries: regional security, as in the Persian Gulf, is weakened to an extent impossible if there had been no credit, and provided real oil prices were low. The dominance of any one factor, of any one of the primary structures, therefore, must remain an open question.

Then there are two unresolved questions about the nature of the state. Even realists who are confident that the state, however liberal its ideology and however determined its promotion of private economic enterprise, is still the final political authority in any political economy are no longer quite sure how precisely to define it, nor how to recognize who is susceptible to its authority.

Consider for a moment the United States. We may be able to agree that the US government is in many sectors of the world economy the most influential authority; and that the US government is the legitimate representative of the state. But can we define that state? Is it just the land, the capital investments and the people found within its acknowledged territorial frontiers? What about the plants owned by US corporations, and the property owned by US citizens, in other countries? Are these not assets that are statistically counted as the stock of US foreign investment, over which the US government, acting for the state, claims some rights? In World War II, American investments owned by British individuals and corporations were requisitioned by order of the British government and sold off to buy arms. In another war, the United States would go further and claim reversionary rights even over ships flying foreign flags if their owners were US citizens. But what then of Japanese corporate investments in the United States? Does the Honda plant in Columbus, Ohio, not 'belong' to Japan? Again, in the last war the US government took possession of Japanese property — even property of US citizens of Japanese origin — claiming it as its own. At the moment, the repatriated profits made in Columbus, Ohio, may make their contribution to the Japanese balance of payments, though any cars exported from there to Canada, say, may contribute to the US balance of payments.

If, as governments have discovered in trying to decide whom they should subsidize, the limits of the state are difficult to define in manufacturing industry, they are even more difficult in the service sectors. In banking, insurance, advertising, films or consultancy, the element of 'footlooseness' is all the greater; the same problems of conflicting jurisdiction arise in even greater complexity. What appears to be happening today is a series of tests of strength between states over different jurisdictional issues the outcome of which are all still unpredictable.

The same fluid situation is mirrored on a small scale with individual people. It is more and more difficult to say with any precision what is a British or a US citizen. Men and women often hold two or more passports, often without the issuing governments being aware of it. Some rights accrue not with citizenship but with residence or domicile; others are subject to arbitrary administrative decisions. To the extent that, as always, in the words of Thucydides, the strong will do what they can and the weak what they must, the common elements of state power and the common limits of state authority are likely as a result to shrink and the differences grow between strong and weak states. It follows that the possibility of general theoretical statements about the nature of the state are apt to become more and more difficult.

For it is also apparent that such uncertainty over the limits of state jurisdiction are far more evident with those states deeply involved in the world market economy; and that they do not exist to anything like the same extent for the Soviet Union or even for the People's Republic of China. This is partly a reflection of the fact that the less involved a state is with the world economy, the less susceptible it is, or its enterprises and subjects will be, to the structural power exercised transnationally over the world economy, in production, finance and ideas and information. And it is partly a simple reflection of relational power exercised by the United States over, say, the Philippines and over China. Although it is never possible entirely to untangle structural power from relational power, it is still very important, in my view, not to overlook or underrate structural factors in any power relation.

Conflicting conclusions

That omission seems to me to be the major shortcoming of the most popular school of thought in international political economy today — the hegemonic decline school. Judging by the literature, and by the trend of thinking in the American academic journals, which, unlike European or Japanese ones, are read worldwide, the majority view — certainly in US academic circles today — is that the disorders of the world economy are mainly the result of a loss of American hegemonic power. The school, though broadly agreed on causes, disagrees on remedies. It divides into two broad wings — a liberal wing and a realist wing. An example of the first would be Keohane's *After Hegemony* (1984); and of the second, Gilpin's *The Political Economy of International Relations* (1987). The liberals tend to pin their hopes on collective action as a second-best substitute for hegemonic leadership. Multilateral decision-making through enhanced international organization is their remedy for the ills of the international political economy. The realists like Gilpin tend to be more pessimistic, to doubt the potential of international organization or of economic co-ordination as advocated by American liberal economists like Bergsten or McKinnon. The best hope, however slim, lies in 'benign mercantilism' — a restrained pursuit of national interests that makes some effort to avoid damage to others, or to the system.

An alternative view, to which I hold and which I believe is held by a too-silent majority of non-American scholars — in the Soviet Union, Europe, Japan and the Third World — disagrees with both the American liberals and the American realists on the causes of world economic disorder, but is probably closer to the realists when it comes to remedies. The disagreement on causes is that the United States has not in fact lost power in the world market economy. As that economy has grown and spread, the source of its power has shifted from the land and the people into control over structures of the world system. But the structural power it has acquired in recent decades has been misused in the service of narrow national interests. While this misuse of power has sheltered the US taxpayer and consumer (and to a lesser extent, workers) in the short run, it runs a serious risk in the long run of weakening both the system and the structural hegemony of the United States. Such is the resilience of the system that the time when the United States will reap the consequences of its misuse of power is still some way off. It may still not be too late to reverse the process.

Consider the evidence for American hegemonic decline. It rests heavily on the decline of the US share of world output (from 40 per cent to 22 per cent) in the thirty years from the early 1950s to the early 1980s, and the decline in the same period of the US share of world exports of manufactures, from 30 to 13 per cent. Now quoting these 'facts' implicitly assumes that the US government's power as an authority in the world market economy is accurately reflected by the ratio of GNP to world GNP, and also by the size of the US share of world exports of manufactures. 'Made in USA' in short is an indicator of power. But this is rather like saying that 'Made at Willow Run' is an indicator of the status of the Ford Motor company in the world market for cars. The product of the home territory, no more than the product of the company's original plant, is not necessarily a good indicator of its present power or status. Nor is it sensible to count only output or exports of manufactured goods, and to ignore the US share of the world market for service industries like banking, insurance, data storage and retrieval, which are now much more profitable and much more powerful sources of influence over others. Of course, the trouble with service industries, as noted above, is that the 'US share' is much more difficult to estimate than the US share of industrial output. Service industries, as noted, are far more footloose. Their transactions are hard to count and their profits do not necessarily come 'home'. Overseas operations may easily be more important to the enterprise than the home market, but deciphering the company accounts to find out how much more important is difficult and sometimes impossible. For this reason it is very hard to say whether the increased competition that US manufacturing industry has encountered from Europe, Japan and the developing countries like Korea and Taiwan is more significant for US power than the coincidental opportunities that have opened up for other US corporations in the rapidly growing and highly profitable service sectors.

Focusing only on manufacturing industry in the late twentieth century may be just as myopic for purposes of political economy as it would have been to focus on the ratio of British agricultural output to total world output in the late nineteenth century, or on the loss of Britain's old export markets for wool to Australia! What is of course true is that, for the United States, giving up its former self-sufficiency in manufactures, like Britain giving up its former self-sufficiency in food, entails taking on new dependence on imports, and therefore new vulnerability — just as Britain became vulnerable to naval blockade in time of war. But, short of war and blockade, the competition among suppliers both to sell cereals to Britain and T-shirts to the United States is surely going to make the risks attendant on such vulnerability rather limited and unimportant.

If we can bring ourselves to escape from the intellectual obsession with territorial states, the power equation looks very different. What matters is the relation between the United States as a state with political authority and the corporations operating in and outside the United States. Some of these were originally, and still are, US-owned by foreign managers. Others are foreign corporations functioning in and selling to the US domestic market, and maybe also exporting from the United States. Washington may have lost some of its authority over the US-based transnationals, but their managers still carry US passports, can be sub-poenaed by US courts, and in war or national emergency would obey Washington first. Meanwhile, the US government has gained new authority over a great many foreign corporations operating inside the United States. All of them are acutely aware that the US market is the biggest prize in the competitive game. My guess, from talking to corporate executives — American and European — is that on balance US authority in the world economy has actually increased, not declined.

In many versions, too, even if the evidence for the alleged decline were relevant, it is grossly exaggerated. This in itself arouses suspicion that there is a vested intellectual interest in the notion of hegemonic decline. To be blunt, it is a very convenient excuse for past failures and present indifference to disorders in the system that bear far harder on other people than they do on residents of the United States.

Take, for example, the base line for the statistics. In the early 1950s, the American lead in manufacturing output and exports was exaggerated by the setbacks still suffered from the war in Europe and Japan. By the 1980s, it would have been remarkable if the same gap still remained. Secondly, there is the content of what is counted as total world output. There are good reasons for thinking that the statistics overstate the increase in the size of the whole cake, and understate that part that is counted as the US share. We know, for example, that as the money economy spreads, goods and services that were formerly made or provided within the home, are bought in from outside — and then, for the first time, show up in the monetarily-countable Gross National Product. (If you cook for yourself, it's a hobby; if you buy a meal from a restaurant or a take-away, it increases the recorded output of restaurants and take-aways.) Since Americans were the first to sell and buy such goods and services, the expansion in the counted totals of GNP was likely to show up as growing faster in Europe, Japan and other less developed countries. Similarly, as US companies led in going offshore in the 1950s and 1960s, their contribution to non-US GNP was greater than the contribution of European and Japanese companies to what was counted as the US GNP. They were also leading in the same 'buying-in' of services and components that could be seen in households, once again expanding what was counted as world GNP faster than the rate of increase in what was counted as US GNP.

In short, the figures themselves are only the roughest of guides. They probably exaggerate the degree to which other economies have really caught up with that of the United States. This is also true of another piece of supposed evidence for hegemonic decline — the slowing rate of productivity growth in the United States compared with, say, Japan. But, as with the rate of economic growth, the leader has such a head-start that it can afford a lower annual increase for many years before the followers catch up — a truth sharply recognized in developing countries even when they have quite striking annual growth-rates.

We can conclude, I think, that the gap between US power and that of any rival state when it comes to exercising influence over the basic structures is still so substantial that no initiative has yet been taken in international organizations that the United States has persistently resisted, while most of the (comparatively rare) initiatives that have been taken by the United States are in fact executed by international organizations.

And, besides the dubious character of the underlying evidence of decline, there is one more curious feature of the debate between the American realists and American liberals. The latter always claim to be the ones who are internationalist in their outlook. It is they who have mostly hoped for reform of one kind or another through international organizations, and have often founded their professional reputations on their familiarity with the same organizations. Yet it is they, and not the realists, who seem more nationalist in their defence of US foreign economic policies. Compared with the realists, they are far less ready to admit that there have been mistakes in the management of the US economy, and in unilateralism in the conduct of foreign commercial and financial relations, and that this may have substantially contributed to the disorders they deplore in the system. Gilpin, for instance, concludes his survey of banking and finance by referring to 'American mismanagement of its own internal affairs and of the international finance system'; concluding that this puts responsibility on the Japanese, although it is hard to see how this can be when the system still largely operates in dollars, responds most promptly to policy shifts by the Federal Reserve Board, and when the United States does not make way for Japan in either the BIS or the IMF. In his next, penultimate chapter (p. 345), Gilpin echoes the conclusions of Calleo (1984) when he says,

Critical problems of the world economy in the areas of trade, money and debt were left unresolved . . . Beginning with the Vietnam War and continuing into the Reagan Administration the United States has become more of a predatory hegemon, to use John Conybeare's term (1985), less willing to subordinate its own interests to that of its allies. Instead it tended to exploit its hegemonic status for its own narrowly defined purposes. [Gilpin, 1987: 345.]

Calleo's explanation lay in the attempt, from the Kennedy era onwards, to finance both an extended welfare state and a costly defence programme without increasing either the rate of saving or the incidence of taxation. The superior structural power of the United States made it possible first, under Nixon, to devalue the dollar, thus imposing the cost of persistent US deficits on all who held reserves of dollars; then under Ford and Carter to tax the system by means of inflation, followed by more devaluation. Finally, under Reagan, even more costly defence spending escalated the budget deficit to record heights. But the United States was able to finance it by pre-empting the savings surplus of the Japanese and reversing the flow of funds so that it was the Latin Americans, on balance, who financed the United States, rather than the other way round.

The negative effects of such predatory, or destructive, use of hegemonic power were multiplied by a marked rise in the unilateralism of US policy-making, causing the pious communiqués of orchestrated summit meetings to ring increasingly hollow. Talk of policy co-ordination and the need for teamwork and cooperation accorded ill with the failure of the United States to even pretend to consult its allies over the Strategic Defence Initiative, or over the strategy for arms control bargaining with the Soviet Union. Confidence in US leadership was equally undermined, not by a loss of power over others, but by lost control over its own tangled web of overblown bureaucracy. As the Irangate investigations showed, there was no unbroken chain of command, no clear locus of final responsibility. Policy was muddled by the divisions and uncertainties in the executive over US policies. For example, an initiative like the Baker Plan of 1985 to mobilize new funds for Third World debtors was universally welcomed but the US administration apparently lacked the necessary will, or power, or both, to follow through with the US banks.

To young people, the most depressing aspect of this continuing debate may be, not so much that the experts disagree on causes and on remedies, but that none are particularly sanguine that their favourite remedies will actually be applied with sufficient vigour to bring about a material change. The liberals have to confess that in the light of past experience the chances of radical reform in international organizations are not after all very good. The realists' expectations are low that either Japan will take over as hegemon or that the US policy-makers will start to weigh damage to allied interests as highly as offending important Congressional constituencies. This general pessimism is very different from the confident visions of the future that were widespread after World War II, or even as late as the 1960s.

I can offer only a few crumbs of comfort. One is that the general pessimism is perhaps a better basis for taking decisions than some of the illusions that were current until quite recently and that are, fortunately perhaps, less current today. One illusion was that either the Soviet Union or else China could lead the way through revolution to a better and juster socialist system. I may be wrong, but the acknowledgement by both great socialist states of the shortcomings of socialist management within their own countries and their new flexibility in dealings with the outside world both suggest that neither seriously expects to supplant the world market economy, only to live with it, hoping to profit from its benefits while continuing to insulate themselves from its instability.

Another illusion was that concerted lobbying and solidarity among the developing countries could persuade the affluent industrialized world to increase aid massively and to change the rules of trade radically in their favour. Echoes are still to be heard of some of that New International Economic Order rhetoric, but the actions of Third World governments tell a different story. Like the leaders in the socialist countries and in the affluent alliance, they are showing far more realism concerning the nature of the problem, and about the potential for change and the advisability of self-help.

Two sources of hope, however slender, remain. One is that American self-confidence and idealism once again reassert themselves, that a new generation, less jingoistic and less narrowly nationalist, begins to dream of a new era of American leadership and hegemonic management, in which the long-run interests of people outside the United States are taken into account for the greater wealth, justice and stability of everyone, *including the Americans*. American history is such a record of temperamental volatility, of U-turns in mood and policy, that this is still no longer impossible — more possible indeed in America than in any other country in the world.

The other source of hope is that, instead of resting supinely in the hope that the United States will cease its predatory behaviour, the Europeans and/or the Japanese, as the most economically important partners of the United States, would begin to be more constructive and responsible in their bargaining with Washington. Self-reliance in defence would be a first step. At present, the Europeans and the Japanese have themselves largely to blame that they have been such a weak and flaccid opposition to destructive hegemony.

Notes

Chapter 1

1. I have used the French word here because the English 'problematic' is also used confusingly as an adjective meaning 'doubtful' or 'open to question'. I would define *problèmatique* as the underlying question or puzzle that gives purpose to a field of study.
2. Some recent texts adopting this method of presenting alternative approaches are R. McKinlay and R. Little, *Global problems in World Order*, London, Pinter Publishers, 1986; R. Gilpin, *The Political Economy of International Relations*, Princeton UP, 1987; R. Barry Jones, *Perspectives on Political Economy*, London, Pinter Publishers, 1983, which, however, excludes the Marxist approach.
3. A further development of the argument was made by Miriam Camps in *The Management of Interdependence*, New York, Council on Foreign Relations, 1974, and in W. Diebold's, *The United States and the Industrial World*, New York, Praeger, 1972, also for the Council on Foreign Relations.
4. *Global Reach* was the title of a popular book on multinationals written in the mid-1970s: R. Barnet and R. Miller, *Global Reach*, London, Cape, 1974.

Chapter 2

1. An illuminating study which brings out this side of Smith's writings is David Reisman's *Adam Smith's Sociological Economics*, London, Croom Helm, 1976.
2. Similar assumptions were made by Knorr in a later book, *Power and Wealth* (1973), in which he tried to distinguish different kinds of power based on control over resources. But it should be noted that the literature of power theory is much more developed than would appear from looking at international economics and international politics. An interesting study introducing the reader to the main contributions to this literature was Jack Nagel, *The Descriptive Analysis of Power*, New Haven and London, Yale University Press, 1975. See also J. Hart, 'Three approaches to the measurement of power in international relations', *International Organization*, Spring 1976, p. 291.
3. Much of this work in sociology owed its inspiration to the work of Fernand Braudel, notably his great two-volume study of *The Mediterranean in the age of Philip II*. Early contributions were by Perry Anderson (1974a, 1974b) and Barrington Moore (1967); recently by Michael Mann (1987) and Jonathan Hall (1986). See bibliography for details.

Chapter 3

1. Such is the title of most recent textbooks on international political economy as: J. Spero's much-used *The Politics of International Economic Relations*, London, Allen & Unwin, 1985; R. Gilpin, *The Political Economy of International Relations*, Princeton, Princeton University Press, 1987; D. Blake and R. Walters, *The Politics of Global Economic Relations*, Englewood Cliffs, NJ, Prentice

Hall, 1983. An exception is R. Cox, *Production, Power and World Order*, 1987.

2. 'Revolution' is a particularly elastic term in the vocabulary of security, needing careful definition before it is identified as synonymous with violence and an absence of security. As the French political scientist, Jean Baechler has pointed out, the term 'revolutionary' can reasonably include members of movements which totally reject the values and goals of conventional societies, and even suicides who practise a lonely, personal kind of rejection of society. Moreover, there have been many bloodless revolutions — like the English Revolution of 1688, the Gaullist Revolution of 1958 or the Turkish Revolution of 1983 — all of which enhanced rather than threatened security. (Baechler, 1975.)

3. On tax issues, see Chapter 4, p. 84.

4. See Jervis (1970); Howard (1983); Gilpin (1981); Waltz (1979); Holsti (1983).

5. The US Senate appointed the Nye Commission in the mid-1930s to investigate the matter. Two classic books were H.C. Engelbrecht and F.C. Hanighen, *Merchants of Death* (1934) and Thayer, *The War Business: The International Trade in Armaments*, 1970. See also: R. McKinlay and A. Mughan, *Aid and Arms and the Third World* (1984) and A. Sampson, *The Arms Bazaar* (1977). Bernard Shaw's provocative study of the arms manufacturer, Andrew Undershaft, in *Major Barbara* is also worth re-reading. (See Bibliography for details.)

Chapter 4

1. See Bibliography.

2. See Chapter 6.

3. Baechler (1975: 56–9). On the importance of changed ideas, from St Augustine to Adam Smith, regarding the legitimacy of profit-seeking, see Hirschman (1977).

4. K. Marx, *Capital*, I, quoted by James O'Connor (O'Connor, 1984: 24).

5. See also Chapter 11.

6. 'Turnip' Townsend was one of the chief advocates of the Norfolk four-course rotation of crops in eastern England. This not only increased yields but enabled more cows and sheep to be kept alive through the winter. The forced emigration of Scots in the eighteenth century has been movingly described by John Prebble in *The Highland Clearances*, London, Secker & Warburg, 1983.

7. Cf. Cipolla (1962), and more briefly, N. Demerath, 'World Politics and Population' in Strange (1984).

8. As most British schoolchildren know, the Mutiny spread because Indians believed that native soldiers, or sepoys, were being ordered by their White officers to violate religious taboos, both Hindu and Muslim.

9. 'Multinationals' as a description of corporations operating in several countries and across natural frontiers is misleading because neither in character nor control are most of them multi-national. They are national corporations operating transnationally. 'Multinational corporations' was a term strategically coined by IBM early in the 1960s. 'Transnational corporation', as used by the UN, is more accurate. See United Nations (1983).

10. Vernon's work also owed something to the thesis of Stephen Hymer, a student of Kindleberger's, published posthumously (Hymer, 1976).

11. Nader (1976). Nader made his reputation as a champion of consumer interests, especially in the car business.
12. Franko (1976) has gone as far as comparing TNCs to the tax 'farmers' of pre-revolutionary France and other pre-industrial regimes. Then, the state 'sold' or privatized the tax-gathering concessions. Franko's argument is that when governments allow management fees or kickbacks on aided projects, they are essentially doing the same.

Chapter 5

1. Neither the ECU nor the SDR can properly be described as a truly international currency. The value of both 'baskets', or weighted mixtures of currencies, depends on the net inflationary or deflationary policies of the constituent governments. Only when some multinational political authority takes responsibility for managing the issue of ECUs or SDRs will these take on an existence separate from their national ingredients.
2. J. K. Galbraith's Money — Whence it Came and Where it Went (1975) tells these stories particularly well.
3. The classic study of European lending policies in the nineteenth century is still Feis (1964).
4. See M. de Cecco, Money and Empire; the International Gold Standard, 1974: and for a clear exposition of the circular movement of funds in world trade before 1914, A.G. Kenwood and A.L. Lougheed, The Growth of the International Economy, 1920–1980, 1983.
5. Judd Polk, Sterling, Its Meaning in World Finance. This point is important because under the paper dollar standard the United States often succeeded in doing the opposite: protecting itself from exogenous shocks and passing the necessity to adjust on to others.
6. Alan Milward argues that European economic recovery was going well in 1947 and that the picture sold to the Congress of Europe that it was verging on economic collapse was grossly exaggerated. That was true, but the recovery could not have been sustained much longer without US help. See A. Milward, The Reconstruction of Western Europe 1948–51, London, Methuen, 1984. Also Kindleberger, 1987.
7. A. Maddison, Economic Growth in the West, 1964, p. 77.
8. The major de facto amendments were the decision (to help Britain) to let countries draw on the IMF who were in balance of payments difficulties on capital account as well as current account, as originally envisaged; and the quiet dropping of the 'scarce currency' clause which put equal responsibility to adjust on surplus countries as on those in deficit. This suited the Americans in the 1950s but made it harder to push revaluation on the Germans and Japanese by the end of the 1960s.
9. A full list with explanations of the reasons for introducing these devices can be found in H. Kaufman, 1986.
10. R. Dale, The Regulation of International Banking, 1986, p. 83.
11. US banks too eventually had to stand losses, as Mexican debt began to be sold off at up to 50 per cent of its full value. But the penalty was both delayed and more covertly paid.
12. Ibid., p. 185. An appendix gives the full text of the second Basle Concordat.
13. One encouraging move towards stiffer and more uniform re-regulation was the British–American agreement to standardize the required ratios between banks' capital and their assets (i.e. loans). This led in December 1987 to a multilateral agreement by member banks of the BIS (Financial Times, 9 December 1987).

14. This was the conclusion reached by Calleo in his study of US monetary policies from Eisenhower to Reagan (Calleo, 1984).

Chapter 6

1. Under the slogan *Siamo sempre con te*, a Hewlett-Packard advertisement in Italy recently proclaimed that customers anywhere in the world could keep in touch with data sources, corporate headquarters and customers by means of their sophisticated communication systems.
2. An excellent and entertaining account of this intellectual transition is to be found in Hirschman (1977). See also Heilbroner (1983).
3. Schumacher (1973), chapter entitled 'Buddhist Economics'. See also B. Woods' biography of her father, *Alias Papa*, (1984).
4. Ibid., Figs. 9 and 10, pp. 64/5. Hamelink's sources for these network pages were J.P. Chamoux, *L'information sans frontiéres*, 1980, and the publications of S.W.I.F.T.
5. This was the main finding of S. Davis's doctoral thesis, *The Grain trade and food security in Mexico, Brazil and Argentina*, London University, 1984.
6. United Nations Centre on Transnational Corporations, various reports on Transborder Data Flows in UNCTC *Reporter*; see also K. Sauvant (1986).
7. Some selected titles are: J. Habermas, *Communications and the Evolution of Society*, 1979; R. Barthes, *Mythologies*, 1973; J. Baudrillard, for a critique of the political economy of the Sign, 1986; R. Williams, *Communications*, 1976; A. Smith, *The Geopolitics of Information. How Western Culture Dominates the World*, 1980; R. Hoggart, *An Idea and its Servants: UNESCO from Within*, 1978; M. Mulkay, *Science and the Sociology of Knowledge*, 1979; K. Popper, *The Poverty of Historicism*, 1960; M. C. Gordon (ed.) *Power/Knowledge*, 1980; M. Foucault, *The Archeology of Knowledge and the Discourse of Language*, 1972; K. Deutsch, *Nationalism and Social Communication*, 1953; J.I. Gershuny and I.D. Miles, *The New Service Economy*, 1983; (see bibliography for details).

Chapter 7

1. Soviet practice is often criticized as unfair in Western shipping circles because the Soviet trade agencies insist on buying imported goods f.o.b. and exporting their own goods c.i.f., thus collecting the insurance premium on both inward- and outward-bound cargoes.
2. As quoted by *The Economist*, 6 June 1987, p. 79.
3. The first big one, the wreck of the *Torrey Canyon* off the British coast, occurred in 1967 and spilled 120,000 tons of crude oil. Much worse, spilling nearly twice as much, was the break-up of the brand new supertanker, the *Amoco Cadiz* off the French coast in 1978. Less damaging, but causing just as much fuss, was the wreck off the Massachusetts coast of the *Argo Merchant* in 1979.
4. That was the ratio as estimated by IMO officials in 1973. By 1983, it had fallen to less than 2:1. See Bongaerts and de Bievre (1987: 146).
5. Claims against Liberian tankers for major oil spills have totalled $254 million, against totals for Japanese- and Norwegian-registered tankers of $22 and $10 million respectively. (Bongaerts and de Bievre, 1987: 155).
6. My own father, Col. Louis Strange, had the peculiar distinction of being the first British pilot to fit a machine gun to his plane — at first he was told to take it off at once — and also the first British pilot to use French artillery

shells on bombs strung up with wire below the wings to bomb an enemy target — the rail station at Tournai. Strange (1933).

7. A similar situation has arisen with Gibraltar. A 1987 attempt to get more competition on European air routes foundered because Spain objected to Britain treating Gibraltar as a 'British' airport when most of the traffic was destined for Spain's Costa del Sol.

8. Another was opened by two very small states, Iceland and Luxembourg, to whom geography gave a chance to opt out of IATA and cut fares by flying a great circle route across the Atlantic.

9. A.P. Ellison and E.M. Stafford, *The Dynamics of the civil aviation industry*, New York, Saxon House, 1974, p. 188.

Chapter 8

1. The corresponding figures for bloc exports were 13 per cent and 32 per cent respectively. GATT, *International Trade 1982/3*, Table A14.

2. US Senate report, February 1973, *Implications of multinational firms for world trade and investments and for US trade and labor*, pp. 278–9; and for Britain, Meyer (1978: 33). See Tussie (1987).

3. Seers (1983: 13).

4. See my argument in Tsoukalis (1985).

Chapter 9

1. The plebiscite of 1935 was the occasion for the early use of an international peace-keeping force. The Saarlanders voted overwhelmingly to rejoin Germany.

2. The International Atomic Energy Agency is a UN specialized agency set up in 1957. For an analytical summary, see Scheinmann in Cox and Jacobson (1973).

3. Quoted in Ebinger (1982: xvi).

Chapter 10

1. B.V.A. Roling, 'International Law in an Expanding World' quoted in Bull (1977: 146).

2. See Strange, 'International Economic Relations' in Twitchett (1971).

3. For this reason the study of what is called 'welfare economics' is not strictly speaking a branch of economic science at all, but rather of political economy. Although there may be economic aspects to it and factors involved in it, it primarily concerns matters of political decision-making — a point well made by Lionel Robbins who in later life regretted that economists had not accepted a clean separation between the two.

4. It may also indirectly benefit the taxpayers in the donor countries. A major cost in defence industry is research and development of new weapons, etc. Each additional marginal sale lowers the average incidence of these development costs, thus making it possible to lower the unit price to the country's own armed forces. This is the logical reason why European countries like Britain and France, with smaller national arms markets than the United States, are so keen to expand arms sales abroad.

Bibliography

Amin, S. 1976. *Unequal Development*. Hassocks, Harvester.

Angell, N. 1909. *The Great Illusion*. London, Heinemann.

Aron, R. 1958. 'War and Industrial Society', *Millennium*, 7, No. 3, 1979.

Baechler, J. 1975. *Revolution*. Oxford, Blackwell, Tr. from the French: *Les Phènoménes Règolutionnaires*, Presses Universitaires de France, 1970.

Baechler, J. 1975. *The Origins of Capitalism*. Oxford, Blackwell.

Barnet, R. and Muller, R. 1974. *Global Reach*. London, Cape.

Barry Jones, R. 1983. *Perspectives on Political Economy*. London, Pinter Publishers.

Barthes, R. 1973. *Mythologies*. London, Granada.

Baudrillard, J. 1986. *For a Critique of Political Economy of the Sign*. Tr. C. Levin 1972, Saint-Louis, Telos Press.

Bell, D. 1974. *The Coming of the Post-Industrial Society: A Venture in Social Forecasting*. London, Heinemann Educational.

Bergsten, C.F. and Nau, H.R. 1985. 'The State of the Debate: Reagonomics'. *Foreign Policy*, Summer.

Berle, A. and Means, G. 1967. *The Modern Corporation and Private Property*. New York, Harcourt Brace.

Blake, D. and Walters, R. 1983. *The Politics of Global Economic Relations*. Edgewood Cliffs, NJ, Prentice Hall.

Block, F. 1977. *The Origins of International Economic Disorder*. Berkeley, London, University of California Press.

Bongaerts, J.C. and de Bievre, A. 1987. 'Insurance for Civil Liability for Marine Oil Pollution Damages', Geneva Papers of Risk and Insurance, April.

Bull, H. 1977. *The Anarchical Society: A Study of Order in World Politics*. London, Macmillan.

Cafruny, A. 1987. *Ruling the Waves*. Berkeley, University of California Press.

Calleo, D. 1982. *The Imperious Economy*. Cambridge, Mass., Howard University Press.

Carr-Saunders, A.M. and Wilson, P.A. 1933. *The Professions*. London, Frank Cass.

De Cecco, M. 1974. *Money and Empire. The International Gold Standard*. Oxford, Blackwell.

Chandler, A. 1977. *The Visible Hand*. Cambridge, Mass., Harvard University Press.

Cherry, C. 1971. *World Communication. Threat or Promise*. New York, John Wiley.

Cipolla, C.M. 1962. *The Economic History of World Population*. Harmondsworth, Penguin.

Cooper, R. 1968. *The Economics of Interdependence. Economic Policy in the Atlantic Community*. New York, McGraw Hill.

Cox, R. 1981. 'Social Forces, States and World Order'. *Millennium*, Summer.

Cox, R. 1987. *Production, Power, and World Order*. New York, Columbia University Press.

Cox, R. and Jacobson, K. 1973. *The Anatomy of Influence*. New Haven/London, Yale University Press.

Dahl, R. 1961. *Who Governs? Democracy and Power in an American City*. New Haven, Yale University Press.

Dale, R. 1984. *The Regulation of International Banking*. Cambridge, Woodhead Faulkner.

Delamaide, D. 1984. *Debt Shock*. London, Weidenfeld and Nicholson.

Destler, I.M. 1986. *American Trade Politics. System Under Stress*. Washington DC, Institute for International Economics.

Deutsch, K. 1953. *Nationalism and Social Communications*. Cambridge, Mass. MIT.

Deutsch, K. 1968. *Political Community and the North Atlantic Area*. Princeton, Princeton University Press.

Diebold, W. 1959. *The Schuman Plan: A Study in Economic Cooperation, 1950–1959*. Published for the Council of Foreign Relations, Praeger, Oxford University Press.

Diebold, W. 1980. *Industrial Policy as an International Issue*. New York, McGraw-Hill.

Drucker, P. 1986. 'The Changes in World Economy'. *Foreign Affairs*, Spring.

Dunning, J. 1985. *Toward an Eclectic Theory of International Business*. Mimeo., Reading University.

Ebinger, C.K. 1982. *The Critical Link. Energy and National Security in the 1980s*. For Centre for Strategic and International Studies, Cambridge, Mass., Ballinger Publishing Co.

Ellison, A.P. and Stafford, E.M. 1974. *The Dynamics of the Civil Aviation Authority*. New York, Saxon House.

Emmanuel, A. 1972. *Unequal Exchange*. Tr. from the French, London, New Left Books.

Englebrecht, H.C. and Hanighen, F.C. 1934. *Merchants of Death*. Toronto, Dodd.

Feis, H. 1964. *Europe the World's Banker 1870–1914*. New York, Kelly.

Foucault, M. 1972. *The Archaeology of Knowledge and the Discourse of Language*. London, Tavistock Publications.

Foucault, M. 1980. *Power / Knowledge*, C. Gordon (ed.), Brighton, Harvester.

Frank, A. Gunder. 1978. *Dependent accumulation and Underdevelopment*. London, Macmillan.

Franko, L. 1976. *The European Multinationals*. London, Harper & Row.

Galbraith, J.K. 1975. *Money — Whence it came, where it went*. London, Andre Deutsch.

Gardner, R. 1969. *Sterling–Dollar Diplomacy in Current Perspective*. New York, Columbia University Press.

Gershuny, J.I. and Miles, I.D. 1983. *The New Service Economy*. London, Pinter Publishers.

Gilpin, R. 1981. *War and Change in World Politics*. Cambridge, Cambridge University Press.

Gilpin, R. 1987. *The Political Economy of International Relations*. Princeton, Princeton University Press.

Habermas, J. 1979. *Communication and the Evolution of Society*, T. F. McCarthy, London, Heinemann Educational.

Hall, J. 1985. *Powers and Liberties*. Oxford, Blackwell.

Hamelink, C. 1983. *Finance and Information*. Norwood, NJ, Ablex Publishing Corp.

Hayter, T. 1971. *Aid as Imperialism*. Harmondsworth, Penguin.

Heilbroner, R. 1983. *The Worldly Philosophers*. 5th edn, Harmondsworth, Penguin.

Hirsch, F. 1976. *Social Limits to Growth*. Cambridge, Mass., Harvard University Press.

Hirschman, A.O. 1977. *The Passions and the Interests*. Guilford, Princeton University Press.

Hoggart, R. 1978. *An Idea and Its Servant: UNESCO from Within*. London, Chatto & Windus.

Holsti, K. 1983. *International Politics*. 4th edn, Englewood Cliffs, NJ, Prentice-Hall.

Howard, M. 1983. *The Causes of Wars and Other Essays*. 2nd edn, London, Temple Smith.

Hufbauer, G. and Schott, J. 1985. *Economic Sanctions Reconsidered*. Washington, MIT Press for Institute for International Economics.

Hymer, S. 1976. *The International Operations of National Firms*. Boston, MIT Press.

Innis, H. 1950. *Empire and Communications*. Oxford, Clarendon Press.

International Energy Agency (IEA). 1986. *Energy Policies and Programmes of IEA Countries*. Paris, OECD/IEA.

Jervis, R. 1970. *The Logic of Images in International Relations*. Princeton, NJ, Princeton University Press.

Johnson, D. Gale. 1973. *World Agriculture in Disarray*. London, Penguin.

Johnson, T.J. 1972. *Professions and Power*. London, Macmillan.

Joll, J. 1968. *1914: The Unspoken Assumptions*. Weidenfeld and Nicolson. (LSE Inaugural Lecture.)

Jonsson, C. 1987. *International Aviation and the Politics of Regime Change*. London, Pinter Publishers.

Kaufman, H. 1986. *Interest Rates, the Markets and the New Financial World*. London, Tauris.

Kenwood, A.G. and Loughead, A.L. 1983. *The Growth of the International Economy, 1920–1980*. London, Allen & Unwin.

Keohane, R.O. 1984. *After Hegemony. Cooperation and discord in the world political economy*. Princeton, NJ, Princeton University Press.

Keohane, R.O. and Nye, J.S. 1977. *Power and Interdependence*. Boston/Toronto, Little, Brown & Co.

Kindleberger, C.P. 1987. *Marshall Plan Days*. Cambridge, MIT.

Knorr, K. 1956. *The War Potential of Nations*. Princeton University Press, Oxford University Press.

Knorr, K. 1973. *Power and Wealth*. New York, Basic Books.

Krasner, S.D. 1983. *International Regimes*. Ithaca and London, Cornell University Press.

Krasner, S.D. 1985. *Structural Conflict: The Third World against global liberalism*. Berkeley, University of California Press.

Lall, S. 1983. *The New Multinationals. The spread of Third World enterprises*. Chichester, Wiley.

Latham, A. 1978. *The International Economy and the Underdeveloped World, 1865–1914*. London, Croom Helm.

Lever, H. and Huhne, C. 1985. *Debt and Danger*. Harmondsworth, Penguin.

Lewis, W.A. 1978. *The Evolution of the International Economic Order*. Princeton, Guilford, Princeton University Press.

Lindblom, C. 1978. *Politics and Markets*. New York, Basic Books.

Little, R. and McKinlay, R. 1986. *Global Problems and World Order*. London, Pinter Publishers.

Lowes Dickinson, G. 1916. *The European Anarchy*. London, Allen & Unwin.

MacBean, A.I. and Snowden, P.N. 1981. *International Institutions in Trade and Finance*. London, Allen & Unwin.

McKinlay, R.D. and Mughan, A. 1984. *Aid and Arms to the Third World*. London, Pinter Publishers.

Maddison, A. 1964. *Economic Growth in the West*. London, Allen & Unwin.

Maddison, A. 1982. *Phases of Capitalist Development*. Oxford/New York, Oxford University Press.

Malthus, T. 1798. *Essay on the Principle of Population as it Affects the Future Improvement of Society*. London, J. Johnson.

Mann, M. 1986. *The Sources of Social Power*. (vol.1. *A History of Power from the Beginning to AD 1760*). Cambridge, Cambridge University Press.

Meadows, D.H. *et al*. 1972. *Limits to Growth. A report for the Club of Rome's project on the Predicament of Mankind*. London, Earth Island Ltd. New York, Universe Books.

Melman, S. 1970. *Pentagon Capitalism*. New York, McGraw-Hill.

Melody, W. 1985. 'The Information Society: Implications for Economic Institutions and Market Theory'. *Journal of Economic Issues*, June.

Meyer, F.V. 1978. *International Trade Policy*. London, Croom Helm.

Michalet, C.-A. 1976. *Le Capitalisme Mondiale*. Paris, Press Universitaires de France.

Mikdashi, Z. 1986. *Transnational Oil*. London, Pinter Publishers.

Miller, J.D.B. 1986. *Norman Angell and the Futility of War*. London, Macmillan.

Moffitt, M. 1984. *The World's Money*. London, Micheal Joseph.

Moore, Barrington, 1967. *Social Origins of Dictatorship and Democracy*. London, Penguin.

Morse, E. 1983. 'The Petroleum Economy: Liberalism Reborn?' *SAIS Review*, 3, No.2, Summer.

Mulkay, M. 1979. *Science and the Sociology of Knowledge*. London, Allen & Unwin.

Nader, R. 1976. *The Taming of the Giant Corporation*. New York, Norton.

O'Brien, R. Cruise, 1985. *Economics, Information and Power*. London, Hodder and Stoughton.

O'Connor, J. 1973. *The Fiscal Crisis of the State*. New York, St. Martin's Press.

O'Connor, J. 1984. *Accumulation Crisis*. Oxford, Blackwell.

Olson, M. 1982. *The Rise and Decline of Nations*. New Haven, Yale University Press.

Penrose, E. 1959. *The theory of the growth of the firm*. Oxford, Blackwell.

Polanyi, K. 1957. *The Great Transformation*. (1st edn 1944), Boston, Beacon Press.

Polk, J. 1956. *Sterling, its Meaning in World Finance*. New York, Harper.

Popper, K. 1960. *The Poverty of Historicism*. (2nd edn), London, Routledge & Kegan Paul.

Poster, M. 1984. *Foucault, Marxism and History*. Cambridge Polity.

Rothschild, K.W. (ed.) 1971. *Power in Economics*. Harmondsworth, Penguin.

Ruggie, J.G. 1983. *The Antinomies of Interdependence*. New York, Columbia University Press.

Sampson, A. 1977. *The Arms Bazaar*. London, Hodder & Stoughton.

Sampson, A. 1981. *The Money Lenders*. London, Hodder & Stoughton.

Sampson, A. 1984. *Empires of the Sky*. London, Hodder & Stoughton.

Sauvant, K.P. and Hasenpflug, H. (eds). 1977. *The New International Economic Order*. London, Wilton House Publications.

Sauvant, K. 1986. *International transactions in services: the politics of transborder data flows*. Boulder, Westview.

Savary, J. 1984. *French Multinationals*. London, Pinter Publications.

Schumacher, E.F. 1973. *Small is Beautiful*. London, Blond & Briggs.

Seers, D. 1983. *The Political Economy of Nationalism*. Oxford, Oxford University Press.

Sen, G. 1983. *The military origins of industrialization and international trade rivalry*. New York, St Martins.

Skocpol, T. 1979. *States and Social Revolutions*. Cambridge, Cambridge University Press.

Smith, A. 1980. *The Geopolitics of Information. How Western Culture Dominates the World*. London, Faber.

Solzhenitsyn, A. 1972. *August 1914*. London, Bodley Head.

Spero, J. 1985. *The Politics of International Economic Relations*. London, Allen & Unwin.

Staniland, M. 1985. *What is Political Economy?* New Haven, Yale University Press.

Stoffaes, C. 1978. *La Grande Menace Industrielle*. Paris, Calman-Levy.

Stonier, T. 1983. *The Wealth of Information*. London, Thames Methuen.

Strange, L.A. 1933. *Recollections of an Airman*. London, John Hamilton.

Strange, S. 1970. 'International economics and international relations: a case of mutual neglect', *International Affairs*, 46, No.2, April, pp. 304–15.

Strange, S. (ed.). 1984. *Paths to International Political Economy*. London, Allen & Unwin.

Strange, S. 1976. *International Monetary Relations*. vol.2 of A. Shonfield (ed.) *International Economic Relations in the Western World 1959–71*. O.U.P.

Strange, S. 1986. *Casino Capitalism*. Oxford, Blackwell.

Streeten, P. 1987. 'New directions for private resource transfers', *Banca Nazionale del Lavoro*, March, Rome.

Thayer, G. 1970. *The War Business: The International Trade in Armaments*. London, Paladin.

Tsoukalis, L. (ed.). 1985. *The Political Economy of International Money*. London, RIIA.

Tussie, D. 1987. 'The LDCs and the GATT'. Mimeo. for International Studies Association, April.

Twitchett, K. 1971. *The Evolving United Nations*. London, Europa.

United Nations Centre on Transnational Corporations (UNCTC). 1983. 'Transnational Corporations and World Development'. Third Report. New York, UNCTC.

Vaitsos, C. 1976. In Gerald Helleiner (ed.) *A World Divided*. Cambridge, Cambridge University Press.

Vasak, K. (ed.) 1982. *The International Dimension of Human Rights*, vol. 2.

Vatter, H. 1985. *The US Economy in World War Two*. New York, Columbia University Press.

Vernon, R. 1971. *Sovereignty at Bay*. London, Longman.

Vernon, R. 1977. *Storm Over the Multinationals*. London, Macmillan.

Vincent, R.J. (ed.) 1986. *Human Rights and Sovereignty: Issues and Responses*.

Wall, D. 1973. *The Charity of Nations: The Political Economy of Foreign Aid*. London, Macmillan.

Wallerstein, I. 1974. *The Modern World System*. New York, London, Academic Press.

Wallerstein, I. 1979. *The Capitalist World Economy*. Cambridge, Cambridge University Press.

Waltz, K. 1979. *Theory of International Relations*. Reading, Mass., Addison-Wesley Publishing Co.

Wheatcroft, S. 1956. *The Economics of European Air Transport*. Manchester, University Press.

Wight, M. 1986. *Power Politics*. Harmondsworth, Penguin. 1st edn, London, RIIA, 1946.

Willetts, P. 1978. *The Non-aligned Movement*. London, Pinter Publishers, and New York, Nichols Publishing Co.

Williams, R. 1976. *Communications*. Harmondsworth, Penguin.

Winham, G.R. 1986. *International Trade and the Tokyo Round Negotiations*. Princeton, NJ, Princeton University Press.

Woods, B. 1984. *Alias Papa*. London, Cape.
Wriston, W. 1986. *Risk and Other Four-Letter Words*. New York, Harper & Row.

Index